How To Bring Up Your
Parents

The Essential Survival Guide
Brought to you in glorious TERRORVISION

Emma Kennedy

Illustrations by KayPiss
(not real name)

FRIDAY
BOOKS

D1381918

First published in Great Britain in 2007 by Friday Books
An imprint of The Friday Project Limited
83 Victoria Street, London SW1H0HW

www.thefridayproject.co.uk
www.fridaybooks.co.uk

Text © Emma Kennedy
Photographs © Jim Marks
Illustrations © KayPiss

ISBN 978-1-905548-57-6

British Library Cataloguing in Publication Data

A catalogue record for this book is available from the British Library

3 5 7 9 10 8 6 4 2

Cover and internal design by e-Digital Design

Typeset by e-Digital Design

Printed by MPG Books Ltd

The Publisher's policy is to use paper manufactured
from sustainable sources

DEDICATION

For my best boys, Ben and Tom, and for
Richard Keith Herring, to whom I owe everything,
not least introducing me to the word 'clacker'.

FOREWORD

At last a guide book that tells us all how to cope with the older generation, for anyone who realises they're turning into their parent, whilst their parents are turning into their kids. Forget Einstein, Emma Kennedy's Theories of Relativity are immutable and unchallengeable and will ring true to anyone who has ever thought their parents were eccentric, embarrassing, overbearing, infuriating but underneath it all somehow totally loveable. Having met both Emma and her parents I can tell you that the apple never falls far from the tree: they're all barmy, but brilliant.

Richard Herring

THANKS VERY MUCH

First up I must thank Hannah Griffiths who encouraged me to start writing a blog. If she hadn't then this book would never have happened. Next, I need to doff my hat in the direction of Clare Christian, Clare Weber and everyone at The Friday Project for asking me to write a book and then for liking the idea I came up with. I must also extend considerable thanks to Carrie Walker, whose meticulous eye for detail has saved me a multitude of grammatical embarrassments, and Amy Snowden. Special awards should go to the team at e-Digital Design and Jim Marks, who not only designed the book and took the photographs respectively, but also managed to control my parents and Poppy at the shoot. Next in line must be Camilla Hornby, my literary agent, a woman so very tall and brilliant that it's impossible to do anything other than look up to her. Nods must also be thrown in the direction of my other agents at Curtis Brown: Sarah MacCormick whose devotion is the stuff of legend and Joe Phillips, a man blessed with the happiest face in the world. Lower down the line, but no less important are those wonderful fellows Dave Gorman and Danny Baker, both of whom saw very early drafts and whose encouragement meant worlds. My old chum Sue Perkins also deserves a pat on the back for letting me write at her house in Cornwall and for keeping me going with the nicest fish curry I've ever tasted. Bended knees are in order when thanking Kate Barsby who provided capable assistance and is very good at chopping wood. I would also like to thank Sharon Powers and everyone involved in *Celebrity Scissorhands*, a voice-over job so exceptional that I managed to write the lion's share of the book in between recordings on a sofa in the reception at UNCLE. Given that this book is loosely based on my blog over at www.emmakennedy.net I couldn't live with myself if I didn't thank the Webmaster, Rob Sedgebeer, who designed the website and helps me when I don't understand how to do links. What I would do without him, I do not know. Thanks on bended knees must also go to everyone who took the time to answer my online questionnaire. Your replies were invaluable. A heartfelt thank you is also reserved for all my regular blog readers, especially the Guestbookers whose daily comments are a constant delight. I would also like to send an appreciative wave in the direction of Jeffrey Noggin and MegaNoggin whose collective stink spurred me into action. Gratitude must also be splattered all over Elizabeth Freestone, Heather Bull, Debbie Chazen, Lucy Austin and Juliet McGill, all of whom sparked off conversations that turned themselves into practical problems. For once and for all, Juliet needs to understand that an egg is NOT a dairy product. Last but not least, my greatest thanks must be reserved for my mum and dad. When I was approached to write this book, my mum had just been diagnosed with breast cancer. If it hadn't been for the exceptional care she received from the doctors and nurses at the Royal Marsden hospital in South Kensington then she might not still be here. But she is and she's doing brilliantly. This book is my love letter to both my parents. I just adore them.

The words from the song Sodomy from the musical *Hair* are reproduced with kind permission from James Rado. The lyrics were written by the authors of *Hair*, J. Rado & G. Ragni.

CONTENTS

Introduction   xi

Identify your parent   1

The science and history bit (because you're worth it)   31

The practical problems section   51

Uncommon ailments   137

Entertaining   147

Leaving home   191

It's a dog's life   211

Sex and other embarrassments   223

Work   245

Miscellaneous difficulties   261

Conclusion   283

Appendix: You and yours   287

INTRODUCTION

Parents are dangerous. Fact. My mother has never made me a meal. My father tells me what I'm getting for Christmas. I like to dance around my kitchen and pretend I'm in a musical. Welcome to my world. I am a 39-year-old only child and I'm going to help you bring up your parents.

Chances are you and everyone you know has at some time or another had at least one parent. It's a chicken and egg thing. But not everyone knows what to do with a parent or how to manage them. This book is your parenting manual and will help you get through any number of blood-curdling moments. Using diagrams, practical examples and specially provided Terrorvision specs, this book will help you dive into the damp, underground hellhole of parental management and, if you follow the steps provided, emerge without an embolism.

Compulsory Attendance Days, holidays and introducing your parents to that crucial new partner – minefields all. But coping with your parents doesn't have to be the Mother of all Migraines. Using this guide, you will learn how to cope with every conceivable conundrum. Drunk too much at Christmas? Fed up of explaining who's who in *Big Brother*? Well, worry no more. Whether it's your mother convinced that eggs are a dairy product or your father claiming to have received a text message from the Queen allowing him to watch the snooker, I will teach you how to head your parents off at the pass and wrangle them into one manageable unit.

From the history of the parent to the molecules that make them, this book provides you with everything you will ever need to know about taking charge of your parents. Learn how to identify your type of parent, calculate how embarrassed you should feel in any given situation and realise, once and for all, that not only can you finally comprehend what your parents are going on about, but that you can control them with a Vulcan-like grip.

How to Bring up your Parents is **THE** essential survival guide.
DON'T GO HOME WITHOUT IT.

GLUE

TERRORVISION

IN CASE OF PARENTS PLEASE PUT ON

YELLOW PLASTIC

GREEN PLASTIC

IN CASE OF PARENTS PLEASE PUT ON

TERRORVISION

GLUE

TERRORVISION SPECS

What you're about to see is DANGEROUS and can KILL. Please make yourself a pair of Terrorvision spectacles before proceeding. Failure to do so may result in instantaneous fatalities, breakdowns and eye blisters.

You will need:

 some cardboard
 some scissors
 some clear plastic squares
 one yellow highlighter pen
 one green highlighter pen
 a metre of silver foil
 glue.

1. Cut out or copy the spectacle template.
2. Attach the template to some cardboard and cut round it with scissors.
3. Cover the cardboard template with silver foil.
4. Take the plastic squares and, using your highlighter pens, colour one yellow and one green.
5. Now glue the coloured squares to the spectacle frame.
6. Put the glasses on and, for extra protection, use the remaining silver foil as a helmet.

You are about to see the different types of parent you may encounter. Try not to be too frightened. If you have not already done so, please put on your Terrorvision Spectacles now.

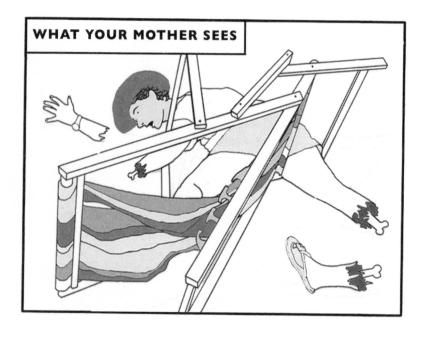

THE PRACTIBOT

Identification

Wiry, neat frame; tendency to wear military style clothing. Thin fingers. Clammy skin. Unnaturally deep belly buttons. Keeps all house and car keys on retractable elastic. Never leaves the house without spare socks, pants, jumpers, trousers, glasses, shoes, wellingtons, waterproof head wear, waterproof underwear, blanket, maps, emergency phone numbers, emergency flares, traffic cone, first aid kit, collapsible stretcher, splints, cherry pipper, melon-ball spoon, nutmeg grater, outboard motor, spare tyre, spare engine, whistle, one bar of elvin lamas bread, sugar-free mint breath-fresheners, a length of rope, sewing kit, torch, crampons, iron, ironing board and a flask of strong beef tea.

Habits YUK

All irritating without exception. Loves recycling. Spends hours turning old newspapers into paper bricks on the off chance that one day they might come in useful. Can become aggressive in supermarkets if someone with a trolley stands in the Baskets Only check-out.

Voice

Low-pitched, droning, nasal monotone that will make you want to rip your ears off. Most likely to talk about parking, one-way systems and the quality of driving in Rome compared with Paris. Identifying call: 'Just in case'.

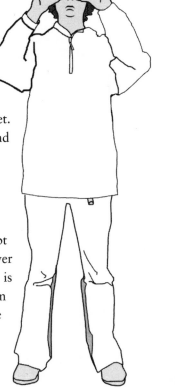

Habitat

Barratt Home three-bedroomed semi with fenced back garden and self-contained garage. Matching three-piece suites a must. Not fond of art but will accept prints of motor vehicles in the toilet. Books in home include maps, atlases and timetables. Favourite book – *London A–Z*.

Food

None of your foreign muck. Refuses to accept fish as a legitimate food group. Will never throw anything out of the freezer, which is packed with Findus Crispy pancakes from the 1980s and blackberries picked one Sunday in 1972.

3

Breeding

Once every two months, strictly by prior arrangement only.

Movements and migrations

Everything they do has to be planned out three months in advance and filled out in triplicate. Long, complicated driving holidays around Britain that involve multiple route planning are a real joy. The more adventurous Practibot may be found camping in Northern France, but only if they've completed a Listen and Learn French Course, which they have played on a cassette inside the car ad nauseam for over three years.

Distribution

Numbers dwindling in the Midlands but breeding pairs are flourishing in and about the Home Counties. Current population estimated at 400 000–800 000. Widespread across the Southern home counties, Practibots are commonly sighted on new housing developments, especially if there's a herringbone driveway.

THE FAFFER

Identification

Almost exclusively female. Constant, anxious expression. Twitchy legs and fingers. Haggard complexion. Always look fatter than they actually are due to their excessive jumper-layering system. Sensible shoes with flat heels to prevent ankle injuries. Zips, hooks and pins to be avoided at all cost. Elasticated trousers essential. Would accept Velcro, although someone at a bus stop once said it caused cancer and that was that. Likes to wear gloves when using public toilets and/or meeting teenagers.

Habits YUK

Believes that anything that could ever happen to the human body is due entirely to the 'change of air'. Ignores technology and doesn't trust CDs. Clings to the cassette as if it were the last chance of civilisation. Terrified of electrical devices and regards tuning a radio as the devil's own work. Although generally passive, can turn on a tuppence. During arguments, may wag finger and push glasses aggressively up nose. Worries about frozen bread, pandemics and limescale. Thinks you can catch AIDS from cutlery.

Voice

High pitched and piercing. Has a tendency to conduct conversations through pets, i.e. will address an entire conversation to the dog rather than the owner. When being driven will scream 'Mind that lorry!' every five to ten seconds, even if you're parked. Swears like a navvy. Identifying call: 'Be careful!'

Habitat

Prefers a house with no sharp corners. Would love to live in hermetically sealed environment. Suffers from arachnaphobia so intense they don't even need to SEE the spider: the Faffer can just SENSE its presence. Hates mess and thinks dust can give you TB. Whenever entering any property always asks 'Is there any asbestos?' Suspicious of bungalows.

Food

Dreadful cooks. Everything tastes of washing-up liquid. Handles chicken like nitroglycerine. If possible, will avoid cooking altogether. May be found boiling eggs in kettles.

Breeding

Don't be ridiculous. Far too dangerous.

Movements and migrations

Male Faffers are rare but can be found standing around in motorway service stations, pointing towards the toilets and saying, 'We're not going until everyone's been!' Faffers enjoy travelling but hate journeys so will often say 'Let's go to Cambridge for the day' and then scream all the way there and all the way back again. Will only allow three tapes to be played on any given car journey – 'Born in the USA' by Bruce Springsteen, 'An Innocent Man' by Billy Joel and 'The Best of Simon and Garfunkel'. That's it.

Distribution

Faffers tend not to form breeding pairs with other Faffers. Often to be found with a Practibot or Generbob. Current estimates two to three million. Widespread throughout United Kingdom. Avoid major conurbations and marshy areas. Encyclopaedic knowledge of all mountain ranges in the event of 'Britain falling into sea'.

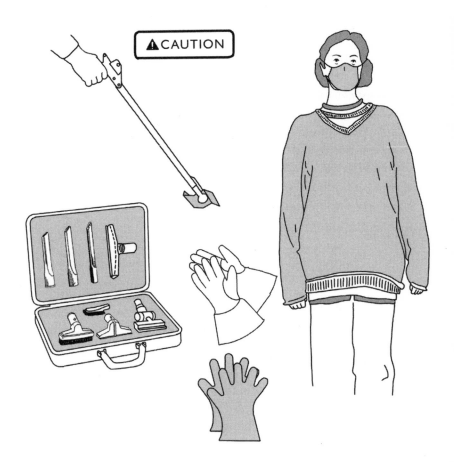

THE WASSERNAME

Identification

Tend to be male. The main distinguishing feature of a Wassername is that they display no interest in you whatsoever. Males may smoke pipes while standing at the bottom of gardens staring at compost heaps. Never not in a cardigan. Preferably with large, wooden buttons in the shape of footballs. Other than that, anything comfy and brown. Slight odour of wet mud.

Habits YUK

Spends hours on end in sheds sawing or chopping bits of wood for no discernible reason. Often obsessed with home-grown compost heaps (see above) and vegetable patches. Sits on stairs at parties and reads the paper rather than talk to anyone. Enjoys any solitary activity like stamp-collecting, alphabetising food cupboards and shitting. Last known conversation with a member of the family was in 1981 following the engagement of Lady Diana and the Prince of Wales. Hides biscuits in pockets.

Voice

Low rumbling indifference sprinkled with boredom. Insists on the correct pronunciations of words at all times. Fillet steak – 'fill-aye'. Mexico – 'Mekk-i-co' and paella must be 'pi-aye-ah'. Sighs a lot, usually when you're speaking. Will address you as 'Colin' even though your name is not Colin, you don't know anyone called Colin and you're a girl.

Habitat

Unsociable creature so favours villages with very few neighbours. All furniture smells of damp cardboard and tobacco. Books on gardening kept down the side of armchairs. Old car manuals also a favourite. No pictures of you anywhere in sight. Instead, keeps album after album filled with pictures of vegetables and pipes.

Food

Mince, mince and more mince. Basically anything brown, shredded and tasteless, and always served with shrivelled home-grown vegetables. Nothing wasted. Likes to use up any bits of unwanted roast chicken or lamb by shoving them into a gravy based gloop and pretending it's mince. Pasta is something they've only read about.

Breeding

Infrequent but filthy.

Movements and migrations

Loves pencil museums. Enjoys driving just under the speed limit on any given carriageway. Buys cars with plastic upholstery for wipe-a-bility. Has a sun cover only for the driver's seat so you have to endure nuclear leg burns during the summer months. Prefers day trips to proper holidays. Life's ambition is to visit every National Trust property within a 200-mile radius and open a centre devoted to mince.

Distribution

Up until 1965, the Wassername flourished throughout Britain. Numbers now dwindling and quite rare. Small concentrated pockets in North East England and the Scottish highlands.

THE GENERBOB

Identification

Stick out like sore thumbs. Look as if they've just stepped out of a time machine. Refuse to accept that hair or fashion has moved on since 1976. Often to be seen wearing iron press T-shirts with 'I Hate Jimmy Osmond' on the front. Females will only wear shoes that 'Princess Anne would wear'.

Habits   YUK

Will think nothing of teasing your friends mercilessly. For example, your friend is leaving. She says, 'Thank you for the tea.' Rather than just smiling and nodding, the Generbob will attack the friend by saying, 'But you didn't just have TEA. You had CAKE as well. What about the CAKE? Does the CAKE not deserve a thank you?' And then laugh at their own stupid joke. Insists on everyone knowing the 'family whistle', only to be used in the event of an emergency or when leaving garden centres. Belches constantly.

Voice

Given to making trumpet sounds with the mouth at random moments and has a tendency to speak French in the middle of sentences as in 'The floor ce n'est pas the bottom shelf.' Other common phrases include '"I don't know" is NOT an answer' and may refer to a particularly inedible meal as 'Another notable success'. Sarcasm is the Generbob's calling card and they pity anyone who doesn't get it.

Habitat

Owns 500 videotapes of recorded animal documentaries. Still uses a Soda Stream drinks machine and can't understand why anyone would want to pay for fizzy drinks. Has a plaque in the hallway that reads 'Proper Prior Planning Prevents Piss Poor Performance'.

Food

When shopping for food, converts everything into shillings as a way of expressing displeasure as in 'Ten bob? For an ice cream?', followed by a dismissive 'Fucking arseholes!' Prefers traditional staples like faggots, dumplings and stews. Distrusts coriander, hummus, avocados and anything proved to be edible after 1980.

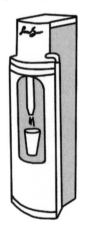

Breeding

Vigorous but very swift.

Movements and migrations

Most likely to be seen in a Datsun Sunny. Male Generbobs like to drive using only one finger at the bottom of the steering wheel. They also like to put their foot down on the approach to humpback bridges. Everyone else on the road is a 'clown'. Steering wheel is also used to wipe bogeys on. Favour Cornish caravan sites to foreign holidays. Tried going abroad once but found 'Spain too Spanish' and never went again. Female Generbobs should not be trusted driving as they are almost always wearing glasses bought at car boot sales.

Distribution

Prolific. Widespread throughout mainland Britain. Have not yet reached the Isle of Wight.

THE MUZZAFUZZ

Identification

Slightly dishevelled. Hair like cave-
men. Wrap-round skirts, flip-flops
and clogs. Cheesecloth tunics.
Badges from political organisations
that no longer exist. For the male,
lots of stripes all going in the wrong
directions and jumpers with holes in.
Tend to look confused and disorientated.

Habits YUK

Overemotional after a drink. Unhealthy obsession with the wheelie bin
and its being full the night before the dustmen are due. Very generous
with everything apart from tinfoil, which they hoard like a mental.
Tend to fall asleep on the sofa with their mouth open. Like to start
telling funny stories but always give up half way through. No anecdote
has EVER been finished. Extreme indecisiveness. Tendency to agree
with things they know nothing about. Similarly, will spend hours
telling people how to do something they have never done themselves.
May hire out community halls for expressive dance sessions.

Voice

Can be slurred, often effected. Hums a lot when thinks no one is looking.
Males may sing 'Pom, pom, pom' to themselves while thinking. When
asked questions, females will often repeat the question three times in
their head before attempting an answer. May suddenly say, 'Did I ever
tell you, you were adopted?' during moments of weakness.

Habitat

Often to be found in ramshackle cottages. Clutter is their middle name. Home-made pots everywhere. Anything made from plastic is forbidden from crossing threshold. Wicker chairs, patterned throws and candles to be expected. May own cats. Whenever there are more than three people in a room, the male Muzzerfuzz feels compelled to get out his guitar and play soft rock. Badly. The more extreme Muzzerfuzz will insist on living next to or above pubs. Failing that, anywhere within walking distance of an off-license.

Food

Mostly vegetarian, although will serve fish-paste sandwiches on long car journeys. Underdone potatoes and overdone cabbage a speciality. Perseveres with home-made bread even though it's denser than lead and the birds won't touch it. Makes rubbish gravy.

Breeding

Tried tantric once but couldn't stay awake long enough.

Movements and migrations

Always holiday abroad. Self-catering villas in France or Italy a real favourite. Tend to wander round churches lighting candles like they're going out of fashion even though you have never seen them go to church in this country, not even once. Usually drive yellow VW Beetles or Morris Minors. Afraid of red cars. Females try to sit with their noses as close to the windscreen as possible. Also drive with their hands in the classic ten-to-two position and NEVER cross their arms over while turning the steering wheel.

Distribution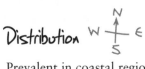

Prevalent in coastal regions and the West. Current numbers range between 750 000 and 1.5 million. Can often be seen at folk concerts and craft fairs but only if they're spelt with a 'y'.

THE BLIVYOID

Identification

The classic sock-and-sandal combo. Male Blivyoids will embrace the too-short shorts and wear them without a hint of embarrassment. Jackets and ties must also be worn, especially when swimming. Females often to be seen in home-made matching shirt-and-skirt apocalypses. Short-sleeved shirts and beige action slacks also a must. Slip-on shoes essential.

Habits YUK

Spends hours taking household appliances apart if they're not quite working and then realise they don't know how to put them back together again. A strange obsession with Holland and everything Dutch even though has never been. Often jingles change in pockets when bored. Likes to eat cakes in supermarkets before getting to the check-out. Leans to the right when farting. Joyless.

Voice

Female Blivyoids will often ask you a question and then talk over your answer. Their chatter is a wall of noise. They refuse to accept that you are over eighteen or gay. The male Blivyoid has a limited conversational range confined to discussing mortgages, repairs, mechanics and plumbing. Confuse playground insults for hip street slang and use it at inopportune moments as in asking one of your friends to 'sit in the back of the car with the rest of the flids' thinking 'flids' means 'kids'. It doesn't.

Habitat

Will only read books with ships on the cover. They insist on the cords of all electrical appliances being kept scrupulously clean. Convinced that children who don't tidy their rooms will become axe murderers. Interested in local history and have produced home-made photocopied fact sheets that are handed out to anyone who comes round. Hobbies include making ecclesiastical vestments.

Food

When in restaurants, Blivyoids think it is their duty to do bad impressions of the waiters. They also like to blow wine corks out of their mouth at dinner guests. Will often serve meals they've 'seen once in a magazine', such as pasta with tinned satsuma segments. Gristle stew a regular. Home-made flapjacks that could be sold to builders to make bricks are served on Saturday afternoons without fail.

Breeding

Functional and methodical.

Movements and migrations

Most likely to be driving a Hillman Hunter. While driving, will read out names of shops and signs on lorries irrespective of whether they are of any interest. Believes that the merest presence of a windbreak will spice up an otherwise miserable beach holiday in Wales.

Distribution

Widespread throughout the Midlands and North West England. Dominant throughout Northern Ireland.

THE GORGADRILLE

Identification

Females only – ski pants with foot straps, worn with wedge espadrilles. Crocheted gillets. Gemstone pendants. Headscarves. Will only wear a T-shirt if it's covered in sequins. A lot of lilac. For the male, high-waisted slacks with the shirt always tucked in. May have a beer belly and facial hair.

Habits   YUK

Gorgadrilles will force food on you and anyone with you from the moment you arrive to the moment you leave. Not happy unless everyone is eating, is about to eat or has something in their hand that they can eat. Thinks everyone with a job should have a briefcase irrespective of what that job is. Loves puzzle books and entering competitions on cereal packets. Thinks playing on a fruit machine on holiday is the height of luxury. May keep budgies and likes to rearrange your furniture when you're out.

Voice

Swears without swearing – 'Blast and bloody bleep bleep' and 'Muggy Moo Mars' are particular favourites. Hates the word 'snog'. Signs off all letters and emails with 'Purrs from the cat'

Habitat

Flocked wallpaper everywhere with patterns of anything edible. Framed pictures of cakes you made as a child hanging in the sitting room. Watercolours of joints of meat a real favourite.

Food

Gorgadrilles will eat anything, but everything MUST be on a plate. Even bananas.

Breeding

Highly sexed. May try swinging and wife-swapping.

Movements and migrations

Insists that A roads are faster than motorways. Can often be seen driving an Austin Princess or a Mini Clubman. America is their favourite destination, especially if they're going to stay with an 'open-minded' couple they've met on the Internet.

Distribution

Found in most cul-de-sacs in the South East and are very common in the Leeds-to-Bolton corridor. Currently believed to be 250 000 in the British Isles, with small migratory communities to be found in Utah and at the Sack and Crack Caravan Site in Weston-super-Mare.

THE MUTTOLAMB

Identification

Any haircut they've just seen in *Heat* magazine irrespective of its suitability. Chunky jewellery, denim skirts, sparkly dresses with wide elastic-band belts. Massive handbags that only body-builders can lift. Muffin tops and camel toes a given. For the male, double denim, converse trainers and one pierced ear. May attempt dressing like a snow-boarder but still smells of antique shops.

Habits YUK

The only person in the crowd who joins in with Morris dancers at village fêtes. Female Muttolambs are convinced their children possess amazing talents for singing and/or acting even in the face of irrefutable evidence to the contrary. Buying in bulk and buy-one-get-one-free offers can induce free-standing orgasms. Uncanny ability to fall asleep within five minutes of sitting in any armchair. Sense of humour like a seaside postcard. Will punch anyone who makes them laugh very hard on the upper arm. Males own massive vinyl record collections and pride themselves on being able to name every single session musician on any *Lynyrd Skynyrd* track.

Voice

Uses the word 'frigging' a lot but doesn't actually know what it means. Females may be convinced they can speak to the unliving and so nurture a breathy whisper when in company. Males swear a lot and refer to things being 'street' while nurturing mockney accents even though they were very obviously brought up in Surrey.

Habitat

Muttolambs love the cities but will live anywhere as long as there's a wet room, a breakfast bar and dimmer switches. Juke boxes and reclaimed pinball machines often found in their garage or sitting room. Commissioned family portraits hang in every room along with every certificate you ever gained from Cycling Proficiency onwards.

Food

Low-fat ready meals or anything as long as it can go in a microwave. May have attempted a proper cooked meal once, but whatever it was it would have darkened the souls of all who ate it.

Breeding

Very, very noisy.

Movements and migrations

Males like to go to music festivals and stand swaying near the front with their arms in the air, their eyes closed and their teeth hooked over their bottom lip. Females love package holidays to Greece or Ibiza or anywhere with cheap cocktails. Flashy cars a must.

Distribution

Massive population in the North with numbers exceeding four million. Also found in the South but clustering round New Towns. Colonies tend to appear within a five-mile radius of out-of-town retail villages, while their density is so severe around shopping malls that a government-controlled cull has been considered.

THE TRAVOLTEE

Identification

For the male, open shirt with the sleeves rolled up, St Christopher medallion, shin-high white socks in summer and dodgy trainers, comedy ties. Sweatshirts that say 'Same Shit, Different Day'. Always wears a football shirt at the weekend. Combed-over hair. Navy blue safari suits for special occasions. Females favour catsuits and polyblend blouses with hypnotic patterns. Green or yellow three-quarter length trousers also a must. Horrific morning breath. When in the house, slippers must be worn at all times.

Habits YUK

A collector of random, arcane facts. They are the only people actually to let Jehovah Witnesses into their house and put the kettle on. Houseflies make them livid. Possess an encyclopaedic memory of every goal ever scored for or against (*please insert name of football team here*). Only get angry on Tuesdays and Fridays. Are convinced that any music played at any family gathering imbues them with the power of dance. Can become terrified if all members of family aren't wearing slippers. Sneeze like dogs.

Voice

Loves saying 'Softly, softly, catchee monkey.'
Operates under the delusion that their telephone answer machine message is hilarious, i.e. 'We are having too much fun to come to the phone, ha ha ha ha ha ha ha. You can leave a message after the BEEEEEEEEEEP! Ah ha ha ha ha ha.' Pathological inability to pronounce the word 'squirrel' correctly. Identifying call: 'Where are your slippers?'

Habitat

Anywhere as long as it's beige. Males of the species enjoy pictures of planets, comets and minor characters from James Bond films. Creatures of habit, they will also have drunk tea out of same mug for thirty years. Female collects ceramic figurines, usually pigs, elephants or serial killers.

Food

Regimented meal schedules. Meat pies on Mondays, spaghetti on Tuesdays, macaroni cheese on Wednesdays, pork chops on Thursdays, fish and chips on Fridays, Chinese takeaway on Saturdays, roast on Sundays. 'Twas ever thus and always will be.

Breeding

All fantasy role play accepted as long as everyone's wearing their slippers.

Movements and migrations

Beaded car seat covers non-negotiable. Consider self-catering holidays with disdain and bewilderment. Will only contemplate hotel holidays with lots of daily organised activities. Very competitive. Usually to be found in a Ford Sierra, the male insists on driving, even if drunk and will ALWAYS wear his leather driving gloves even if he's topless and shoeless. Females spice up car journeys by singing the musical *Les Miserables* from start to finish.

Distribution

Population appears stable, although breeding between wild and domesticated Travoltees has created confusion just south of Bangor. Although found all over the British Isles, densities are low in fen areas and in any town that doesn't have a karaoke bar.

THE MARVO

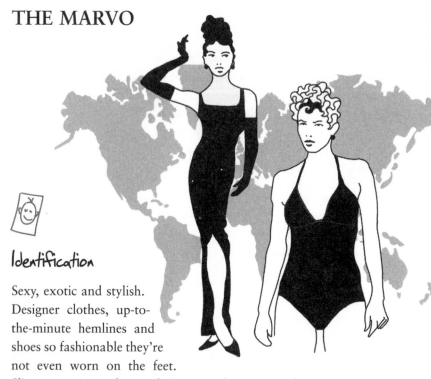

Identification

Sexy, exotic and stylish. Designer clothes, up-to-the-minute hemlines and shoes so fashionable they're not even worn on the feet. Slim, attractive and tanned. Cutting-edge noses and trend-setting foreheads. Devastate all who come before them. Can induce weak knees and spontaneous combustion.

Habits   YUK

Brilliant at everything, this astonishing breed can actually shit diamonds. Accomplished and suave, the Marvo wants for nothing. Swimming pools, helipads and falcons fill their every waking hour. Can whittle entire houses from the trunks of trees and lick their own elbows. Have been known to cure the blind.

Voice

Hypnotic. Like velvet chocolate in a honey glove. Too laid back ever to raise their voice, may say, 'Drugs? Want me to get you some?' or 'You want £25 for a prostitute? Here's £50. Get two.' May also wander in and announce, 'I've just discovered the cure for cancer' with the comfy nonchalance of someone picking their nose.

Habitat

Converted windmills, barns and abattoirs. Everything made from reclaimable and sustainable materials. Totally eco-friendly. All shelves smothered in awards. Supports conservatories for the homeless and steam rooms for orphans.

Food

It's langoustine this and quinoa that. Everything organic, picked or killed within twenty minutes of cooking. Everything made from scratch including pasta, ketchup and olive oil (requires three years' notice).

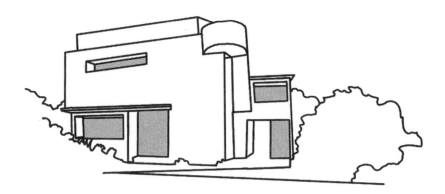

Breeding

Possess sexual charisma so intense that anyone who looks at them can become pregnant. Even men.

Movements and migrations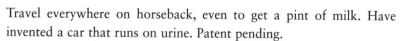

Travel everywhere on horseback, even to get a pint of milk. Have invented a car that runs on urine. Patent pending.

Distribution

Beyond rare. One breeding couple was once spotted in a coach house in Notting Hill. Other than that, unheard of.

So now we know what we're up against. But before we get our hands dirty with the nuts and bolts of the parental flat pack, let's stop a minute and try to understand where parents have come from and how they've been dealt with. Parents have existed since the dawn of time and, sadly, for most of that time they've had the upper hand. But with my help, you can change all that, so let's look now at some Parental Factoids.

Parents can be compounded into a very simple equation:

Maths!!

$$\frac{M \times B (Ph^3 - A)}{42}$$

Scientists working at the University of Slobodov during the 1950s discovered that if you multiply Ego (M) with Genetic Survival (B) by a factor of Laziness (Ph) to the power of three minus Panic (A) and divide that by the optimum age (42), you will have a parent.

Studies revealed that most adult males and females are driven to become parents not because they like each other but because the urge to continue the genetic line is as overpowering as a hungry leopard. Add in the fact that most adults can't be arsed to look after themselves in late middle age, coupled with a genuine terror of not having someone who can give you a kidney, and the reason to procreate is as obvious as a bucket of beetroot.

Before becoming a parent, the biological and chemical make-up of the male and female is exactly the same as for you or me, but as soon as a child is produced, fundamental changes take place at a cellular level. After birth, a chemical, Ramafoxenin, is released by the liver into the blood stream. In the female, this induces constant feelings of panic while the male experiences a sudden urge to put up shelves. The Ramafoxenin then binds with red blood cells to form a new organ, the Procnall Bladder, which sits just behind the left lung.

This then works in conjunction with the appendix (which lies dormant until you become a parent) to produce feelings of superiority and inadequacy in equal measure. It is this constant balancing act between feeling that your child might just be the greatest thing that ever walked the earth and an underwhelming sense that your child will only ever work at a supermarket check-out that creates the sort of parent you will be. It's not called the nervous system for nothing.

Procnall Bladder

But the Procnall Bladder isn't the only biological change that your parent will experience. Brains, up until you have a child, are uncomplicated organs. In the pre-parental brain, there is a sense of balance between the cerebellum and the cerebrum. From the moment a child is born, however, the brain is thrown into turmoil. The limbic system, which controls survival instincts and emotions, swells to ten times its original size. It remains engorged for the next eighteen years or until you leave home. At that point, the limbic region reduces only to be replaced by a swelling in the parietal lobe that confuses the sense of spatial awareness. As soon as you have left the parental home, therefore, your parent will have uncontrollable urges to invade your space on a constant basis and stare at you. A lot. But this isn't the only uncontrollable urge that your parent will experience.

Ivan Petrovich Pavlov was a Russian psychologist obsessed with gastric juices. Best known for his experiments with bells and dogs, Pavlov also conducted controversial clinical experiments on his parents. Pavlov's parents, Varvara and Peter Pavlov, were used to investigate conditional reflexes. These are the body's physical responses to situations without recourse to critical thinking.

Pavlov asked his mother to drive a car. While she was driving, Pavlov sat in the front passenger seat. Every time Varvara put her foot on the brake, Pavlov noticed, she would suddenly thrust her left arm out across Pavlov's chest in an attempt to protect him, even if they were only driving at ten miles an hour. Realising that his mother associated braking with danger, Pavlov began blowing a whistle every time Varvara placed her foot on the brake. After three weeks of conditioning, every time Pavlov blew the whistle, his mother, irrespective of where they were, would fling her arm across his chest. Pavlov could blow his whistle anywhere – standing in a bus queue or sitting on the toilet – it didn't matter. Whenever he blew that whistle, out came his mother's arm. Pavlov had managed to initiate a reflex action through the creation of a stimulus. His mother's sensory neurons reacted to the sound of the whistle and immediately initiated a muscular response. In his mother's brain, the whistle was the brake.

When it came to his father, Pavlov became aware that ten minutes after eating any meal, Peter would let rip with a fart of gargantuan proportions. For this experiment, Pavlov blew a trumpet every time his father broke wind. Again, after three weeks, every time Pavlov blew the trumpet, his father farted. In fact, the conditional reflex was so strong that if Pavlov played a tune, his father was able to accompany him. Hence the expression, 'I have trumped'.

Pavlov's experiments were revolutionary. They proved that parents' motor neuron responses are involuntary and, more importantly, that they're as easy to train as dogs. Pavlov conducted further research into the conditional reflexes in parents and discovered the following:

- *The Salivean reflex* (mothers only) – the uncontrollable urge to wipe dirt off your face using spit and a bit of tissue

- *The Zittilles reflex* (mothers only) – the compulsion to get your head in an arm lock and squeeze the blackheads on your nose

🦋 *The Phono-Tickerus reflex* (fathers only) – occurs when any teenager is on the telephone, inducing finger-tapping on the wristwatch while pulling an 'I'm paying for this' expression

🦋 *The Muconcarpeter reflex* (mothers only) – the merest sound of a shoe on a carpet initiating screams of 'Shoes! Shoes! Shoes!' and the sudden production of slippers.

But it's not just the biology of parents that we need to examine. In order to gain a more thorough understanding of the parent as a species, we need to study the laws of physics that govern them.

A physical law is a scientific generalisation based on observations of physical behaviour. Below are listed the ten laws of physics that apply to parents. Ignore them at your peril.

1. *The Anthropic Principle* states that the conditions necessary for the development of intelligent life will be met only in certain regions that are limited in space and time and will not include the inside of your mother's head if there is a small, attractive dog in the room.

2. *The Bore Magneton and the Bore Radius* states that the quantum of magnetic movement concerning you and your threshold of interest will be diminished within five square feet of any family gathering that lasts for over 48 hours.

3. *The Casimir Effect* is a quantum mechanical effect in which two objects placed close to each other will

experience an attractive force in the absence of other forces where the other forces are your parents and the objects are you and someone your parents don't like.

4. *Einstein's Constancy Principle* states that there can be nothing faster than the speed of light except the speed with which your father will get a stain out of the sofa before your mother sees it.

5. Copernicus stated it was the sun, not the earth that was the centre of the universe. *Neither are correct. You are.*

6. *Event Horizon* – the radius that a spherical mass must be compressed in order to transform it into a black hole, or the radius at which time and space switch responsibilities. Once inside the Event Horizon it is fundamentally impossible to escape to the outside. In other words, no, you can't get out of the family Christmas.

7. *Faraday's Fourth Law of Electrolysis* states that at the age of fifty, your mother will start complaining about growing a moustache.

8. *Kirchoff's Fourth Law* – an incandescent parent under high pressure will produce a continuous spectrum of complaints.

9. *Kirchoff's Loop Rule* –the sum of potential differences encountered in a round trip around any closed loop is infinite. In short, stuck in a car in a one-way system in a small market town with no map and a mother desperate for the toilet will cause explosions.

10. *The Magnus Effect* states that parents, once on the move, will drag you everywhere, especially if it's round a National Trust property.

So that's the science. Let's now look at the history. (OLD STUFF)

THE DAWN OF MAN

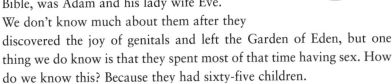

What came first? The child or the parent? Whatever you believe, early man's reliance on religion makes the argument moot. Original Sin has a lot to answer for. The first set of parents, according to the Bible, was Adam and his lady wife Eve. We don't know much about them after they discovered the joy of genitals and left the Garden of Eden, but one thing we do know is that they spent most of that time having sex. How do we know this? Because they had sixty-five children.

Is it any wonder that one of their sons, Cain, killed his brother Abel? Of course it isn't. If Adam and Eve weren't changing nappies or getting someone off to school, they were having more sex to make more babies. Never mind that their eldest son was smashing in his brother's skull, the only thing Adam and Eve had time for were each other's erogenous zones. These are the facts. Sixty-five children. It's in the Bible. I am merely the messenger. So Adam and Eve's terrible parenting skills bring us neatly to Rule Number One of Bringing Up Your Parents.

I'm going to write it in extra large letters so that you don't forget it.

NO MATTER WHAT YOU DO, EVER, EVEN IF YOU KILL YOUR BROTHER – IT'S ALWAYS YOUR PARENTS' FAULT

The main problem with Original Sin was that parents lived under the fervent misapprehension that children were the source of all evil. The fact that it was Adam and Eve, the parents, who were the cause of all the trouble was conveniently swept under the carpet; every child born was inherently bad, and unless they were subjected to rigorous beatings and puritanical teachings, the door to Hell's gate would forever be ajar. With this in mind, children were subjected to all manner of cruelties. Swaddling was a perennial favourite – wrapping babies into restrictive parcels so that crooked limbs could be nipped in the bud. But swaddling wasn't just about keeping younglings on the straight and narrow: an illustration from a seventeenth century almanac reveals that swaddled babies were actually used as badminton rackets.

Swaddled babies make handy badminton rackets

Fruit was another problem for our religious predecessors. Because Eve had partaken of the delights of the apple, fruit was considered dangerous and children were forbidden from eating it. Children, denied the essential vitamins that fruit provides, were riddled with scurvy, rickets and constipation. Not satisfied with keeping their children properly malnourished, parents then used to treat the ensuing childhood illnesses with medicines made from worms, snails' shells and powdered white dog turds.* 'Pity the children', said Jesus. And he was right.

*This is true. I read about it in a book: *Antiques and History of Child Care* by Sally Kevill Davies.

THE DARK AGES

Even though man had discovered things like the wheel and wooden spoons, matters did not improve for the younger members of the family. During the early seventh century, a German blacksmith called Witlin Probert discovered, quite by accident, that if you melt down a seven-year-old, you can actually make base metal. This led to centuries of abuse where each family was required, by law, to give up one child at the age of seven who would then be melted down and turned into horseshoes.

Children during this period of history had their hands tied – often literally because they were sometimes spit roasted to get their parents through lean winter months. Just like owls, parents gave birth to a multitude of offspring. Not because they liked children but because they were easier to catch than bears. Children's only chance of survival was to stab their parents while they were sleeping. That was as good as it got.

Recipe for base metal!
1 seven year old child (melted)

THE MIDDLE AGES

The Middle Ages were an unsettling time for child and parent alike. Spain had gone mad and made a three-year-old boy their King. The Spanish Infanta's first decree was for a bag of biscuits to be made Archbishop , his second to declare war on France. England was rattled, and to prevent the 'madnesse' spreading, King Edmund passed new laws that prevented a child ever becoming King of England, carving teeth or looking at parsnips.

Power struggles began breaking out in Colchester and, led by a bold eight-year-old, Lambit Tarcup, an angry mob of children managed to storm a farmers' market in Culpepper. Roused by Lambit's precocious rhetoric to 'bringe kaos and notte go to bedde', hoards of pre-teens pelted their parents with root vegetables for three days. Determined to quell the youngsters' riot, King Edmund rode to Culpepper with a small army and broke the children's barricade by releasing a score of puppies into their ranks. The King was unflinching in his punishment and ordered Lambit to be hung. He then ordered the other children to draw him (one picture remains – see below) before having him quartered.

But it wasn't all going the parents' way. Modern copies of *The Canterbury Tales*, by Geoffrey Chaucer, end with 'The Parson's Tale'. But there was actually a 25th tale, 'The Younge Scampe's Tale', which was cut at the last minute due to legal reasons. In it, Chaucer celebrates an infamous incident.

Sadly only extracts remain…

Whilom ther was dwellynge in London
A poore childe with parentes maddon
Whit was her smok, with likerous eye
Hir hayr col blak silk, with rybon for tye
"Lo childe!" cryde the Mother, fulsome and fatte
"Com washen dyshes and trym beefe. No blat
Lik a smalle lambe shalle I heare whilst ye chore
For if I heare one blat I'll selle ye to whore."
Than is the younge lass meet by the Father
"Lo Childe!" quoth he, alle drunken and lather,
"Runne faste lik the ratte who flees from the knife
"And place bette on hoss and don't telle the Wife."
"Com Mother, Com Father." quoth gentlee the childe
"And sup from this cuppe filled with unction alle milde.
A potion for bothe, to soothe and make gentil
I mayde it from pees and crabbe and greene lentile.
Drinke up parentes two, ye wille not regrette
And this kindeness I sho ye wille never forgette."
Thus drinketh the two, and fore veree long
Bothe Mother and Father were fallen upon
The ground where they laye stiffe and quite deade
"Oh dear, "quoth the childe, "I haff made my bedde.
And nowe I shall lye in it and laughe tille I crye
For the childe lives on and the parentes do dye."

Gruesome perhaps, but far from shocking. It's what children had to do to avoid being sold to Egyptians and being crushed down to make pyramids. Yes. That is what happened.

a sad, sad tale

THE RENAISSANCE

New worlds were being discovered and artists could now draw hands, but still the misery of childhood rattled on. It was the age of fads and fashions, and parents, distracted by the allure of the potato and the frisson of tobacco, didn't give their children a second thought. But the demand for anything new didn't just lead to neglect. In 1622 Thomas Middleton wrote a play, *The Changeling*. It was an overnight sensation. The 'changeling', was a fairy child substituted for a human baby, and suddenly everyone wanted one. Children all over England found themselves tied to mulberry bushes or pinned on willows and then left 'to turne faerie'. Tragically, many succumbed to the elements and died from hypothermia, while others were snatched by eagles, but a lucky few were saved by a remarkable woman who, single-handed, turned the tide of children's fortunes forever.

parents didn't give their children a second thought

Matilda Yesterday was, on the face of it, an ordinary woman. Contemporary articles report her as being 'plaine, with muche fleshe, crook o' nose, stoope of back and slighte smelle o' pisse, in shorte, a rare beautie'. She lived in a modest dwelling within sight of Hampton Court where she worked as a 'muslin mayde', churning milk to make cheese. Towards the end of 1622, when the craze for 'changelings' was at its height, Matilda came across a tree 'filled of strange fruite'. The 'strange fruit' were babies, all left to be turned to fairies. The young cheese maid was so moved by their wailings that she felt compelled to lift them down and take them back to her lodgings, where she cared for them by feeding them on cheese shavings and butter lumps. By the end of that year, Miss Yesterday's Orphanage was infamous. Not only did she now have

eighty-four babies under her care but they were the fattest babies in England. News of her endeavours soon reached Court, and she was summoned to an audience with the Queen. Official records describe the encounter thus:

'Of Ms Matilde Yes'erdaye, a mayde. Summon'd to the presence of her gloryous Majestie Queene Elizabethe in the year of 1623. Prayse Godde. On fyndyng babes in woodes and other brambles, this mayde dide give them comffort. Oure Magnyfycente Queene dide expresse wonderment at suche devotione and mayde gifte of patronage in the summe of One hundrede golde coynes. Prayse be.'

So influenced was society by the plight of the changeling babies that parents began actively taking an interest in their children. There was a small blip in the ointment when Matilda was caught giving her young charges draughts of laudanum and arsenic to 'mayke sleepe com more quickly', but cut the woman some slack. Everyone's allowed to make mistakes. Children were now the centre of attention. But that came at a price.

THE RESTORATION

Children were now top of the agenda. Parents were falling over themselves to produce the perfect child. Births were now celebrated with the gifting of 'layettes', a hamper of clothes, toys and equipment deemed necessary for a newborn's needs. Parental devotion was now so fashionable that the more excessive layettes became status symbols. Compare the contents of this modest layette issued in 1763 by the Cranston Foundling Hospital, a charitable institution for distressed womenfolk:

A lump of soap
One candle
2 swaddlebands
5 calico clouts (nappies)

… with this extravagant layette as prepared by the Duchess of Gisborne for her son Godric:

7 linen biggins (bonnets)
62 silk clouts
12 cot blankets
4 bootees (golden soles)
6 knited petticoats
5 fancy bibs
4 nightgown (chilprufe)
Powder box
Snuff box
Jack in the box
One kite
The Bishop of Leeds
A pony
25 sailors
The village of Penton
Brace of pheasant
Collar of brawn

Silver Chamberpot
12 ruby brushes (soft)
Quart of ale
3 prostitutes
Portugal
2 velvet matinee jackets
1 whipping boy
1 Mad woman in attic
A quantity of gravel
18 bleeding cups
2 kneeling stools
4 puking bowls
Small stuffed bear

Appearance was everything, and the desire for perfection didn't just extend to the material. Children were now expected to be beautiful, and if they weren't then corrective devices were applied. Splints constrained legs, corsets cramped chests, and iron sheaths were screwed onto noses to improve profiles. Wooden collars and back-boards were worn to improve posture, and parents would think nothing of forcing children to stand all day, some boards even bearing spikes so that any form of relaxation was impossible.

Coffee had recently come to England, and there was a widespread belief that giving it in large quantities to children would improve their learning. A letter to the famous diarist Samuel Pepys from his sister laments that 'after the giving of five quarts of coffee, your nephew Thomas failed to so sleep for the best part of a fortnight'. Thinking that this new state of 'alertness' was to do with an expanded mind rather than an overdose of caffeine, children were often placed in harnesses hung from ceiling beams. This enabled the parents to go to bed while their children remained awake. Hanging from the ceiling they were unable to get into 'mischeef'; not only that but a surgeon, John Owen Cooper, discovered that if you hung two children over a beam and then attached the ends of the harnesses to your ankles then 'a bad backe would awake much refreshed'. Children were beginning to have a purpose.

Nose sheaths 1771

THE VICTORIANS

The Victorian era couldn't have started better for children. The young Queen had bagged herself a looker in Prince Albert and couldn't get enough of him. One cock ring and nine children later, and it was all about the kids. It was Sunday walks here and perambulators there, unless you were very poor, in which case your children could just look forward to being poisoned by lead. But, rich or poor, everyone loved their children. Or at least they did until Prince Albert died and, like an end-of-the-line steam engine, it was all change. Racked with grief, the Queen decided that if she wasn't going to get any, then she was damned if anyone else was. The backlash against sex had begun, and while the sovereign railed against 'arousing' table legs and 'whorish' ankles, the frontline of the Queen's assault was reserved for everyone's favourite hobby: masturbation.

The Queen bagged herself a looker in Prince Albert and couldn't get enough of him

The Victorians were obsessed with stopping their children masturbating. Children couldn't even scratch themselves without arousing suspicion. Special 'fluid tongs' were designed so that boys could urinate without having to touch their own penis. Not only that, but button flies were removed from the front of trousers and replaced with fastenings at the rear so that there could be no chance of lightly skimming any part of the penis with a finger while getting dressed. So worried were some parents that their charges were within millimetres of damnation that they actually had their sons' arms amputated. Rather a lifetime of eating with your feet that a moment of onanistic madness. And to make doubly sure, they had their sons fitted with 'penis boxes' which obscured the offending member from sight and thought.

But for the poorer members of Victorian society, penis boxes were unaffordable so they stopped their children having unholy moments by plain knackering them out. The Industrial Revolution was a devastating time for children of the poor. Child labour became the norm, with children as young as five being forced to work in the flax mills and lace factories that were springing up all over the country. Starting at six in the morning, many wouldn't finish work until nine at night, and only a lucky few could expect time off for lunch. Forced to stand for hours on end, many developed physical deformities and, as a result, were disabled for life. Poor things. Still, at least they weren't wanking. And that was the main thing.

Penis boxes
— only for the
rich members
of Victorian
society

THE MODERN REVOLUTION   *HOORAH!*

Ironically, it was the hardships suffered at the end of the nineteenth century that were to reverse children's fortunes once and for all. Reformers like Lord Shaftesbury, who pushed to reduce children's working hours, and Seebhom Rowntree, who loved children so much he invented fruity chewy sweets, were starting to make an impact. Children could now no longer be abused without consequences. But it was the birth of the teenager that was to be the real breakthrough.

In post-war Britain, children were about to have their brains melted by the crazy drug Rock, and also Roll. Suddenly, no one wanted to like or be like their parents. It was time to rebel, and if you weren't sporting a haircut that would embarrass you in later life, you were nobody. Running wild, turning bad, smoking and puking on your shoes – these were the new hopes and dreams. Teenagers were now so very revolting that if they weren't pregnant or spaffed out on crack, parents thought they had a prodigy. And so we find, for the first time in history, that children have the upper hand. All your parent longs for is for you to be nice to them. Oh! How the tables are turned!

The
Practical
Problems
Section

So you've got some parents. But what do you do with them? Before we look at the practical problems, let's set out some ground rules. You can apply these in any given circumstance. Always remember that dealing with your parents is as easy as crossing the road. That road may be a busy five-lane motorway , but with a bit of nifty footwork and a splash of good fortune, your spongy fontanelles can avoid being crushed by the parental juggernaut.

So here are the three Golden Rules:

* **SARCASM WILL GET YOU EVERYWHERE**
* **SUDDEN-ONSET DEAFNESS IS BRILLIANT**
* **IF IN DOUBT, JUST IGNORE IT**

I have two parents. One is called Hysterical Mum Brenda. The other is called Welsh Dad Tony. Before we get cracking, let's take a few moments to meet the family.

Hysterical Mum Brenda

A classic Faffer, HMB is only a hair's breadth from danger at any given moment. Talking in a voice that only dogs can hear, terror is everywhere, and it's her job to make sure that everyone knows it. Crazy schemes are a speciality and, when combined with an unshakeable belief that she's NEVER wrong, you've got accidents waiting to happen. Unusual for her breed in one respect – she is completely incapable when it comes to practical skills. She can't cook, she can't drive and she treats tap water with suspicion. An armchair feminist, she believes that all men are awful but has been married, very happily, for forty years. When questioned on this discrepancy, she always replies 'Your father doesn't count.'

completely incapable when it comes to practical skills

Welsh Dad Tony

A Practibot through and through. His anecdotes on the merits or otherwise of the St Ippolyts bypass are the stuff of legend. Thorough and meticulous, this Practibot won't do anything unless it's been discussed, dissected and reassembled for at least five days. Obsessed with parking, road works and rush hours, WDT won't go anywhere unless a two-hour margin for error has been factored in and, once executed, will be talked about in a military style debrief for anything up to 72 hours. Brilliant at cooking, his crème caramels can induce mass hysteria. A skilled linguist, WDT can ask for two beers in eight languages.

can ask for two beers in eight languages

Poppy, My Most Excellent Beagle

Look at this dog and remember her face. Feel yourself being sucked into her vortex? Experiencing the urge to give her treats? Yes. That's because she is EVIL. Poppy is a five-year-old beagle with warts on one ear. Hobbies include trotting like a pony, walking sideways like a crab and masturbating. Obsessed with food, this ravenous hound has stolen loaves of bread, packets of biscuits and (her particular speciality) bags of apples. Canny and inventive, she's taught herself how to push a chair across the kitchen to the kibble jar, how to tip over the pedal bin and how to use a plastic bag to open a low set of drawers so she can gain access to a pot of vegetable peelings. She is my mother's pride and joy. I regard her with nothing but suspicion.

I regard her with nothing but suspicion

These are the members of my family. Using WDT and HMB as our template, let's now look at some common tricky scenarios.

COMPULSORY ATTENDANCE DAYS

CADs are unavoidable. Whether it's Mother's Day, birthdays or that enfant terrible, Christmas, your hands are well and truly tied. It would be very easy to begrudge the amount of time you have to devote to CADs, but look at it this way – everyone you know is ALSO obliged to roll out the carpet of attendance so you're not missing out on anything. My advice is to relax, give in to it and remember that it will all be over within 48 hours. Think of CADs as a quick and violent bout of diarrhoea – it might not be pleasant at the time, but you will always feel better afterwards.

The trick to CADs is quite simple:

TRY NOT TO HAVE AN ARGUMENT WITH ANYONE, EVEN THAT FAMILY MEMBER WHO NEVER HELPS OUT WITH THE WASHING-UP AT CHRISTMAS

And always bear in mind that:

IT DOESN'T MATTER HOW BORED YOU ARE, YOUR PARENTS FIND YOU FASCINATING

CADs are powder kegs waiting to blow. Chances are at least one member of the family is going to get drunk. If you've got a Muzzerfuzz, that's a given. Add into the mix a board game that someone's taking WAY too seriously and you've got an incendiary device that could obliterate a family of four. So wipe every slate clean and make like the Swiss. The more neutral you can be, the less likely it'll be that you'll experience the volcanic force of a CAD gone pear-shaped.

CADs are times to make your parents just about as happy as they ever will be. They love it when you come home because it reminds them of when you were seven and still thought everything they said was reasonably significant. Unless you've got the terrible parental combination of a Double Wassername, you are guaranteed to be welcomed in with open arms. Think of CADs as banking goodwill. If you can pull this one out of the bag, you'll be in a stronger position to ask one or both of them to help you clear your drains.

So let's work through some on-the-button experiences between HMB, WDT and me.

Scenes from a Mothering Sunday (in no particular order)

Celebrating the Mother in all her forms is no bad thing. Perhaps you've bought her a card. Maybe you've got her some flowers. What is certain is that you've had to go home and spend all day with her. But what sort of things can happen? Let's take a look.

NUMBER ONE
'Where's my eyeliner! Tony! Where is it?' screams HMB with a sense of panic only previously experienced by the crew of the *Titanic*.
'In your hand.'
'Oh.'

NUMBER TWO
HMB, me and WDT are dancing to 'Automatic' by the *Pointer Sisters* in the sun lounge. Poppy, My Most Excellent Beagle, looks on with disdain.
'Look what you done to me, I'm totally at your whim, all of my senses down.....badabadabeebop,' sings HMB.
'Do you think I'm just brilliant at dancing?' says WDT, swaying with confidence.
Everyone stops and stares at him.
'No.'

Remember card for Mom

NUMBER THREE

'This has been a lovely walk hasn't it?' says HMB, smiling.
small kerfuffle on the floor to our left
'Aaaaaaaaaaaaaaaaaaaaaaaaagh!' scream all three of us, looking down
to see a wood pigeon being ravaged by a sparrow hawk. Right there!
hawk sees us, flies off
'Aaaaaaaaaaaagh!' we all scream again.
*wood pigeon flails on its back, turns its head towards us and stares at us
with one yellow eye. The sort of stare that will haunt you till the end of days*
'Aaaaaaaaaaaaaaaaaaaaaaagh!' we all scream. And run off.

NUMBER FOUR

'I'll just go and see if that wood pigeon's still there,' announces WDT,
brandishing a heavy implement. 'If it's suffering, I'll deal with it.'
HMB grips chest and nods
'Oh Tony!' shouts HMB, after he's left the room.
'Yes?' shouts WDT back.
'Don't catch bird flu!'
'All right!'

NUMBER FIVE

'The pigeon is dead.'
'Oh no,' say I.
'Did you kill it?' asks HMB, clutching at her jumper.
'No. The sparrow hawk is eating it. Anyway. Lunch is ready.'

the infamous pigeon fiasco!

NUMBER SIX

'Your great grandfather was a Romany gypsy,' says WDT, pointing at
an old black and white photo.
'What? A proper one?' say I, raising an eyebrow.
'Oh yes. He played the drums and everything.'
'Is that what Romany gypsies did then? Play the drums?' asks HMB.
'I thought they sold pegs. They cornered the peg market. They were
peg entrepreneurs.'
'No,' says WDT, 'he didn't sell pegs.'

'What? Not even one?' says HMB, furrowing her brow.

'No.'

'No wonder this family has never made any money,' sighs HMB, staring out of the window. 'Bad genes.'

NUMBER SEVEN

'I keep thinking about that pigeon,' says HMB, whispering.

'Nature in the raw,' says WDT, folding his arms.

'It's a shame *Planet Earth* weren't there to film it,' nods HMB. 'Or Tony Robinson.'

'You mean Bill Oddie,' say I.

'No,' says HMB emphatically. 'I mean Tony Robinson.'

draw your own conclusions to fade

THE SOLUTION

OK. So there's a lot here. Let's break it down. Obviously, the day is dominated by the incident of a wood pigeon being ravaged to death in front of our tender eyes. Now something like that isn't going to happen every day, but it's an incident that helps us understand our parents in two ways. First, the Dad will always be quietly pleased when things like this happen because it allows him to go out and give the impression that he's almost useful. Second, it allows the Mum to come over a bit Jane Austen.

Note how I mostly keep my mouth shut throughout. In moments of intense family experiences, you will generally come out on top if you (a) play dumb and (b) just let them get on with it. Your objective, every time you find yourself back in the parental home, is to do as little as possible. Parents like it when you come home and will be willing to do everything for you. So just sit tight. In any perceived crisis, parents expect NOTHING of you. So don't disappoint them.

The more alert of you will have noted HMB's mention of bird flu.

мotner's dials are always set to worse-case scenario. WDT just agrees with her here, of course. He's not stupid. Learn from him.

Mother's Days are the catalyst for the annual trawl though the old family albums. You've heard all the stories every year for about as long as you can remember, but don't let that put you off. Consider it Quiet Time, where you can reflect on your immediate ancestral past, marvel at how you look so much like your mother's cousin Pauline and enjoy either parent's theories on why the family is not what it might be. Parents feel constant guilt that they're not Sir Alan Sugar. Don't bother putting them right. You've got to work your arse off because your parents couldn't be bothered. So let them worry.

Mother's days are the catalyst for the annual trawl though the old family albums

Most parents don't quite understand television or anyone on it. Anything that can't be wound up with a key is going to cause them problems. I make a mistake here by attempting to explain that my Mother has become confused. Never do this. Mothers refuse to accept that they're wrong and when questioned switch to Automatic Bullshit, a tide that not even the Thames Barrier can stop.

Acceptable conversations during a parent's birthday

It's almost too obvious to see written on a page but, for the love of God – keep it simple! There are plenty of safe topics of conversation that are never going to get you into trouble. These can include:

- The weather
- How nice the garden's looking and
- Steaming vegetables rather than boiling them (blind them with science).

But whatever you do, make sure YOU'RE IN CHARGE. Let one parent take control of the conversation and you're in more trouble than a virgin at a whorehouse. Let's see what happened to me at the 65th birthday of WDT.

'Do you think I look like Camilla Parker Bowles?' asked HMB, staring at me over the dinner table.
'Camilla Parker Bowels,' I corrected.
'Yes,' said HMB, looking very concerned. 'But do I?'

We had gathered en famille centre ville for the official celebrations of the 65th birthday of WDT. 'I'm an old-age pensioner! I'm an old-age pensioner!': that was his catchphrase. We had been chatting about the forthcoming royal wedding and I had just finished telling them about my brilliant idea for a spinning dead Diana (if it's tastefully done, it's fine) when HMB blurted out her worries.

I stared at her. She couldn't look less like Camilla Parker Bowels if she tried.

'You couldn't look less like Camilla Parker Bowels if you tried,' said I, to prove my point.
'Hmmm,' said HMB, not convinced. 'The thing is, we met the Keppels.'
'As in Judith Keppel who won the million?' said I, wanting to know where all this was going.
'Yes,' said HMB.
'But not Judith Keppel,' said WDT, who is an old-age pensioner. 'She wasn't there.'
'No,' added HMB, 'she wasn't there. And the thing was, I really looked like them.'
'Hang on,' said I. 'You just thought you looked like Camilla Parker Bowels, now you look like the non-Judith Keppels. What is this?'
'Well, it's obvious isn't it?' said HMB, looking straight at me. 'I'm clearly not who I think I am.'

'Mum,' said I. 'This isn't *The Prince and the Pauper*. Camilla Parker Bowels isn't really you, and you're not really Camilla Parker Bowels. Plus, you look nothing like Camilla Parker Bowels.'

'And your grandfather was the spitting image of Renoir,' said HMB. WDT nodded.

'In fact, when we went to Renoir's house, I told them he was my grandfather,' said HMB, smiling proudly. 'I said, "Renoir est mon grandpère"!'

'They all went nuts,' added WDT, nudging me.

'I'm not surprised,' said I. 'Using the present tense of the verb "to be". That's just shocking. Anyway. How old are you, Dad?'

'I'm 65!' said WDT, because he was a bit giddy. 'I'll get my pension next week!'

'Ha ha ha ha ha ha ha!' yelled HMB suddenly. 'I'm married to a pensioner!'

'Ha ha ha,' said WDT, throwing his arms in the air. 'I got four cards this morning,'

'Did you?' said I, in a slightly strangled tone.

'Yes,' added WDT. 'And three of them were from strangers.'

I kept quiet at this point and just stared.

'When I say strangers,' explained WDT, 'I mean people I know.'

'Hmm,' said I, thinking that through. 'If they're people you know, then they're not really strangers.'

'You know what I mean,' said WDT.

'Hmm. Anyway. What do you want for your birthday, Dad?' said I, moving swiftly on from the non-card thing.

'He doesn't want anything!' shouted HMB.

'No,' said WDT. 'I don't want anything. Apart from a *Spiderman* DVD.'

'*Spiderman* DVD?' said I.

'And a *Spiderman 2* DVD,' shouted HMB.

'Yes, and a *Spiderman 2* DVD,' said WDT. 'But honestly I don't want anything.'

'Perhaps I can get a stranger to get those for you,' said I.
'I don't understand,' said WDT.

Nothing new there then.

THE SOLUTION

Ugly. No two ways about it. Note how I tried to parry HMB's theorems with corrections and questions. This was my mistake. Questions fan the flames of any conversation topic that has been introduced at random by an out-of-control parent. JUST DON'T ASK THEM! Note also how I try TWICE to steer the conversation back onto an approved topic – asking your parent's age and what they want are perfectly acceptable questions at this stage of the game. But in this scenario, it's clutching at straws. The damage has already been done. Both parents are ripped to the tits with excitement. This is going to be a very long day.

Watching a sport that one of them doesn't understand

As often as possible, apart from Christmas when it's unavoidable, the general rule when you're back in the parental home must be NEVER WATCH TELEVISION WITH YOUR PARENTS. Not only will one

don't even mention the offside rule...

or both of them provide a running commentary that will render pointless having the television on in the first place, but it's an absolute certainty that if it's a sport or a reality TV show that they've never seen before, then everything will need explaining. Let's take a look at an incident that took place during the Winter Olympics 2006.

'What is this?' asked HMB, gesturing towards the television with the smell of disdain.
'Curling,' said WDT and I, in unison.

'Why is it in the Olympics?' continued HMB. 'It's just a bunch of men flash-mopping the kitchen floor.'

'It's like bowling,' said WDT. 'But on ice. Or pétanque. But on ice. And not so thrown. That's what it is. It's mostly just on ice.'

'It's a very technical sport,' said I, folding my arms.

'What's technical about flash-mopping the kitchen floor?' asked HMB. 'I could do that. Why aren't I at the Olympics?'

'Limpics,' said I. 'Please use its proper name.'

'Hang on a minute,' added WDT, throwing HMB a puzzled look. 'When have you ever flash-mopped the kitchen floor?'

'That's not the point,' said HMB, throwing her face into an arrangement that some would call imperious. 'If I wanted to flash-mop the kitchen, I would. And if I did, I expect I would be brilliant at it.'

WDT and I exchanged a look.

'It's a shame,' continued HMB, 'Because in many ways I'm denying the nation a Sporting Heroine.'

'Do you think you could pick up one of those stones?' said I, turning to look at her.

'Oh no,' said HMB.

'And could you slide on one slippy shoe?' asked WDT.

'Oh no,' said HMB.

'Yeah,' said I. 'You're a regular Kelly Holmes.'

'I am;' said HMB, 'now where's Poppy?'

'She's eating a bar of Imperial Leather,' said WDT, running off to stop her.

'See?' said HMB nodding. 'We're a family of achievers. Now what's on the other side?'

THE SOLUTION

The Bulgarian scientist Kopter Klimniks wrote that 'The physics of parents dictate that whenever one of them sees something they don't understand, they will instantly be better at it than any-one but, crucially, only in their own mind.' It was true in 1704 and it's still true today. This is a classic example of HMB turning non-compre-hension into unfulfilled glories. We're used to seeing this sort of sporting crowing from the male parent, of course, but I wanted you to see that the ladies are more than capable of living in the land of the trophy dead.

What is interesting here is how I bond with WDT in our subtle derision of HMB's physical prowess. This was a good move. It operates on the age-old premise of Divide and Conquer but is done in such a way as to be barely perceptible. It allows me to come in with a good dash of sarcasm – remember, sarcasm WILL get you everywhere – which, here, successfully draws the discussion to a close. You will know when the offending parent has backed down because he or she will always try and shift focus away from themselves. Using the dog, as HMB does here, is a masterly move, but I'm not fooled for a minute. Oh no.

Totally unrelated topics related to your birth   WHAT?!

During any given CAD, there is nothing that is going to come up in conversation more than any story connected to your birth . It's going to come up so often that you can expect anything and everything to spin off the back of it. You need to stay alert during these episodes. They can easily catch you unawares. Here's a typical example.

'I had to walk. WALK! For four hours!' screamed HMB, gesturing with her hand. 'The midwife just handed me over to two other pregnant women and told them to walk me round until I was ready to give birth. Then, after four hours, she came up and told me that I'd better hurry up and have this baby because she was going off shift.'
'Then your waters broke,' said WDT, because he knows this story inside and out.
'Then my waters broke,' nodded HMB, wagging a finger at her nether

regions. 'And the midwife came in, handed a sanitary towel to Tony and told him to clean me up.'

WDT shook his head but looked a bit proud at the same time.

'And your father was useless at the birth. All he did was stand there going "Oooh, look at the colours! The colours!" Bloody useless.'
'The colours were good,' said WDT.
'The whole thing was a shambles,' concluded HMB, who then stopped and looked out of the window for the moment.
'Still,' she added as an afterthought. 'It was the right way to do it.'
'Oh yes,' said WDT, who then thought about that for a minute.
'Talking of callow youths,' said WDT, after a bit more thinking, 'I went to Waitrose yesterday and two girls were on the meat counter. The meat counter. And I said, "Have you got some braising steak?", and they looked at each other and didn't know what I was talking about, and then one of them said, "Oh hang on mate, I think we got some up the back" and then went off and came back with a plastic pack of meat that was so dark I thought it was liver. So I said, "No thanks, I'll get some from the shelves." Girls. On a meat counter. It's not right is it?'
'No,' said HMB, shaking her head.
'But girls! On a meat counter!' said WDT as if nothing in this world would ever make sense.

THE SOLUTION

You wouldn't know it, but I was in the room with both HMB and WDT as this conversation was taking place. I was caught napping when the sudden shift came into play and, as a result, I'm nowhere. Don't make the same mistake as I did. ANY story about your birth can kick off conversational tangents that will leave you reeling. Be prepared. I shouldn't be too hard on myself in this instance as WDT's anecdotes can fell a horse at ten paces, but that to one side, the minute HMB started up with the birth thing, I should have been on my guard.

Parents telling stories that go nowhere *Bla, bla, bla...*

Parents feel it's their duty to talk without stopping for the entirety of your CAD stay. This is because they can never quite believe that they'll ever see you again. This, of course, can be extremely draining. I'm not saying that every time your parent opens his or her mouth it's going to be boring, but let's allow the facts to speak for themselves. In this next example, note how WDT works with HMB. It's a sort of Anecdote Tag that you can do very little about. You're outnumbered and the odds are stacked against you. But that doesn't mean you have to come out of it with a fat lip.

'Ohhh,' heaved HMB, who was sitting perched like a starving eagle on the edge of my sofa. 'I had an awful dream about Poppy.'
'Wait till you hear this,' added WDT, touching me on the knee.
'Just awful,' reiterated HMB, and shoved her glasses back up the bridge of her nose for emphasis.

WDT nodded and flashed me a grin.

'In my dream,' began HMB, 'I was walking along and I came across a ditch. Poppy,' she said, pointing with some urgency in the direction of that Most Excellent of Hounds, 'was buried in it. BURIED in it.'

WDT shook his head.

'And there was this evil cat who was sitting and smirking. Smirking! So I didn't know what to do. Because I had to get Poppy out. And thank God, I found a spoon.'
'A spoon?' said I, raising an eyebrow.
'Yes. A spoon,' said HMB, nodding with something of the look of the wild about her.
'A spoon!' repeated WDT.
'And I dug her out with it.'

The evil cat

HMB then sat back on the sofa and raised her arms as if nothing in this world or the next would ever be as plain and simple again.

No one said anything.

'And?' said I, because this story had been built up and thus far, I had not got what I paid for.
'No,' said HMB, folding her arms. 'That's it.'
'A spoon!' said WDT.
I want my money back.

THE SOLUTION

I think I did the best I could in the circumstances here. A lone parent telling a pointless story is easy to deal with – I refer you to the third Golden Rule – If in doubt, ignore it – but

Post cards!

when you've got both parents, all story guns blazing, then you've got about as much chance as a one-legged donkey in the Grand National. The trick here is not to even begin to try to understand what your parents find interesting. You may as well go for a diving holiday on the sun. In these situations, cut your losses and get the hell out.

Christmas

As CADs go, this one is the Daddy. It's the marathon of obligation, and if you turn up on Christmas Eve psychologically unprepared, then you are going to crash and burn. First and foremost – don't make the mistake I made in 1988 when I came home from university and was a bit of a smuggins because I thought I knew how to make brandy and champagne cocktails. A dash of too much here, and a sugar cube too many there and next thing I know, WDT is lying face down in the hall with his forehead up against the front door and HMB, thinking it's bedtime at three o'clock in the afternoon, forgets where I am and inadvertently locks me in the front room for six hours. I had to urinate into a vase. It wasn't pretty.

The rule then at this most crucial of CADs is:

 ## STICK TO WHAT YOU KNOW

Introducing any new element into the mix at Christmas is a disaster waiting to happen; whether it be a new board game or a new haircut – IT'S JUST NOT WORTH IT.

The week before Christmas is always a perilous one for my family unit. When I say 'family unit' I really mean Welsh Dad Tony, who is pathologically incapable of keeping anything secret. Let's examine an event that took place in 1979.

It was five days before Christmas, and I'm standing in the dining room conducting an experiment with an After Eight and a Brazil nut – namely, putting them in my mouth at the same time to see if they go together. Conclusion – quite good. Just as I was about to repeat the experiment, WDT taps me on the shoulder. I turn and look at him to see his finger on his lips, the International Mime for 'Sssssh. Or your mother will hear.' With a gesture for me to follow him, I put down my snack mixer and trot out after him through the back door, past the coal bunker and into the garage. In the garage, there's a large tarpaulin that seems to be draped over an indiscriminate shape.

'Do you want to know what's under that?' says WDT, eyes dazzling.

finger on lips – the International Mime for 'Sssssh'...

I shrug my shoulders. I'm still thinking about the minty nut frankenstein snack and wondering when I can get back to it.

At this point, WDT, sensing that he's on the verge of a big one, leans forward and pulls off the tarpaulin with a flourish. And there before me is a bright green, brand new, lady's racing bike. It's the most beautiful thing I've ever seen.

'Do you like it?' says WDT.
I stare at him.
'Dad,' say I, 'it's not Christmas yet.'
He stares at me.
'Hmm,' he says, 'don't tell your mother.'

But I did and didn't he catch it then. Weeeee-oooooh.
And this of course brings us neatly to one of the Essential Lessons of bringing up your parents :

DIVIDE AND CONQUER – DOB IN YOUR DAD

Snitching outside the family unit is, of course, despicable and worthy of an Amish-style Shunning, but when it comes to your parents, the earth's polarity actually REVERSES this rule, making it an essential part of your life as the child. The male parent will often do anything for a quiet life and nothing terrifies him more than the thought of being in trouble with the wife for anything he's done with regard to you. So make like a maid and milk it. You will gain the upper hand every single time.

Distant relatives

Brad's dinner?
(must find out who Brad is)

It's the three-line whip. An overseas relative is coming to dinner and woe betide you if you're not there. It doesn't matter if you've only met them once, twenty years ago. They're kin. You miss this one at your peril. Parents set great store on maintaining family ties and are keen to instil a sense of tribal pride. Offspring's natural thermometer on this matter is, sadly, set to Zero Interest, although, paradoxically, on meeting said distant relative that rises to Excessive Fascination as soon as the photo albums come out. This is a temporary state so don't panic. Normal half-arsed disdain will be resumed shortly.

I got a call from HMB.

'You haven't forgotten, have you?'

It was at that point that I realised I had forgotten and had managed to forget it so well that I didn't have the first clue what it even was.

'Brad's dinner,' said HMB.
'Brad?' said I, racking my brains for the
Brads in my life. (Conclusion – none. Surely?)
'Your cousin Brad. From America.'

THEM ——→ US
(too far to care)

It was at this point that my stomach lurched back to that moment in 1989 when I and my best friend Bee found ourselves standing on a wooden porch in a small town in North Carolina.

'This is like the Waltons,' said she. 'But gone all wrong.'

We had done that thing you do when you've just finished being a student and had decided to travel across a continent without a credit card or any immediate funds. We'd slept in toilet blocks and on forest floors, but as the dollars and cents crept out of our pockets, we were forced, for the latter stages of our trip, to stay with any random relative we could lay claim to. Bee had found a 'second cousin of my dad's' who worked in the tobacco business. He had an enormous house with a bar in the basement, which Bee and I, rather rudely, had drunk dry one evening while trying to smash his son's record on a truck-racing computer game. The experience had been lavish.

But now it was my turn, and I had dragged Bee off the beaten track to the house of a robust woman who laid claim to a tenuous connection with my father: 'They used to send me chewing gum,' WDT would tell me with a sense of pride.

'You remember Brad,' said HMB, punctuating my reverie. 'You stayed with him didn't you?'

'Yes,' said I, remembering it only too well. 'But I only saw him twice. Once when I arrived and then six days later at two in the morning . He woke me up to watch a video with him.'

'He did what?' asked HMB

'I was in bed and I woke up. And Brad was standing over me and staring. I said, "Hello". He said, "Do you want to see a movie?" So I said, "Yes, all right then." And I got up, followed him to his room and he stuck on *Texas Chainsaw Massacre*. It's his favourite film. So yes, I do remember him. THAT Brad.'

'So don't forget. He's coming for dinner today. And he's staying over. Are you going to stay too?'

'Why not?' said I. 'Perhaps I can get my revenge and wake him up to watch *Who Will Love My Children*?'

'Good. So don't be late,' insisted HMB.

'Did you hear what I just told you?' said I.

'And put a skirt on,' answered she. And that, ladies and gents, was that.

THE SOLUTION

The reason I've picked this out as a problem is so we can discuss HMB's behaviour in this scenario. Note how she doesn't flinch one iota on being told that her daughter has had a strange man staring at her while she's sleeping only to get her up to watch one of the more notorious slasher movies of our times. Surely this goes against every Faffer grain? In normal circumstances, she'd be in an advanced state of panic, but (and here comes the science bit) the fact Brad is a distant relative and requires entertaining immediately cancels out any concerns for the safety of her own child. In the land of the distant relative, misplaced social etiquette is king. Just accept it. If he wants to chop you up and wash you down with a nice chianti, your mother's going to let him.

HOLIDAYS

do I HAVE to go?

Holidays with your parents can actually be enjoyable up to your twelfth birthday. In slow-developing boys, that enjoyment window can even extend into their sixteenth year. But for most children aged thirteen and up, the concept of the family holiday is a horror so intense it would make the sight of a demonically possessed woman crawling at you at speed seem as threatening as a fish finger. Let's be honest, as soon as you've hit your difficult teenage years, your tolerance levels for staying in a tent where the only entertainment is some piss in a bucket becomes non-existent.

There's only one thing you can do as a teenager on holiday with your parents and that's wander around looking miserable. In fact, the more stunning the landmark, the more disinterested your face will be. Blackpool Illuminations? Whatever. Taj Mahal? Toss off. Your only scrap of hope is to find other teenagers on holiday, join forces and lump yourselves into a permanently mortified mass. Whether it's your dad running about in horrific trunks or your mother walking around with potatoes in her handbag, the family holiday is a torture so dreadful that even if your parents had arranged for you to go to Mars, meet proper aliens and have a go driving the Millenium Falcon , you would still think it was shit. That is just the way it is.

But as you get a bit older, you enter into trickier territory. For starters, you are no longer revolting as an individual, and suddenly the idea of a holiday that has been arranged and paid for by someone else doesn't seem so bad. In fact, it seems brilliant. But hang on, here's the catch – it means spending anything upwards of a week with your parents. And this time, you can't skulk off and play endless games of table tennis or hang around at the back of toilet blocks in the hope that someone's managed to half-inch a litre bottle of cider.

The problem here is one of expectation. Your parents, no matter how old you are, will always be as keen as mustard to have you tag along on any jaunt. My advice here is very clear:

JUST SAY NO

... unless they've rented a lovely villa in Italy and it's got a pool, in which case how quickly can you get to a bureau de change? This may seem harsh, but having conducted experiments under laboratory conditions I can now reveal that, irrespective of your age or profession, you will revert to your revolting fifteen-year-old self within three hours and 47 minutes of going on holiday with your parents. For the sake of everyone, leave it alone.

Let's look now at some common pitfalls that can be easily avoided.

So you've been on holiday without them

Always dangerous. Parents need to know every last thing you do on holiday, including your bowel movements. A friend of mine was always given a Poo Chart to fill in by her father whenever she went abroad. Here is her Poo Chart from a trip to the Greek island of Karpathos in 1986.

So you've arrived home and the parents have come round. See if you can spot the very obvious mistake that I make in the following real encounter.

'So what was the house like?' screamed HMB.

'Well,' said I, thinking that question through to its logical conclusion. 'It was very nice but, I don't know, there was a slightly spooky vibe. You know, like maybe some sort of evil spirit lived there.'

'You mean like a stuffed monkey in a cupboard?' asked HMB, in a heartbeat.

'Sorry,' said I, 'a stuffed monkey? In a cupboard?'

'Yes,' said HMB. 'Very evil. Very. Evil.'

'Have you ever come across a stuffed monkey in a cupboard?' asked I.

'Oh no,' said HMB, with a sense of massive relief. 'Oh, no.'

'But if you did,' probed I, 'then that would be very evil would it?'

'Oh yes.'

'Hmm. But what if the house belonged to a taxidermist. Or a lover of monkeys? In those circumstances, you would expect to see a monkey in a cupboard. Surely?'

'If I found a stuffed monkey in a cupboard,' began HMB, leaning forward to emphasise the point, 'then I would call your father, tell him to pack the bags and we would leave immediately.'

'But hang on,' interjected my dad, who, despite all evidence to the contrary was actually in the room. 'It's only a stuffed monkey. And I would have worked out all the day trips. And I would have written out all the directions. In pencil, admittedly.'

'I don't care,' said HMB, wagging a finger. 'I'm not staying in any house that has a stuffed monkey in its cupboards.'

'Oh well,' sighed WDT, folding his arms. 'At least we'd be on time for the flight home. I'm trying to think of something that would be quite evil if I found it in a cupboard. A dismembered body part would be quite bad. As would a voodoo doll with pins. Especially if, by some trickery, it had my name on it. In that case, and that case only, and perhaps only then after the walls had started bleeding and voices were telling me to stab people in the neck while chopping garlic, then I might think about giving up my holiday and going home. But to be honest, if the weather was nice and there was enough wine to go round, then I think I'd put up with even that. Cup of coffee anyone?'

THE SOLUTION

Well, it's obvious, isn't it? I made reference to something that was almost bad. It's a schoolboy error. Parents are like bats when it comes to picking up tiny references to near-unpleasant experiences. They don't even need to hear them. They can sense them through their over developed Bad Things radar. You can have this surgically removed (see left).

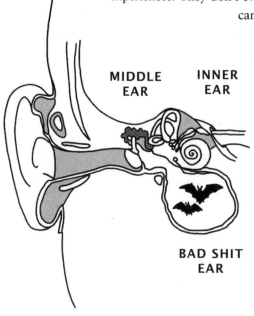

MIDDLE EAR

INNER EAR

BAD SHIT EAR

But what's the point? It's not available on the NHS, and medical studies on the procedure's effectiveness have been inconclusive at best. No. The best policy is just never to say anything that could be construed as a negative experience. Especially when talking about your holidays. Unleash that monster at your own peril.

LETTERS HOME

It goes without saying that every time you go on holiday, they want constant updates, so the odd postcard is going to keep their happy clocks ticking over. HMB always writes pages of letters when she's on holiday. Let's have a look at one of them now and see what it can teach us about the Parental Psyche.

My dear love,

We had a good night in Paris, caught the TGV to Dijon, picked up the car and headed south for Cluny which is approx half an hour from Trambley where we are staying for two nights. It is in the middle of forested hills and quite isolated with only farms and a few cottages spread miles apart.

The apartment is filled with beautiful art and pottery and various marble mantels and fireplaces which the owner has made (he restores sculpture). The bathroom is filled with soothing, perfumed unguents, strangely shaped tools for massage, oils and candles. Since I never use such things, I've been squeezing bits on my hands to give the impression that I have not ignored the generosity offered.

(At this point in the letter the following has been written in big, bold caps by WDT)

BATHROOM TOUR LASTED HALF AN HOUR - D

Well, *(continues HMB)* then the drama began. We were both very tired and in need of showers and hair washings, etc. I couldn't have a bath as it was a hip bath, nearly four feet high but I managed to use the shower fixtures to wash my hair. I then went into the bedroom to dry my hair. All I was wearing was a white T shirt which had some nylon in it and clung rather tightly to my Jordan bosoms. As I had the hairdryer going I was unaware of a woman, a STRANGER (!), entering our apartment.

Tony by now was in the shower. The shower must be clearly visualised. It was enormous - bow shaped and fully see through. Tony being deaf couldn't hear that a STRANGE woman had entered. She started calling 'Excusez-moi! Excusez-moi!' as she stood, mouth agape at Tony in the shower. Just as she started to back out, Tony turned - full frontal - and froze in terror like a museum exhibit.

I meanwhile, suddenly aware of an intruder, clasped my hands over my Jordans (luckily I had my knickers on) and stood behind her. The poor woman's head was spinning like something out of the Excorcist between the Jordans and your poor father's penis. No one under 60 should have to see my Jordans.

It seemed that our ever-so-slightly eccentric hostess had previously shown this young woman around our suite of rooms, had taken their luggage - which now could not be found and so - you have a French farce.

Our hostess is a charming copy of Edith Piaf. She spoke fluent English, was an artist and a philosopher and everything concerning the house was 'organic'. This did not narrowly relate to growing and eating food but was a complex philosophy which included not locking doors. 'Nothing is locked here,' she said.

Then things took an Alice in Wonderland turn when we discovered a connecting door to another guest's room, but it had a key on our side.

By now it was 10.30 and we wanted to go to bed but the thought of all the unlocked doors (we were in the middle of woods) prevented us. With a leap of hope, we started to quietly turn the key to the connecting room. But Madame was a sadist! The key did not function. It was a malevolent trick! As we were bent over trying to quietly lock one door we were suddenly horrified. A man 6 feet tall with a look of the Nosferatu about him opened the door and stood silently staring at us.

'Pardon,' we said in French.

'Nein,' came the reply. 'Das ist mein zimmer.'

'Parlez vous anglais?'

'Nein!'

As we couldn't remember our German, Tony tried to explain our worries about the lack of locks. 'Yah. Nein clefs' There then followed a rather sinister one-sided conversation in German which obviously had something to do with locks. He held us in his gaze, body slightly bent and head over to one side then quietly closed the door on us. We then looked for at least TWO chairs to put in front of THAT door. We didn't sleep well.

Will write again soon.

Love Mum and Dad.

There then follows another patch in capitals, which reads:

1. COFFEE AND 2 CROISSANTS
2. BOWL OF FROMAGE FRAIS AND STRAWBERRY COMPOTE
3. HALF A MELON
4. BREAD, JAM, MORE COFFEE
   ALL FOR 41 EUROS A NIGHT!

THE SOLUTION

Wow. Just wow. Obviously you can't stop your parents writing to you. That's a given. But what can we learn from this experience? When dealing with your parents, it's important to have ground rules and boundaries. What HMB needs to know here is that there is NEVER any given circumstance in which you have to know ANYTHING about your parent's genitals. TOO MUCH INFORMATION.

We know HMB is a Faffer so we can expect her letters to focus on potentially terrifying events. She doesn't disappoint, but note how Practibot WDT brings his agenda to the table. The bathroom tour, he's at great pains to tell us, has lasted for exactly thirty minutes. He will have timed it. So he knows. And look at the urgency at the end. Does he want to tell me he's having a nice time? Does he want to tell me his version of the story? No. He just wants to tell me that they're getting a good financial deal. I once had a postcard from WDT that just read: 'Hello Em. Near Macon. Can't Lock Doors. Love Dad.' Can you smell the theme? Practibots cannot bear or cope with anything that sniffs of communal living. Doors must be locked. It's pretty obvious that the lack of security has chilled WDT so he's clinging to what he knows. Let him.

Just in case

So now it's your parents' turn to go on holiday. This kicks up a whole new dustball of problems. Not least the granite-chiselled belief that they will surely die and leave you all alone in this world with no one to look after you. To this end, there is always a checklist of a ritual that needs to be covered before they can even think about putting their suitcases in the car. Twitch back your curtains and let's have a peek.

'Twas the night before their holiday...

'Our wills are in the red box,' HMB had phoned to tell me.
'And the life policies are in the grey file on the table,' said WDT getting in with the fun on the party line.
'And don't forget to send that thing to the Land Registry,' said HMB.
'Oh yes,' chimed in WDT, 'don't forget that.'
'But only if we die,' emphasised HMB, just to make sure that I was prepared for the very worst.
'You're not going to die,' said I, through slightly gritted teeth. 'You're only going to Normandy. It's hardly Afghanistan.'
'Don't be so cruel!' wailed HMB. 'This might be the last time I speak to you!'
'I've got the E1-11,' WDT piped up, because he had just remembered that.

Will

Life Policy

'I have no idea what an E1-11 is,' said I, fading fast.
'Oh you've got to have an E1-11,' explained WDT.
'So they can fly our bodies back for free. I'd hate to put you to that expense.'
'Don't worry,' said I, breezily. 'If you die I'll just bury you on the beach. It's what you would have wanted.'
'And your father's turned off the water ,' said HMB, ignoring me. 'So the house won't flood.'
'We're getting up at three in the morning,' said WDT.
'Blimey,' replied I. 'What time's your flight?'
'Midday.'

'But you only live thirty minutes from the airport,' said I.

'Doesn't matter,' said he.

'Do you want to come?' HMB then asked.

'No thank you,' said I. 'I'm working.'

'Go on,' said HMB.

'I'm working,' say I.

'Oh, go on,' said HMB.

Repeat to fade.

THE SOLUTION

This is what happens, without fail and in that exact order every single time my parents go on holiday. Once I saw a list that WDT had written two weeks before they were leaving. At the bottom it said 'Phone Em'. 'Why have you written that on your To Do list?' I asked. 'So I don't forget,' said WDT. Yeah. Like that's ever going to happen.

Like a Black Mass barn dance, the same gruesome steps have to be gone through. My parents' attitude towards holidays is similar to any-one else's attitude towards open heart surgery. Pleasure doesn't come into it. Holidays must be treated with the same solemnity as a First World War soldier about to go over the top. You're on to a losing battle here. Just the mere thought of being in a different time zone to you will create a morbid chemical imbalance. So leave them to it. You've got two weeks without them. Now THAT'S a holiday.

14–28th August

Mum and dad on holiday!!!

DANGEROUS TIMES

For most parents (apart from the Wassername, who couldn't care less), every day is a day in which you might die in a freak gardening accident. If you've got a Faffer in the mix, you can times that Fear Factor by a million. It doesn't matter how many times you tell them that just because you've got a hangover it doesn't mean you've got meningitis, they will always and I repeat ALWAYS assume you are in constant peril.

This can cause considerable stress and tension, which can in turn cause lack of concentration, clumsiness and, in extreme cases, potentially ironic accidents. All of this can be avoided, however, if you follow these simple rules.

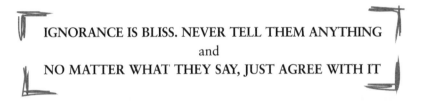

IGNORANCE IS BLISS. NEVER TELL THEM ANYTHING
and
NO MATTER WHAT THEY SAY, JUST AGREE WITH IT

The main problem with parents is that every encounter you have with them is going to be fraught with danger. And that danger doesn't have to assume a physical form. In fact, the greatest danger you will face when it comes to your parents is entirely psychological.

As you are growing up, your parents are in charge, but when you leave the parental home, it creates a vacuum that everyone but nature abhors. For your parents, it's like being given the sack. They will experience a sense of loss, confusion and worthlessness. You, on the other hand, will be jumping for joy stunned in the knowledge that not only can you now eat sweets in the week but you can do what you want when you want and with whomsoever you want to do it. Freedom, however, comes with a price. You have now got to do all those things that magically got done when you weren't looking. Contrary to popular belief, broken gutters and dripping taps do not get fixed in the night by elves . Your parents did it. And now it's your turn. Or is it?

A bored parent is a dangerous parent, and if you're clever you can use a parent's boredom to your advantage. The more you can give them to do, the better. Left to their own devices, mothers will panic about everything from insects to pandemics and start talking about near-death experiences, while fathers will develop cunning streaks that, if allowed to go unchecked, could result in them taking up golf . And no one wants that. But most importantly, if you want a stress-free existence, someone has to do the worrying for you, and this is where your parents come back in. Who better to put in the hours of worry required for modern life? So let's now look at that theory in practise.

WARNING

A bored parent is a dangerous parent

Your mother thinks she's on to something

Mothers can be delusional. Not like Howard Hughes, who liked to walk round his house wearing boxes of tissues for shoes, but like a paranoid dormouse, they see danger everywhere. Mothers also like to think they're prepared for every eventuality and will have come up with a small but perfectly formed plan that will ensure the survival of them and their families. This is quite good and could help you in the event of a nuclear air strike or an outbreak of the ebola virus. To this end, although your mother's paranoia is almost certainly like something you'd expect from a crazy lady who lives on a broken sofa outside a chip shop, you should maintain a healthy interest. The fact that she worries about shit means you don't have to. So let's look at a real event. Pay particular attention to HMB's practical conclusions. What would you do? And how would you deal with it?

'The last time I was on the Eurostar,' said HMB, sipping serenely on a cup of tea, 'I was sitting opposite a millionaire Iranian antique dealer.'

'How do you know that?' said I, smelling suspicion on the wind.

'Because he told me,' said HMB, casting me a patented look. 'Plus, he was holding a Rothschild catalogue.'

'A Rothschild catalogue? Like Littlewoods for posh people?'

'Sort of,' explained she. 'They were selling off some antiques. Anyway, he was on his way to Paris to buy some of them.'

'Nice,' said I.

'I got him to show me what he was buying,' continued HMB. 'I took one look at it and told him I knew where it came from. "Damascus!" I said. That came from Damascus. And he said, "How do you know that?" And I said, "Because I have seen *The Omen*."'

'Yes,' nodded I. '*The Omen* is standard watching for everyone on the *Antiques Roadshow*. That's basic.'

'And then his wife, who was with him,' continued HMB, 'asked me if I thought that the British government would be any good at dealing with disasters.'

'An Iranian on a train asked you that?' said I, eyes narrowing.

'Yes. And I said, "No. Of course not. Our government are useless at disasters. That's why you should always carry a screwdriver."'

'Pardon?' said I.

'A screwdriver. To get you out of trouble. And the Iranian lady asked me how a screwdriver could help in a disaster and I said, "Simple. You can use them to get down manholes."'

'Brilliant,' said I.

'Yes,' nodded HMB. 'And if you go down that man-hole that's just off Tottenham Court Road, you can follow the tunnel all the way up to Belsize Park.'

EMERGENCY SCREWDRIVER

'Genius.'

'Thank you.'

'I never knew you carried a screwdriver. This is a revelation.'

'Here it is,' said HMB, in triumph, holding a big, yellow screwdriver aloft. 'So do your worst Tony Blair.'

THE SOLUTION

So your mother's carrying a screwdriver. Think of it as the sewing kit for troubled times. Although she may be over-reacting, you should see that in the event of a disaster, being able to walk from Tottenham Court Road to Belsize Park might be no bad thing. If you live in London. The fact that my parents live in a nice market town in Hertfordshire makes my mother's solution slightly problematic, but let's give her the benefit of the doubt.

That's a great idea... Note how I encourage her at every stage. This induces feelings of certainty in my mother that allow her to think that she has come up with something that might just work. She hasn't of course, but in her mind she is saving us all which, in turn, means a quieter life for everyone. So, whenever your mother comes up with a glorious hairbrainer – embrace it.

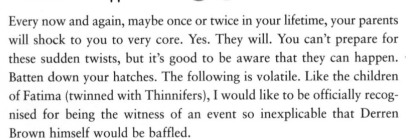

Miracles do happen

Every now and again, maybe once or twice in your lifetime, your parents will shock to you to very core. Yes. They will. You can't prepare for these sudden twists, but it's good to be aware that they can happen. Batten down your hatches. The following is volatile. Like the children of Fatima (twinned with Thinnifers), I would like to be officially recognised for being the witness of an event so inexplicable that Derren Brown himself would be baffled.

In many respects, by publishing the following real life event, I should prepare myself for the steady drip of pilgrims who will want to come and pay homage and buy plastic figurines and gawdy pictures of me which, depending on how you hold them, make my eyes blink. I'm no expert on miracle etiquette, but I expect an official delegation will want to come and have a chat. I'm not sure who the official delegation will be, but I've heard they're a bit like Insurance Assessors and that there are a lot of forms to fill in. But it'll be worth it. For I, TV's Emma Kennedy, have witnessed a miracle.

The miracle that I witnessed took place at 8 am on Sunday morning. The phone rang. I picked it up.

'Hello Em!' said the voice, which by using the part of my brain associated with memory, I deduced to be my father, WDT.
'Um hum,' said I, with a mouthful of toast.
'Just to let you know,' began Welsh Dad Tony, 'that we're going to be late.'

The toast fell from my mouth. My body went limp. My pupils dilated. I shook my head. Surely I was hearing things?

'Excuse me?' said I, looking at the phone as if this was some sort of sick joke.
'We're running late. We'll be at yours about half an hour late.'

I put the phone down and stared into the middle distance. All about me there was the afterglow of an Other-Worldly experience. Had I just heard that right? Had I really?

Let the Official Miracle Notes show that on Sunday the 28th day of the month of February in the year of 2005 the parents known as Welsh Dad Tony and Hysterical Mum Brenda were one half-hour late.

THE SOLUTION

Get down on your knees and pray.

Right royal excuses

If you're holding a delicate object like a piece of crystal or a baby's soft head, put it down. Do it now. I've got something shocking to tell you. Sometimes, parents can't be bothered with you. I know this flies in the face of everything I've told you up to this point. But it's true. It mostly afflicts the male of the pairing and tends to be seasonal. In fact it usually happens on a Saturday. When the football is on. During these bleak episodes, don't expect to get any sense out of your male parent. Chemicals in their brains have made them strangers to reason. There's nothing you can do about it. What is fascinating, however, is the lengths the male parent will go to in order to watch hour after hour of commentated sport. Let's examine a classic display of sneakiness and cunning.

'So the Queen just rang,' said WDT, tres nonchalant.

'Did she? The Queen you say?' said I.

'Yes,' said he. 'She said I could watch the snooker.'

'She said you could watch the snooker? Interesting. So that's in her constitutional duties is it? To phone up random subjects and proclaim that they can watch a minority sport that strangely attracts millions of viewers?'

'Well, she's good like that,' said he, looking out of a window.

'And you're sure about this are you?' quizzed I. 'That the Queen, the Queen of Enger-lund. She actually rang you?'

'To tell me I could watch the snooker. Yes.'

'Hmm. You see, that's what's puzzling me because I didn't hear the phone ring.'

'Ah well, that's because she didn't strictly call me,' said WDT, holding an explanatory finger aloft.

'I see,' said I.

'She actually texted me.'

'Did she now?'

'Yes.'

'She texts you a lot does she? The Queen?'

'Yes, she does.'

'And what does she say?'

'"R U watching the football? C U at the horses." That sort of thing.'

'"C U at the horses"?'

'Yes. And "U can watch the snooker. 1 rules it."'

'Hmm. It's funny isn't it, because you never see the Queen with a mobile?'

'That's because it's in her handbag. She doesn't carry money, although she sometimes has a tenner for when she's in church. But apart from that one tenner, she carries no money. So in her handbag, that she always carries, she's got two things – keys to Buckingham Palace. And her mobile.'

'You wouldn't be lying to me, would you Dad?' said I, crossing my arms.

'Who me? Noooooooooooo!'

I hope the Queen is on a good talk plan.

U can watch the snooker. I rules it

THE SOLUTION

Tissue. Thin. We know he's fibbing his arse off, but one is amused. Therefore, he gets house points. Dads always THINK they're funny, but we know they're not. On the rare occasion when they do manage to entertain, tread carefully. Give them an inch and they'll take a mile. Note here how I refuse to acknowledge that WDT has actually been quite witty. If he got the merest whiff that I thought he was funny, we would never hear the last of it, so play it straight like a spirit level. And then let him watch the snooker. He's earned it.

The moral a-maze

I think it's now been well established that HMB is nuts. So when it comes to philosophy, we're not going to be hanging on HER every word any time soon. Or are we? It's not impossible that a Faffer can sometimes make perfect sense. I know it sticks in the craw to even contemplate it, but every now and again, you may need to accept that your mother might know what she's talking about. Sunday evenings are, traditionally, a time for a post slap-up slump in front of any random BBC big budget family programme. Non-taxing you might think. Well, think again…

'What's this?' said HMB.
'*Planet Earth*,' said I. 'it's the new natural history thing.'
'Couldn't they have thought up a jazzier name?' said HMB, settling back into a large cushion.
'Ummm,' said I, because it was difficult to know how to proceed with this one. 'To be honest, I think their hands are tied a bit. Because the programme is about the planet. The Planet Earth. The clue is in the question.'
HMB then pulled one of her special faces and added, 'No one's got any imagination these days. If I was in charge, things would be a lot different. I'd call it Organic Pizzazz. Or something.'

The elusive snow leopard was the subject of the show we watched, and within moments I was in difficulty.

'I hate the snow leopard,' said I, as the mum leopard chased after a baby goat and almost caught it. 'I hate the way it tries to kill the baby goats. I love the goats .'
'It's got to eat, Em,' said WDT, because he knows these things.

But then the mum leopard trotted back to her cave to be greeted by a hungry baby leopard who seemed crushed that, yet again, there was no dinner.

'Oh no,' said I, as the baby leopard pulled the saddest face available in the snow leopard repertoire. 'Now I love the snow leopard. But wait. I love the goat too. I don't know who I love the most. This is impossible.'
'Thank goodness,' said WDT, moments later, as they showed the mum

leopard dragging back a dead goat. 'Now we've seen a goat escape and the leopard get fed. That's perfect.'

'I'm glad they didn't show the mum leopard catching that goat,' said I. 'That would have raised issues I'm not ready to contemplate.'

'Watching this programme is like a moral maze,' pointed out HMB, chewing on a finger. 'I've worked it out though. The snow leopard catches a goat but we didn't see her catch it. So that was all right. If you don't get to know the goat before it's killed, it's kind of OK. I always think it's the height of rudeness to eat anything you've been introduced to.'

Natural history programme-makers – take note.

THE SOLUTION

I know it's a terrifying prospect. But HMB is correct. It IS rude to eat anyone you've just met. Allow yourself fleeting thoughts that your mother might be the new Plato.

Birthday presence of mind

'That will NEVER happen to me!' We've all said it and then it does. And what then? You're in the shit right up to your ear lobes. That's what. I am talking, of course, about that most ghastly of events, forgetting a parent's birthday. It goes without saying but this natural disaster is to be avoided at all costs, not least because YOU WILL NEVER HEAR THE LAST OF IT, NO, NOT EVER, so let me help you with a small contingency plan that might just pull you out of the quicksand. In the following problem I've woken up oblivious to the day's significance. At 11.30 am I've received a phone call from WDT, who whispers down the phone 'It's your mother's birthday.' My heart's just stopped, and ice has frozen my blood. What did I do next?

'Is this a Christmas card that you didn't use?' said HMB, opening her birthday card from me and staring at the smiling lady surrounded by snow.

'No comment,' said I, twiddling my fingers inside my pockets.

'And where's my present?' continued HMB, fixing me with a penetrating stare.

'I'm getting you a Rigby and Peller bra. But you need to come with me.'

'Why do I need to come with you?' said she.

'Because you have to let the Breast Wizard see your tits' said I.

'Breast wizard?' asked WDT, pricking up his one good ear. 'Is that an official job title, like?'

'Yes' said I, nodding. 'The Breast Wizard comes into the changing room, but only after you have disrobed down to your waist – think the shopkeeper in Mr Benn but with an unnatural interest in breasts – that's what the Breast Wizard is like. Exactly.'

'Nice,' said WDT, who was hanging on my every word.

'So the Breast Wizard comes in and stares at your tits.'

'Nicer.'

'Tony!' shouted HMB, slapping him on his forearm.

'And stares and stares until the Breast Wizard is able to tell you exactly what size bra you should be wearing. So the Breast Wizard might say "34 C/Difficult D". I should make it clear that at no point does the Breast Wizard get out a tape or touch you in any way.'

'An opportunity lost,' said WDT, who received another thump.

'Then the Breast Wizard vanishes. In a puff of smoke.'

We all then sat and thought about that. *We're off to see the Wizard!*

'So that's what you have to do. You have to visit the Breast Wizard who will give you a bra.'

'We're off to see the Wizard!' sang WDT, who was beyond perky.

'No. You're not coming,' said HMB, shooting him a stare.

'Why not?'

'Because you haven't got breasts.'

'I've got nipples,' proffered WDT, pointing to his chest.

'The Wizard has no interest in nipples,' said I. 'Just breasts.'

'I wonder if the Wizard takes on trainees?' mused WDT and wandered off, juggling an imaginary pair of bosoms.

'Thank you SO much Emma,' said HMB, leaning forward to touch me on the arm. 'A trip to the Breast Wizard! I'm being spoiled ROTTEN!'

THE SOLUTION

Yet another potentially fatal scenario avoided. Note how I've zoomed round to the Pezzers gaff. This instantly creates feelings of appreciation within the maternal unit and makes you look like you've gone to some sort of extraordinary effort. Parents generally regard ANY visit home by you as a red carpet event that is probably putting you to great inconvenience, so prey on these thoughts by throwing in phrases like 'Well, I SHOULD be working today but... ' They'll fall for it every time.

Next, let's pay attention to the fact that I've rummaged through my desk and found an old Christmas card that can double up for a birthday card. I just about get away with it, but be aware that some cards won't be suitable – although condolence cards can just about be used but only if you write 'Sorry about how old you are, Ha Ha' inside. Cards made out to you and signed by other people should be left well alone. Even the most stupid of mothers will probably notice that they're not for her.

I've had no time to buy my mother a present. Let's get that out in the open. But I neatly sidestep the issue by thinking up a present that we can only get AFTER the birthday itself. The PROMISE of a present (but one that makes it look like you've intended it all along) will suffice. Note also how I talk at length about the nuts and bolts of what will be involved when we go to get the present. This is crucial if you want to maintain the illusion that you've been planning this for upwards of six months. Does your mother really need to know that you just thought it up in the car on the way? No. She doesn't.

IOU: birthday present

The day of reckoning

Dark storms are gathering. Rats are leaping from ships and solar eclipses are portending endless evil. Why? The day has finally arrived. You've turned into one of your parents.

cue a zillion screams of the living dead

In many ways, there is little you can do to avoid this. Like male pattern baldness, it's inevitable. But just because you know its happening doesn't mean you can't control the symptoms. If you are aware of the first tell-tale signs of a parental metamorphosis, you can, in some instances, stem the tide. Perhaps it's a tendency to jangle change in a pocket, or a sudden compulsion to visit a National Trust tea shop; whatever that first step on the crumbledown stairway to Hell is, get ready. Because it's coming. I experienced my first symptom a few months ago. I'll come clean. It caught me unawares. Let's have a look at what happened and we'll chat about it afterwards.

'Did I tell you about the conversation I had with the man from the Gas Board?' asked HMB, who had come and sat next to me on the sofa. I had just started watching my favourite quiz show ever, *Deal or No Deal (genuflects)*, which must always be watched in TOTAL silence. That's just giving it the respect it deserves. Occasionally, if it's a much-loved contestant, or the game is particularly tense, I will accept the odd 'Ooooh' here or a 'Don't deal!' there, but persistent, low-level chatter is absolutely forbidden.

If you've been living on a desert island or work for a living, *Deal or No Deal* is a game in which twenty-two boxes contain twenty-two different sums of money and one person has to eliminate three at a time in the hope that they can keep the larger sums still in play. After each round, the contestant receives a call from a mystery banker who makes an offer to buy the contestant's own box. The longer you keep in the higher sums, the larger the offer becomes. It's a game of random luck, but somehow, for forty minutes every weekday afternoon, it becomes more important than gravity.

'No,' said I. 'Don't talk to me now. It's *Deal or No Deal*. Thank you.' And that was my first mistake.

'*Deal or no Deal*?' asked HMB, settling in. 'What's that?'

'It's a game.'

'What sort of game?'

'It's about the boxes. And what's in the boxes. And they have to take out three of them at a time and then the banker makes an offer.'

'An offer for what?'

'For the box in front of the contestant.'

'But they've all got boxes. Does he buy all the boxes?'

'No. Just the box in front of the one sitting down at the table.'

'Why does he want to buy a box?'

'Because he does.'

'Well, how much does the box cost?'

'That's the point of the game. It can cost 1p or £250 000 or any sum in between.'

'£250 000? For a box? Is he mad?'

'He doesn't really buy the box. It's a device. Anyway! Be quiet now. And let me watch the game. It's just constant buzz with you. It's like being trapped in a tube with a thousand mosquitoes.'

'Who's that?' sad HMB, pointing at the screen and ignoring me.

'Noel Edmonds,' said I.

'And who's that?'

'Mumtaz, she's the contestant today.'

'Ask me the question, Noel,' says Mumtaz.

'What question?' asked HMB.

'Mumtaz,' begins Noel with that penetrating stare of his, '£8000. Deal or No Deal?'

'Is that what she's won?'

'No deal,' says Mumtaz, and the crowd goes wild.

'Has she just won that?'

'No. She didn't deal.'
'Didn't deal what?'

slight bout of VERBALAX

grip cushion till knuckles go white

Cut to three hours later and I found myself round at my friend Heather's house. She was watching *Lost,* a big-budget American drama.

'Why are they worried about numbers?' said I.
'They're special numbers,' said Heather in what some would call a classic mutter.
'What's special about them?' said I.
'It's too complicated to explain. They're just special numbers. They keep cropping up.'
'Cropping up where?'
'On the island. On doors. And things.'
'What things?'
'OK!' shouted Heather. 'That's it. You're going home now. No talking during *Lost*!'

And somewhere, in the distance, a dog howled.

THE SOLUTION

I know I said we could chat about this afterwards but I can't. I'm too depressed. So you've turned into your parent. Give up now. Your life is officially over.

Near misses

As your parents get older, you have to contemplate that one day they might die. Parents start casually mentioning that they're not long for this world as soon as they hit retirement age (for Faffers you can expect daily reminders of their oncoming demise from forty onwards). All mentions of wills, funeral arrangements and other morbid subjects should generally be tolerated but politely ignored. They're only doing it to make you come round for Sunday lunch, so treat it as the ruse it is. But there's one thing you must give your full attention to and that's the basked glory of a near-fatal miss.

I'm sitting with my mother, Hysterical Mum Brenda, and my father, Welsh Dad Tony. They've just returned from a holiday.

'I didn't mention in my letter', squealed HMB. 'But I almost died.'
'When you say "almost died"' asked I, 'do you mean "grazed your knee" or "had a slight cough"?'
'No,' said she, with a tremor of truth. 'I mean I "actually almost died". Didn't I, Tony?'
'She did, yes.' For it was WDT.
'Hang on a minute,' said I, 'is this going to be another one of your exaggerated stories? Nothing terrible EVER really happens to you. The thought of anything truly bad happening to you is an almost impossible concept. Like cheese in the crust.'
'How DO they do that?' whispered WDT.
'Well, it did. We were in a restaurant', began HMB. 'Weren't we, Tony?'
'We were. Restaurant. Yes,' said he.
'And I had a stew. And the meat was ever so large. Wasn't it?'
'Unnaturally so.'
'And I had one bit in my mouth and then the next thing I knew, half of it had sucked itself into my windpipe. I couldn't breath.'
'She couldn't breath. Proper like.'
'So I had to get up. And I was standing. And choking.'
'Choking.'
'And Tony had to get up and perform the Heimlich manoeuvre.'
'I hit her on the back. And then I did the manoeuvre.'
'Because your father's a trained first aider.'
'Oh yes.'
'And the bit of meat shot out of my throat.'

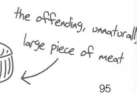

the offending, unnatural! large piece of meat

'Shot out.'

'Your father,' announced HMB with something of a fanfare, 'saved my life.'

There was then a silence as I took that all in.

'Oh Dad,' said I. 'That was your ONE chance.'

'Ohhhh!' screamed HMB. 'Ohhhhh! You are AWFUL.'

'Heh, heh, heh,' giggled WDT.

'Jeez Loueez,' said I, sitting back. 'You had a narrow escape. Imagine that. Ugh. I can't think of anything worse than choking on your dinner. What a waste. Of dinner.'

'Oh that's nothing,' declared HMB. 'Listen to this. We met this couple at the airport. And we got talking and they'd been to a wedding where the groom had started choking on a pickled onion. The bride, in a panic, got a fork and tried to spear out the pickled onion!'

'Madness,' said WDT, shaking his head.

'Spear it out! With a fork!' shouted HMB, making the appropriate hand gesture. 'But of course, that just made it worse. Anyway, the ambulance driver arrived. Saw the groom was dead but didn't like to say.'

'Because it was a wedding,' explained WDT.

'And he didn't want to ruin everyone's day. So he picked up the corpse and did the Heimlich manoeuvre on it. Out shot the pickled onion. Blinded the grandmother in the eye.'

'Stop it!' said I. 'You're making this up.'

'God's honest truth. Groom dead. Grandma loses an eye. Terrible. Still, I nearly died. didn't I?'

'Yes, I suppose you did,' said I, giving her a small cuddle.

'So are you coming to lunch on Sunday?'

Every time…

THE SOLUTION

Never eat pickled onions at weddings.

Age Shall Not Wither Her

HMB's birthday is a well of mystery so deep that not even diminutive adventurer Dame Ellen MacArthur could fathom its depths. When it comes to knowing your mother's age, you might get lucky. Some mothers, they're rare but they do exist, are quite happy for their family to be able to pin down accurately how old they are. But what do you do if you haven't got the first clue whether your mother is still a spring chicken or is an old-age pensioner? And no. You can't cut her in half and count her rings. That's trees. Just watch. And learn.

CARDINAL SIN! ASKING A WOMAN HER AGE

'How old is your mother?' asked my friend Tom, flicking through the travel section of the *Sunday Times*.
'There's no way of knowing,' said I, stuffing a chicken with lemons. 'She changes the rules every year. Sometimes she operates the always-say-you're-one-year-older-than-you-are rule, then it's two years, and then, without any warning, she switches to two years younger. So, you know, your guess is as good as mine.'
'Doesn't that make special birthdays a bit difficult?' asked he, leaning over and stealing the grapes I had set aside for a sauce.
'Yes,' said I. 'I waited three years for her 60th and then found out we'd already had it, except no-one knew.'
'Hmmm,' said Tom and went back to reading about trekking holidays in Outer Mongolia.

It was, of course, the birthday of HMB. WDT had phoned me two weeks previously to ask whether I was going to go to their house for the day in question. 'No,' had said I. 'You come to me. That way I can decide when to put the vegetables on.'
'What time?' had asked WDT, with a strain in his voice.
'Well, working on the constant premise that you will always turn up an hour before I want you to then let's say half past one. That way you'll turn up at half past twelve.'

Two weeks later and they turned up at ten to eleven.

'You're early,' said I, sweating cobs that I hadn't even thought about putting the chicken in the oven.
'Yes,' said WDT. 'There's going to be road works on the A1.'
'Going to be?' said I, with a frown.
'Yes. There's going to be road works in two weeks.'
'So you set off early in anticipation of road works that aren't starting for another two weeks?'
'Yes,' said WDT, who looked very pleased with himself indeed.
'Good. Well. Glass of wine?'

The lunch was a roaring success (WDT had made raspberry crème brulées that might just be the finest pudding I've ever tasted), and everyone was on fine form.

'So how old are you?' asked Tom when all was eaten and done.

WDT looked up, a moment of fear and excitement dancing in his eyes. A mighty hush descended on the table.

'How old do you think I am?' said HMB, fixing him with one of her special stares.
'Ummm, 56?' said Tom, after a swift kick from me.
'Ohhh! Ohhhh! You lovely man!' squealed HMB, with an ear to ear grin. '56! I'm 63!'

Ker-ching.

THE SOLUTION

Easy when you know how. In this practical problem, preparation is everything. Not only have I prepared the food, but I've prepared Tom. When you need to find stuff out about your parents, NEVER ask them yourself. You'll get nowhere. So get someone else to do it for you. And the less well known that someone is to your parents, the better. In fact, if you're introducing someone new to your parents, you can get them to ask ANYTHING. So in this scenario, I've used Tom (a) to ask quite specifically how old my mother is, but crucially (b) to follow up with an age so well below what we all suspect her to be that (c) she'll be delighted, show off and spill her real age like the guts of a just slaughtered cow. Peasy.

Stormy weather

If you've got a Faffer, anything and everything can and will become a crisis. Whether it be the terror of a lump of coal on a carpet or the devastation of a shattered soufflé, the Faffer is ready to make a mountain out of any tiny molehill. But nothing will induce a sense of heart-stopping panic more than the prospect of terrifying weather. I make one mistake in the following. Keep your eyes peeled and maybe you can tell what it is.

'We can't leave the house!' said HMB who had phoned me at 8 am that morning. 'It's practically a hurricane !'
'Hang on,' said I, clawing hair out of my eyes. 'The bad weather is in Scotland. You're in Hitchin. In Hertfordshire.'
'I know that,' said HMB, whining. 'But it is quite windy. You never know.'

We had been planning a Family Day Out, which, with WDT at the helm, is nothing short of a military operation – 'I've been to the library and copied a map of Cirencester,' he had told me three days previously. 'Now I know where the car parks are.'

The reason for our trip to Cirencester was that I had been given a painting by an artist called Camilla Clutterbuck, who, besides winning the prize for best name ever, is also quite brilliant. She had painted a picture of Poppy, which was being shown in a gallery in Cirencester.

She asked me if I would like to go to the opening and whether I would like to bring Poppy with me. Of course, I agreed.

The Poppy portrait

'Oooh, yes please,' said HMB, when I suggested, in a moment of madness, that perhaps the whole family would like to come too. In fact, it would suit me down to the ground to have the Pezzers along as I had to go and see a friend in Stratford who was in a play. 'I shall kill several birds with one stone!' thought I. 'I shall go to Cirencester, pass the dog to the Pezzers like a hairy, biscuit-loving baton and zoom to Stratford where I shall watch the matinée of said show, see friend, pat her on back, then zoom back to Hitchin where a feast shall be awaiting me. And also the dog.'

And it was all going so well. But then came the winds to the North and the alarmist weather reports telling people in Scotland not to leave their houses.

'I know your geography is bad,' I said to HMB, 'but you're nowhere near the Highlands. Plus, by driving to Cirencester you're actually moving even further away.'
'But what if the car gets blown over?'
'Mum,' said I, fingers creeping up to grip the bridge of my nose, 'it's a little bit windy. I'm hard pressed to even refer to it as a breeze. It's hardly *Twister.*'

Seven phone calls later, after WDT had spoken to the Environmental Agency to cross that T, and I had spoken with Camilla who was 'on the spot' in Cirencester to dot that I, and HMB relented and agreed to make the journey of potential death. But only on condition that everyone told everyone else that they loved each other before we set off.

The net result of the to-ing and the fro-ing was that we were now two hours behind schedule. The plan had been to arrive in Cirencester at 10.30, go to the gallery, take Poppy for a lovely walk, find a rambling country pub for lunch and then I would scamper away to Shakespeare country. Instead, I arrived in Cirencester at 12.30, got lost, found the gallery with the help of a man with a bucket, looked at the painting, ate a biscuit and wondered where the Pezzers were. They arrived at 1.30 with a flourish. HMB swept in and, when asked by the very pleasant gallery owner if he could get her anything, screamed 'My husband has a psychosis about parking. Honestly, I'm getting a divorce!'

I then turned to WDT and said 'Where are you parked?'

He replied, 'I don't know, I forgot my map' and just stood looking ashen. The matinee I had bought £30 tickets for started at 2.30. Looking at the map, Stratford didn't look too far away from Cirencester so at 1.45, when I asked the gallery owner 'How long will it take me to get to Stratford?' and he said 'Ooooooh, a good hour', I threw the dog's lead into HMB's hand and legged it.

I arrived half an hour late for the play, missed most of the first half and then wondered why my friend didn't appear to be in the play at all.

'Did you like my dance at the beginning?' said my friend when she met me afterwards.
'Mmmmmm,' said I, and changed the subject sharpish.

THE SOLUTION

Nothing wrong with a little white lie...

Did you spot the mistake? Yes. Easy wasn't it?
I invited them in the first place. What was I thinking of? Day trips with your parents need to end at the age of twelve. Anything after that and you're staring at a blackboard of depression. And pain. Endless pain.

Taking on the World

So some of you, let's say the parent sympathisers among you, might be wondering what HMB has done to deserve her hysterical moniker. Are you quite mad? Has nothing I've said penetrated your blind noggins? Well read the following and then let's see where you stand.

I got a postcard from HMB. She's not on holiday, neither has she been anywhere for a day trip. What I'm saying is, the need for a postcard was a curious one. The postcard itself was a moody affair, a dark sepia scene of a cityscape that was gloom itself. Flipping the card over, I noticed it was a picture by Mark Kessler. It was called 'The Final Hours'. Remember, the clue is in the question.

I then turned my attentions to the block of text, which, because of its impossible spidery-like scrawl, could only have come from one person: Hysterical. Mum. Brenda.

'DO NOT PUT THIS ON YOUR BLOG!' it screamed. Underlined three times, no less. HMB meant business. I was intrigued.
'Dear Emmy,' it began. 'Stop criticising Bush on your Blog! It's danger-ous! US Fascism is a reality – as bad and evil as the Third Reich. You can't fight it – just survive it. Don't make yourself a target. The US is taking revenge on Europe and the Euro...' (*What? Taking revenge on the Euro? Anyone?*) '...by devaluing the dollar and making Euro exports too expensive.' (*Ahhh – I see. Yes. That IS evil.*) 'It will get worse yet. DUCK AND DIVE!' (*DUCK underlined. But this time only twice.*)
And then, 'Anyway, see you soon. Kisses for Poppy. xxx.'

I rang her immediately.

'So I got your postcard,' said I, sounding a little like Mae West.
'Sssssssssssssssssssshhhhhhhhhh!' hissed HMB. 'They might be *listening*!'

'Have you,' I pondered, 'been taking LSD?'

'What do you mean?'

'Well, it's just the, how shall I put it?, the timbre of your postcard is verging on the mental.'

'I certainly am not mental!' declared she.

'Welllll...,' replied I.

'Emma,' punctuated my mother. 'I am NOT mental. Duck Emma! And dive! But mostly just keep quiet. Sssssshhhhh!'

And with that she put the phone down. And off I went. Ducking and also diving.

THE SOLUTION

Am I wrong? Of course I'm not. The woman lives in a bubble of perma-terror. If you've got a Chicken-Licken parent convinced the world is about to end, there's no reasoning with them. Just smile and nod and offer to send them on a ten-day intensive survival course. That should keep them quiet.

No matter how small

When it comes to living life on the edge, parents can and will ensure that anything and everything can have perilous undertones. Parents have incredible skills for turning anything into a crisis. Or at the very least, making it seem that the universe as we know it is about to end. When it clearly isn't.

'Well, it was a disaster!' boasted HMB, flicking my arm with one tiny hand while nudging WDT with the other.

I looked at WDT, who made the internationally recognised face for 'Can you believe it?'

'We were at the front of the queue,' said HMB.

'Front of the queue,' said WDT.

'And the lady said we could go through,' said HMB

I'm hearing double...

'Go through,' said WDT.

'And off we go, up the stairs.'

'Up the stairs.'

'Sorry,' said I. 'Is there an echo in here? Can one of you tell the story and the other one remain silent? Thank you.'

'So we go up the stairs,' rattled on HMB. 'And I'm at the front.'

HMB now began giggling and was clutching my forearm as if this was just about the funniest thing that had ever happened. Ever.

'And everyone's following me. And I go up. And I go up. And I go up. And everyone's behind me. The entire audience. And I get to the top of the stairs. And there's nothing there. And I see this guy and I say "Excuse me, where's the theatre?", and he looks at me and he says, "What theatre?"'

'What theatre!' chimed in WDT. 'Can you imagine?'

'So I turn round and shout, "It's not up here. We'll have to go back!"'

'She was like the Pied Piper of Hamlin!' said WDT.

'We all had to come back down. Ah ha,' said HMB. 'Ah ha ha ha ha.'

'Ha ha ha!' joined in WDT.

'WHAT a disaster!' underlined HMB.

There was then a period of silence during which there was much shaking of the heads from both parents.

Tumbleweed moment

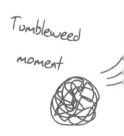

'Is that it?' said I.

'Yes,' said WDT. 'Want some crisps?'

'But where's the disaster?' said I, puzzled.

'Well it was ALMOST a disaster,' said HMB.

'Mum,' explained I. 'A disaster is when people die. Or when aeroplanes crash. Or when prize cows get run over by trains. You just went

up some stairs. And then came back down them again.'
'But you almost didn't have an audience,' said HMB as if that were self-explanatory.
'Yes,' said I thinking about that. 'That would have been a disaster. Cheese and onion please.'

THE SOLUTION

The big puzzler here is just how much both parents have loved their brush with danger. To you and me, having to go up some stairs only to have to come back down them again would be nothing more than the mildest of irritants. Not for HMB and WDT! That's been the highlight of their day. So what does this teach us? That retired parents are unbelievably bored and, contrary to popular belief, they should never live in bungalows.

A DEFINITE NO-NO

Power tools and mothers don't mix

It's almost too obvious to mention, but if you want to use power tools, don't do it in front of your mother. The following speaks for itself. Poppy, My Most Excellent Beagle, had been away for the weekend.

She packed her overnight bag on Friday and trotted off to the home of Hysterical Mum Brenda and Welsh Dad Tony, where she is spoiled rotten and has every whim indulged.

'I was up at a quarter to four with her last night,' said WDT, stifling a yawn.
'What for?' said I, crossing my arms and staring down at Poppy who tried to change the subject by lying on her back and waving her legs in the air.
'I thought she wanted a wee but she just wanted to run round the garden.'

'I can't believe you fell for that old trick,' said I. 'That's her Speciality Move.'

The Pezzers had come to kill two birds with one stone. First, they were returning that Most Excellent of Hounds. Second, WDT had arrived armed with a hedge-trimmer with which he was going to attack the monster that was taking over my front garden.

'Can I have a go?' I said, staring in wide-eyed wonder at the hedge-trimmer and all its glory.

'No,' said WDT, cutting through the errant hedge with green-fingered zeal.

'Why?' said I. 'Is it very dangerous?'

'No,' said WDT, looking back at me. 'It's too much fun.'

'Give Emma a go!' intervened HMB, with a sense of impending fury. 'Don't be so selfish, Tony!'

'Yes!' said I, jumping on that bandwagon. 'Don't be so selfish, Dad!'

'But it's quite hard as well!' retorted WDT. 'You've got to know what you're doing! Your hedge could end up looking like a French collaborator!'

'Give her a go!' yelled HMB.

'Yeah!' yelled I. 'Give me a go!'

'Well, all right!' shouted WDT. 'But don't say I didn't warn you!'

'Hang on a minute!' screamed HMB. 'Is that thing safe? Is it? Is it safe?'

'Yes it's safe!' screamed I.

'No!' screamed HMB. 'It's NOT safe! It's not safe, Tony! Take it back! Don't let her use it!'

'It's not safe, Em!' cried out WDT. 'Don't use it!'

'It IS safe!' yelled I

'NO!' screamed HMB. 'It's NOT safe! Oh God! Tony! Tony! Stop her! It's NOT safe!'

'Give it back!' wailed WDT. 'Give it to me! That's it! That's it! OK. We're safe. We're very safe!'

I'VE GOT THE POWER

small moment of quiet. And then...

'Oh God, NO, Tony!' retched HMB. 'Don't use it! It's NOT safe! You could have your arm off! NO! Put it down! Turn it off! Don't even TOUCH it!'

Apparently half-cut hedges are all the rage this season.

THE SOLUTION

Some mothers are like well-tuned Ferraris in that they can go from 0 to one hundred in less than six seconds. Here HMB displays her top-of-the-range status. Your mother will ALWAYS take your side over your father's and, in normal circumstances, this is a productive cow that's permanently ready for milking. But in this instance, the maternal need for you to never be in any danger has gone into over-ride and spack-attacked any plans for a bit of razor-edged fun. Conclusion – do not operate heavy machinery while under the influence of your mother.

Smashing the boredom threshold

There is nothing more dangerous than a bored parent. You may as well hire a Boeing 707 and try to fly to Rio with 300 hungry lions sitting in economy. Try asking THEM if they want beef or chicken. A bored parent can be unpredictable

BORED PARENT = DANGER

and volatile. The danger here is that they start thinking. And when they start thinking, they get ideas. Bad. Very bad. A parent with an idea is as unstable as a split atom. So do you take to your bunkers, slam on the locks and wait for the all clear? Or is there something you can do about it? Let's have a look.

'Have you thought about what you want to do for Christmas?' HMB said, screaming in through the front door of Kennedy Towers.

'No, Mum,' I said, feeling my energy sap in her very presence. 'I haven't, but then it is only September the eighth.'

'Oh,' said HMB, looking downcast. 'That's very disappointing. I just wanted something to think about. I'm VERY bored.'

'Worrying,' said I.

'I always get in trouble when your mother's bored,' sighed WDT. 'I got put in the book this morning because I went shopping and didn't come back for forty minutes.'

'Clearly he was up to no good,' declared HMB.

'I'm sorry,' said I, brow furrowing, 'what's this book?'

'The book,' explained WDT, 'in which your mother logs every misdemeanour.'

'Pardon?' said I, baffled.

'Yes!' said HMB, with a sense of pride. 'Every time your father does something wrong – it goes in the book!'

'"That's going in the book",' said WDT. 'That is her catchphrase.'

'So today he went missing for forty minutes,' said HMB. 'He was obviously up to no good.'

'No, I wasn't,' said WDT. 'I was buying your mother conditioner. And I went to the corner shop but they didn't have separate shampoo and conditioner, so I had to go to the supermarket and get it there.'

'A likely story,' said HMB, arms folded.

'But I came back with the conditioner,' pleaded WDT.

'How convenient,' said HMB, throwing him a sarcastic nod. 'But never mind that. This morning there was only one window open at the train ticket office. One window!'

WDT sighed a little and hid behind a newspaper.

'AND it was half term. AND it was just after ten when the false rush hour starts!'

'False rush hour?' asked I.

'Yes. To get the cheaper tickets. And they had ONE window open! Not only that, but there were FIVE inspectors standing on the platform doing NOTHING! So I said, "What are you going to do about it? There's only one window open!", and the man said, "Everyone has to have a 20-minute break", and I said, "There's supposed to be three people working there!", and he said, "Staff cuts", and I said, "Staff cuts? This is HITCHIN! Not Ely! We're only twenty minutes from London. I can imagine that at least 500 people get on a train at Hitchin. 500! And we've only got one window open! It's a disgrace!" And then I fixed him because I said, "Have you ever been on the French trains? They are excellent!" And he looked sheepish. Because he couldn't answer that. You know what men are like. They can't give you a direct answer. So he said, "You should see what the French trains are like on the branch lines!" And I said, "Excuse me. The SNCF is excellent. Anyway we're not talking about French trains. The French trains are the best in the world. But look here. At least forty-five people are standing waiting. And there's more people coming in. Would this happen in France? No! It wouldn't!" And that rattled him so he said, "Well, I suppose I could get an inspector to serve behind the window", and I said, "Oh really! And you're ONLY just thinking of doing that NOW?" And then he said, "On the Swiss trains, some of their seats aren't even bolted down!" To which I gave him a look and said, "I think we've had enough discussion about trains in other countries. The issue I'll be raising with customer services is how it is that we have staff cuts at Hitchin station when there are five inspectors standing about doing NOTHING!" That told him. And then I said, because the line used to run by WAGN and now it's run by FCC, "FCC! Fucking the Customers Constantly!"

YOU MAY WANT TO MAKE YOURSELF A CUP OF TEA FOR THIS PARAGRAPH

'Oh dear,' said I. 'And what were you doing while this was happening, Dad?'
'Hiding behind the ticket machine ,' sighed WDT.
'I wish you knew what you were doing for Christmas. I had a dream that you got married,' HMB said, changing the subject dramatically.

'That wouldn't have been a dream, Mum,' I said. 'That would have been a nightmare. A nightmare, I might add, that has no hope of ever coming true.'

'You'll never guess who to,' she said, ignoring me.

'I have no idea,' I said, giving Dad one of my special looks.

My mother stared at me smiling, glazed over, and then turned to my Dad and said, 'Who was it, Tony?'

'I don't know,' said my Dad, crossing his arms, 'I wasn't watching.'

'I need new curtains' said I, gesturing towards the window.

'New curtains?' asked HMB. 'Oh I can make those! Tony! Car! Fabric! Let's go!'

THE SOLUTION

Like a binged-up teenager, the bored HMB is just bouncing about looking for a fight. Note how she whips herself into a small frenzy but is unable to remain focused on one subject. This is where you can come in and douse the flames with a well-timed distraction. The general rule is that if your bored parent has reached critical mass (as happens here with her monologue about the trains), you can sweep in, drop your information cluster bomb, sit back and wait for the legs to blow off. I like to use the tried and tested certainty of a home improvement. The merest mention of curtains stops HMB in her tracks and instantly gives her something to focus on. You don't always have to suggest chores that need doing round your house, of course, but trust me, it works every time.

Sting in the tail

Nothing presents more of a terrifying chill to a Faffer than the inescapable dangers of a small insect. If it's buzzing or has flapping wings, you increase that fear by a factor of ten. It is important during moments of tail-spin madness that you keep your head. Most of the time they're just trying to suck you into the vortex.

'Just a spider SITTING in a web is dangerous,' began HMB. 'What with climate change, you can't be so sure of what's in your garden. Now, you don't know who's lurking ready to spit at you. Or crawl into your knickers. Or kill you.'

'Crawl into your knickers?' asked I. 'That's something you're terrified of is it? That a spider might crawl into your knickers?'

'It's not something one would look forward to,' replied HMB, with a sigh. 'No. But then no-one wants a spider crawling into their vagina. Or even worse, into the small, dark hole at the back. That's itchy enough as it is. The problem is, webs have changed. They're not like they used to be. Nowadays they're all a bit three-dimensional and some have tunnels. I find a general rule is – the more spectacular they look, the more terrifying the spider. And the more intricate and clever the web, the greater the chance of them jumping into your knickers. I had one on my breast once. It leapt up from my thigh.'

HMB stopped, and shook a little at the memory.

'Apparently,' said I, 'it's scientific fact that every human will eat four spiders during their lifetime.'

'Stop it!' yelled HMB. 'That can't be right. No one's going to eat a spider!'

'No. They crawl into your mouth when you're sleeping. That's quite common.'

'Oh that's terrible,' cried HMB, putting a hand to her mouth. 'But then again… Hmmm. Perhaps I could start selling Anti-Spider Face Masks? I wouldn't charge much. Because it's providing a service. You know, like plastic gloves. They're the first line of defence against anything unspeakable. So like plastic gloves. But for faces. I suppose you could use them for scorpions as well. Italian scorpions are notorious. They've got Tunisian relatives. So they're hot ones. Not cold ones. You don't need to bother with the cold ones. They don't come after you so much.

But the hot ones are permanently LIVID.'

'You seem to know a lot about insects,' said I, eyes narrowing.

'It's important to know your enemies,' replied HMB, with a wag of a finger. 'Take the bee. No bother. The bee is our friend. If a bee is troubling you, just step aside and let it get on with its business. But if it's a wasp! Well! Everyone should spend ten minutes everyday doing wasp exercises. I find that French fly-swatters are best. They have more bounce and flick. You need to practise on imaginary wasps. Get your wrist in. But wasps must be annihilated.'

'They're not that bad,' protested I. 'Besides, wasps only sting you if they think you're prey or you've upset them.'

'Nonsense!' declared HMB. 'That's just a myth perpetrated by wishy-washy naturalists. The wasp has been bred for war. What use is a wasp? What does it do? Nothing. Apart from eat the wood in my loft and make very pretty hives. No! The wasp is fair game. You should feel no remorse for the wasp. And then there's centipedes. VERY dangerous. They can give you a horrid rash. And the worrying thing about centipedes is that there's nothing to stop them crawling into your knickers when you're using the toilet. You can't let your guard down for a minute. I think I should set up a Ninja training academy against dangerous insects. And sell Anti-Spider Face Masks. And the wasp swats. Oh, wait. I don't like moths. You never know when they're going to flap in and die on your light bulbs. One flew in my face once. They're like demon spirits. Can't trust them. There's something "of the night" about them.'

'That's because they're nocturnal creatures,' explained I.

'Exactly!' said she, tapping the arm of her chair. 'Up to no good! But going back to wasps, there were some wasps in the garden yesterday. And they stalked Tony until they stung him. Plus they fit exactly the description of the killer wasps that had come in from Africa on the Eurostar. We need to be alert. They're getting organised. Crawl into your mouth at night do they? Hmm. £4.99 for a family set. I think that's VERY reasonable.'

... and the most useless insect award goes to ...

THE SOLUTION

Hwwwhooooooo. Crazy. Crazy. Crazy. What we need to take note of here is the Pezzer's love of anything that whiffs of a conspiracy. I have no doubt that HMB genuinely believes that an evil insect force is lying in wait to take down the human race. The best course of action here, then, is to parry all concerns and treat the insect world with a bored nonchalance. That way you starve the fever and keep the matter contained. But don't tell her about that time you opened a banana and a big red spider fell out. Ever.

It's bird flu!

Chicken's off the menu

If your parents had a top ten list of terrible things that could ever happen, a global pandemic is going to be right up there. It was bad enough when glandular fever was doing the rounds when you were in the sixth form. But then the fact that a 17-year-old was listless, grumpy and slept all day wasn't anything out of the ordinary. The prospect of a full on airborne plague, however, takes matters to a different level. In times of peril, the parent needs to protect and survive. Dads can develop Bunker Brain, a neurological condition that compels them to stock up quietly on tinned meats and candles. Mums, however, have a more hands-on approach to impending doom and like to suck themselves down a spinning plughole of panic. Examine the following.

'Oh!' cried out HMB, hand to her forehead. 'Did you see that big picture on the front of the *Guardian* this weekend? It was of a policeman standing guard over the spot where that bird flu swan died!'
'Yes, I did see that,' replied I. 'And it puzzled me. What was he doing? Waiting to arrest passing jelly-legged birds?'
'We need an evacuation plan,' continued HMB. 'And we mustn't eat chicken!'
'You can't catch bird flu from eating chicken. You have to get off with

spores

a swan. Or a duck. You know, proper kiss it like. With tongues.'

'But that's just not true!' yelled HMB. 'A duck only needs to cough in your direction to give you bird flu. You're going to need to check your pockets for crumbs before you leave the house. Birds with flu will be attracted to you. They're like the living dead. And then they'll quack on you or something worse and they'll give you flu. And then you'll die.'

'But surely birds with flu don't have much of an appetite?'

'Yes, but they have to eat something and they can't get their own meals because they're too ill. Therefore they will seek out pockets full of crumbs.'

'I can see you've given this a lot of thought,' said I, with a wry smile. 'It's not FUNNY, Emma,' chided HMB. 'This is a very SERIOUS matter.' 'Hmm. Though I expect it'll be quite easy to spot a bird with bird flu. Male birds will be the ones complaining that no other bird has ever been as sick as them. And there'll be showy displays of sneezing and possibly dry retching. Female birds are the real danger because they'll just be getting on with their day. Although some breeds of geese will cluster in front of television shops. Especially if *Richard and Judy* is on.'

'I love *Richard and Judy*,' noted HMB, for the record.

'Exactly,' said I. 'OK. So let's imagine you've found a bird with bird flu. What do you do? Stand in a doorway? Or get under a desk?'

'That's nuclear bomb attacks,' said she, shaking her head. 'No. I'd use bird speak. You know *whistle, whistle, whistle* 'bird flu' *whistle*. You've got to get the right whistle of course. And then, if it nods, either hit it with a brick or run a mile. Probably run a mile. Because of the spores.'

'Spores? Birds aren't like mushrooms. That's not how they work.'

'Yes! Spores!' yelled HMB, eyes widening. 'You can inhale them! The flu gets absorbed by the feathers in the skin. And when the wind blows the feathers about, it spreads the spores. That's what's so fatal.'

'But what would you do if there was a proper outbreak? And it was everywhere? What would you do then?'

HMB heaved a sigh and shrugged, 'Well, I'd have to get out a balaclava and put it on. That's the only solution. That and wearing a cardboard mask. And I'd carry a weapon with a pointed edge. Like a javelin. If anyone comes near me, then I can swing it about. Keep them away. And then spray them with disinfectant .'

She stopped, sighed again and wrung her hands.

'Actually,' she began again. 'I'd probably just paint a big, red cross on the front door and tell everyone to fuck off.'

Good luck, Britain.

THE SOLUTION

If I were you, I'd photocopy this problem, stick it behind some glass and provide a hammer so you can smash your way back to it in an emergency. It seems so obvious now we know how, doesn't it? So start investing in balaclavas and javelins. Their stock's going to go through the roof. We might all be about to die in a spore-based outbreak but at least we can try to make a few quid on the way down.

At your inconvenience

It's rare, but sometimes your parents like to let slip that they might not be the squares you take them to be. Generally, parents will keep secret any behaviour deemed bad by an independent panel of experts. This is because they don't want you to know that anything they've done is just as terrible as anything you've done and, in some instances, ten times worse. Any intel you can gather of parents behaving badly is like striking gold. Keep it to yourself and then smash them in the spleens when the timing's right. When it comes to slim advantages, this one keeps you on your toes.

'I was involved in a strange and slightly dangerous toilet shenanigan today,' said I, having phoned HMB for a round-up of the day's activities. 'We were filming in a pub and I needed to Ten One. That's TV parlance for Going For A Whizz.'

'Interesting,' commented HMB. 'Ten One. Yes.'

'So off I go to the toilet, and I should say that I'm still in my costume, which is an oversized camouflage tracksuit.'

ENGAGED

'That's a look,' said she.

'Yes,' agreed I. 'So I go into the toilet. And following the first rule of Public Toilet Etiquette, I go to the cubicles with open doors first. Imagine now, with the power of your mind, that there are two cubicles in the ladies toilet.'

'Is that all? Disgraceful,' said HMB.

'And that one door is shut. And the other is open. But the open door has a sign on it which says OUT OF ORDER. OK?'

'Yes.'

'So in this instance, you leap forward to rule number two, which is, if the cubicle with the door open is unusable, then you see if any of the cubicles with their doors shut are, in fact, free.'

'I tend to stand and listen for urine. Or wiping noises,' informed HMB. 'Thank you. You CAN do that, but I favour the light press against a closed door to see if it is, as you suspect, locked and therefore occupied. So this I did. And discovering that the door was locked I stood back, folded my arms and stared at my shoes.'

'Yes,' said HMB. 'I don't like to catch a lady in the eye when they come out from a toilet. There's something a bit shaming about it.'

'So at this point, another lady comes into the toilet and follows the exact same procedure, culminating in the light press on the closed cubicle door. Finding it locked, she then turns to me and says "Is someone in there?", to which I nod without smiling. Then, and I can't stress how quickly this all happened, another lady comes in, ignores the open cubicle totally and just goes straight for the door press. So now, and I'm recapping here, the

OUT OF ORDER

closed toilet door has been pushed three times in under a minute. At which point, the occupant, probably a little disconcerted...'

'Well, yes,' butted in HMB. 'Nothing worse than a wee interrupted.'

'A little disconcerted... calls out in a small, plaintive voice, "Give me a minute! I've only just got here!"'

'Nothing unusual in that.'

'Well, you would think not. But the lady who came into the toilet last took great exception, huffed and, before I could bat one, lazy eyelid, stormed back out of the toilet shouting (in my direction I might add) "Fucking mouthy bitch! You film people are all the same! You think you're it!"'

'What? She shouted that at you?'

'Yes! I wasn't even SPEAKING! And she called me a mouthy bitch!'

'Were you a bit terrified that she was going to come back with her mates and do you over?' asked HMB, with something akin to a glint of excitement.

'I was a bit,' confessed I. 'Because to look at, she WAS at the rougher end of the Lady Scale.'

'I would have stayed in the toilet for the rest of the evening,' said HMB, with a tremble. 'Especially if I was wearing an oversized camouflage tracksuit. That's just asking for trouble.'

'Yes, except, I HAD to go out. Because we were filming.'

'And you'd only gone for a Ten One. If you'd stayed in there they'd think you'd gone for a Ten Two.'

'Probably,' said I. 'But I decided to head matters off at the pass. So I Ten Oned, went out into the public bar and found her.'

'You never did!'

'I did. And blow me if she wasn't the bloody barmaid!'

'No!'

'So I go up, and she's sucking furiously on a cigarette and surrounded by a livid circle of thick-necked gentlemen and similarly spread ladies. And I say, "Excuse me. Did I offend you in any way? Because if I did, then I apologise", to which she replied "Mouthy bitch!" At this point I remember that I am not, like the character I am playing, some sort of street-fighting hard nut but a mild-mannered actress who needs some sort of face to earn a living. And to this end, I edged away slowly, a bit like when David Attenborough tries to get away from gorillas, clutching the top of my oversized camouflage tracksuit as I went.'

'Terrifying,' said HMB. 'Although I've had incidents in toilets, of course. When you first went to university, your father and I used to go and sit at the bottom of the garden, cry and get pissed. And one night, after crying and drinking two bottles of wine we walked down to the Italian restaurant. I go to the toilet on arrival. A woman comes out of the cubicle. I grab her, cry out "Ohhhh! What a beautiful ghost!" run out of the toilet and walk all the way back home again.'

'Where was Dad?' asked I.

'He was still sitting at the table. He'd ordered lasagne . He didn't know where I was. He had to send a search party into the toilets. So he pays the bill, walks home and then can't get in because I've taken the keys and passed out on the floor in the hall. I actually had carpet in my mouth.'

'Hang on a minute. This happened twenty years ago and I'm only hearing this for the first time?'

'Well,' said HMB, with a dismissive tone. 'You don't need to know EVERYTHING do you?'

Au con – very – traire.

THE SOLUTION

be prepared like a boy scout

So the trick here is to soak up the volatile information like a sarcastic sponge, store it in your memory banks and be prepared to blurt it back in their faces whenever you're being told off for doing anything remotely similar. In this instance, my mother will NEVER be able to tell me off for sailing past the drunk post again. If she does, she's going to get it.

THE FAMILY IN CRISIS

Part and parcel of being a member of a family is that, every now and again, bad things happen. These are the times when you couldn't be more glad you've got parents because, in a crisis, most of them will excel. When you were little and you'd just broken your leg because your brother dared you to bounce down the stairs on a space hopper, it was your parents who, somehow, stopped you from puking your lungs up with fear AND made you feel quietly smug that you'd now got a leg in plaster. This is what they're good at. Watch and learn. Because at some point, the tables are going to turn. Unlike Captain Scarlet, your parents are not indestructible. I repeat, NOT indestructible. And this means, that at some point in the future, their quality will start to deteriorate. But unlike a pair of old shoes, you can't take them back or ask for a refund. You're stuck with them.

So what do you do? A game I sometimes like to play with HMB is pointing into old people's homes and then casually asking "Do you like THAT one?" I inevitably get thumped for this, but it's a gentle of way of raising the issue before it turns into a weeping sore. Having said that, I'm with the Italians on this one. When the Pezzers are too old to look after themselves, they're moving in with me. I drove them mad for eighteen years and I would consider it rude not to allow them the opportunity to return the favour.

But let's not get bogged down in a morbid fascination with illness and death. Because it's not just bodies that can go wrong; stuff can too. And sometimes the stuff that goes wrong needs to be complained about. In my experience, parents, especially the females, are genius when it comes to complaining. Like cheese, parents get better at complaining with age. My mother is now so adept at complaining that she's only got to show up at her local supermarket and they're queuing up to give her her money back. I challenge any of you to find a better complainer than my mother. She is a phenomenon. I am so confident that nobody could out-complain her that if you could find anyone who comes even close to complaining as brilliantly as my mother, I'd give you my dog. Like a wind farm, you need to work out a way to harness all that complaining power to your advantage. Read on and become enlightened.

The other thing guaranteed to set your parents into a sticky spin is CHANGE. Remember their faces when you told them about the existence of DVDs? Ever seen them use a mobile without staring at it for five minutes? No. Of course you haven't. New things can disorientate and induce nausea so, like a bomb disposal expert, you're going to need to tread carefully.

Rotten times come to us all, but remember that a proper parent will be able to turn ANY incident into a disaster and still come out of it smelling of roses. In this section we'll touch on the more delicate matters of death and illness, but I'll also show you how doom and also gloom can be seen as an opportunity rather than a setback. Let's start by examining a minor tragedy that HMB turned into a triumph.

Your Mother Thinks She's Been Really Clever

This happens more often than any of us would like. There are two defined schools of thought about how to deal with this problem – ignore it or indulge it. Let's look at what happened when we suffered a loss in the family. Keep a close eye on HMB during this one. What would you have done?

'The engine's gone!' cried WDT, who had rung me in something of a lather.
'Have you called the AA?' said I, because they are the fourth emer-

gency service. Everyone knows that.

'Yes, and it's gone! Gone!' wailed WDT, who's had that car for ten years.

'Oh, Em,' he whispered on. 'When they came to take it, they put it on the back of the tow truck and the arm of the machine went through the windscreen.'

He stopped and I heard a catch in his throat.

'I had to turn away. It made me weep.'
'Oh, Dad,' said I, because we've had a bereavement. Pure and simple.

And so it was that I found myself speeding up the A1 to take WDT and HMB to a garage where they would road-test a new motor.

'Are the spheres in good working order?' HMB asked a skinny youth in a blue overall as we arrived.

I looked at her and narrowed my eyes a little.

'Spheres?' said I.

'Yes. Spheres. The spheres,' she said, waving a small hand in the direction of the rear end of the car.

'Oh, yeah,' said the youth. 'Everything's working.'

HMB nodded and slid up to me. 'He won't try and pull a fast one on us now,' she whispered, nudging me in the ribs. 'He knows that I know about the spheres.'

So, safe in the knowledge that HMB had secured the respect of the motoring trade through her knowledge of small, but crucial engine components, the Kennedy family all piled into a car and span off for a test drive. It was at this point that HMB displayed her car know how to the full.

'Are you comfy, Tony?' asked HMB.
'Oh, yes,' said he.

'Are you comfy, Emma?' asked HMB, looking over her shoulder at me.

'Yes thanks,' said I.

'Well, that's that then. We'll take it.'

My parents are now the proud owners of a Citroen Xantia. Rounds of applause please.

THE SOLUTION

So – what would you have done? Write down your answer now in the space provided.

_____

This is a textbook display of bluffing from HMB. I'm guessing she's overheard WDT (who does know his engines) during a strained conversation with a car mechanic in which 'the spheres' were discussed in full. What might seem to you to be a desperate attempt to impress a youth with bum fluff and a greasy handshake is actually, in this situation only, a very astute move. Think it through – WDT is in no state to negotiate anything with anyone. He loved that car, and seeing the windscreen smash in front of his hurting eyes has pushed him over the edge. You can count him out right now. He's no good to anybody. But HMB knows this and, because she is now the Parent In Charge, feels duty bound to grab the baton of the second-hand motor and run with it.

This is busking at its best. But has she pulled one over my eyes? Of course she hasn't. See how I make an extra effort to question her knowledge of the spheres. This sends her a clear message that I know that she knows as much about the spheres as an elephant knows about the production of acetate as a side-product of plastic.

It's important to give your parents a sense of self-worth. They have to feel as if they're achieving something, and nowhere is this best played out than in an arena in which they know nothing. So the lesson to learn here is: if your dad's car has been killed by a tow truck and your mum smells an opportunity to flash fag-ended conversations about like a hound with a hare – let her. Sometimes you can end up with a very good bargain.

Proper ill

oops

It's a sad inevitability that, in the general scheme of the universe, your parents will die before you. It's just another example of how very selfish they can be. That to one side, when a parent falls ill, it can be extremely traumatic. Keep yourself as healthy as you can during this time as you will need all your strength, not least to support the parent who isn't ill, who will be having a far worse time of it than you. Role reversal is common during extended periods of dealing with illness, so don't be surprised if you find yourself asking your father just when, exactly, he intends to clean up his room or chiding your mother for speaking with her mouth full. This is all perfectly normal.

But just because you're walking through the darkest of days, it doesn't mean that light has nowhere to shine. In 2005, HMB was diagnosed with breast cancer, which we all found devastating, but after the initial shock had worn off, we settled into a pattern of coping that involved taking fun where we could grab it. Let's look now at an incident that took place a few weeks after HMB had had surgery.

'I start my radiotherapy the week after next,' said HMB, thumbing through a copy of *Grazia* magazine.
'I know,' said I.
'They've got to give me some tattoos,' said she.
'Pardon?' said I. 'Not permanent ones though?'
'Yes,' said HMB, looking up. 'The doctor said I'd have to have them cosmetically removed. I'm not sure I want them done. I can't spend the

rest of my life walking round looking like a builder. Or Robbie Williams.'

'They'll be the size of pin heads,' interjected WDT, who was looking through some binoculars at a long-tailed tit .

'Pin heads?' said I. 'Well then, what are you worried about? You'll barely see them. And it's hardly as if you're planning to go into topless modelling when you're finished.'

'God forbid,' mumbled WDT.

'Tony!' said HMB, leaning over to give him a sharp shove. 'That's not the point. I'll have tattoos. I don't want tattoos.'

'Yes,' said I, sensing exasperation central, 'but you have to have them done because otherwise the radiotherapists won't know where to do the zapping. They have to line these things up. It's very precise.'

'Very precise,' repeated WDT. 'Ooooooh. A little blue tit.'

'That's not the point. I don't want tattoos.'

'OK,' said I, leaning back in my chair. 'Let's say you've been abducted.'

'Fat chance,' said WDT.

sideways glance

'You've been abducted by a desperate band of Tattooists. They've got you holed up in an underground Tattoo parlour and you've got to have one tattoo. Or die.'

'Well, that's hardly ever going to happen, is it?' said HMB.

'It might' said WDT. 'Stranger things have happened.'

'Like what?' challenged HMB.

'There was that boy. Who was brought up by wolves. That was quite strange.'

'Come on,' said I, interrupting. 'One tattoo. Or die. You've got to have one. What tattoo would you have?'

'Easy,' said HMB, without a moment's hesitation. 'Three words – I. Was. Right .'

sighs all round

THE SOLUTION

This demonstrates nicely how, even in the face of a lengthy course of unpleasant treatment, HMB's mind is never far from her Faffer status. Faffers will never accept that they are wrong. This makes them impossible to argue with, so my advice is – don't bother. Note though, how I steer HMB towards the path of getting something done that she doesn't want done by planting a small seed of something far worse into her line of thinking. This is always the best course with most parental types. If they're stubborn and won't do something that needs to be done for their own good – just get them to imagine a worse scenario. You'll bring them round every time.

an apple a day ...

Maintaining a healthy parent

So your parent has had an illness. Fingers crossed that that illness has been treated and you're all enjoying the salad days of postoperative recuperation. But don't think for one minute that you can take the pedal off the metal because parents, like old cars, need a lot of maintenance. Many of the common diseases that parents fall prey to could be avoided altogether if they hadn't indulged in a middle-age spread so, if you want your parents to bask in the wrinkled glory of a ripe old age, there's one thing you can nag them about ad nauseam – keeping down their weight. Dads are usually more receptive to this sort of thing and can wander off and dig up a vegetable patch to get back their six-pack, but with mums it's a more delicate matter. You can't just blurt out 'You're fat and you're going to die.' That would be quite bad. No. Assume the scientific approach and results are sure to follow.

'So what you do,' said I, sounding very knowledgeable, 'is work out your body mass index. And that tells you how much of your body is fat. That way you can work out whether or not you're overweight .' 'I've got news for you,' declared HMB, who was looking rather pleased with herself. 'Someone's worked out a new way of figuring your body mass index. I read about it in *The Guardian*. What you do is you get your longitude and latitude...'

'Sorry?' interrupted I. 'Your longitude. And your latitude?'

'Yes. Longitude and latitude.'

'How, exactly, are longitude and latitude going to help you find your body mass index?'

'Well, she'll know exactly where she is for a start,' piped in WDT. Because he was sitting quietly in the corner. That is his job.

'No!' announced HMB, with a shake of her head. 'I mean the other thing. Logarithms! You've got to work out the log of it. You know. You have to do that cunning thing.'

'Yes,' agreed WDT. 'It's called multiplication and division, love.'

'No wonder I had to bank off maths,' sighed HMB.

'Bunk off. Not bank,' said I.

'Bunk off, then. But do you know, they never missed me all those years. Not once.'

'I don't know where maths goes in your mother's brain,' said WDT, crossing his arms.

'What you don't want to accept, Tony,' began HMB, 'is that I am a sort of genius. The mathematical paradigm invented by some man is all wrong. I bet we're older than we think we are. I bet I'm 200 years old.'

'How do you work that out?' said I, licking my lips as to where this was going.

'I mean who says it's a seven-day week with twenty-four hours a day? Who says it is? Twenty-four hours a day is ridiculous. If you get up between nine and ten, then you ought to go to bed again between four and five. I think days are a lot shorter than we're being led to believe. No! We should have twelve-hour days!'

'But that would mean some days are just all night time,' suggested I.

HMB stared out the window and thought about that for a bit. Then, with a theatrical flourish of her arms, 'Well so what? You have a dark day. You have a light day. When we lived in caves, we got up any old time. All right, admittedly everyone had a much better sense of smell in those days. But my point is made.'

'Anyway,' said I. 'Your body mass index?'

'Yes. Well, I'm only four pounds overweight.'
'And did you work that out by doing your logarithms?'
'No. My doctor told me.'

Great.

buy diet book!

THE SOLUTION

It's the sort of classic Faffer display that top flight behaviourists can only dream about. But let's scratch the surface and sniff a little deeper. Note how I've brought up that most sensitive of issues with a dredge-net of a statement. By keeping the matter generalised, I avoid the inevitable wailing and weeping that would follow a blunter approach. The rule to getting your parents to do anything is always

MAKE THEM THINK THEY THOUGHT OF IT FIRST AND LET THE SMUG TIMES ROLL

And then, and only then, chuck out all the biscuits.

Parent skills

Now I don't want you to get the wrong idea and think that parents have nothing useful to offer. Far from it. Some of them are brilliant at complaining. And not just about you or your lifestyle choices. No. I'm talking about constructive complaining on your behalf to anyone who's made the wheels of your day-to-day existence clog up with rankle grease. If you're lucky enough to have one of these special breeds of parents who loves complaining, it's perfectly acceptable to exploit them. Put them to work. It's like making a broken donkey smile again.

'Bloody Freeview box !' said I, within my mother's radius.
'What's wrong with it?' said she, coming over to stare at it.

'I don't know!' said I. 'But it's really playing up. Sometimes I can get all the channels and then all the Channel 4 ones disappear. And then the ITV ones go as well. There's no rhyme or reason to it.'

'And this is something you've paid for?' asked HMB, edging closer.

'Yes,' said I, with a small whine.

'Well, that's not acceptable. If you've paid for it, then it needs to work. That's the Sale of Goods Act. It's got to be reasonably fit for its purpose.'

'But I don't know who to complain to,' explained I. 'Do I complain to Channel 4? Or ITV? Or the government? They're the ones who are making us all go digital!'

'If they want everyone to go digital,' pontificated HMB, 'then they need to sort this out. This is a shambles!'

'Yeah!' agreed I. 'It's all digital this, digital that. And I can't even get ITV2!'

'Absolute disgrace,' pronounced my mother, shaking her head. 'Right. That's it. We need to complain. Who's in charge of digital pixies?'

'Sorry,' said I, bending my head towards her. 'Digital pixies?'

'You know, the tiny things pictures are made of.'

'Pixels?'

'Yes those. Who's in charge of them?'

'Freeview I suppose,' said I, with a shrug.

'Oh!' exclaimed HMB. 'Do they really exist? I thought they were a metaphysical concept. This is a bit like the film career of Julian Sands – you know it exists but you don't who to complain to, to stop it.'

'He was good in *Room with a View*,' muttered I. 'But anyway, yes, they do exist. Maybe they've got a Customer Support Helpline? Oh look – here it is, written on this piece of paper.'

'Give it here!' gestured HMB, with purpose.

'No Mum! Don't! You'll just be shouty and complainy.'

'Give it here!'

'Oh, all right then,' said I, handing the number over.

'Is this Freeview?' barked my mother to some poor wretch. 'Well listen here. My daughter's box doesn't work. Sometimes

American idol
Sat 8pm!

she gets Channel 4. Sometimes she doesn't.'

'And ITV2!' said I, in the background.

'And ITV2!' shouted HMB.

'I can't watch *American Idol*!'

'She can't watch *American Idol*! Now, what I want to know is, what are you going to do about it? Or am I going to have to report you to Trading Standards? Mmm-hmm. Yes. Hmm. I see. Emma, have you upgraded your aerial?'

'What? No. I didn't know I had to.'

'She didn't know she had to,' snapped HMB.

'Ooooh,' mumbled I. 'Ummm, actually I didn't think about the aerial thing.'

'Right. I see. Thank you! Well!' declared HMB, handing me back the phone. 'That's that sorted! You need to upgrade your aerial. Good!'

'So there isn't a problem with the Freeview box at all?' asked I.

'No. It's your aerial. But you'd think they'd tell you these things wouldn't you? I might write to my MP...,' tailed off HMB and off she wandered to find something else to have a fight about.

THE SOLUTION

I've had a lucky escape here. But let's shatter the technical fourth wall and examine the techniques I employ to mobilise the complaining blunderbuss. Note how, yet again, I unveil the problem with a casual aside. The less you can make it look like you want your parent's help, the more likely they are to offer it. It's like magnets . Parents are instantly attracted to anything they think you don't want them near. A more astute individual would have questioned the fact I have the number of the Customer Support Helpline already written down, but not HMB. She's got the smell of fresh blood in her nostrils and is going to threaten someone with the Trading Standards Office if it kills her. Beware though, because a parent who lives to complain is a potent force and should be unleashed sparingly, not least because sometimes, like above, it might be all your fault.

Weird science

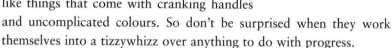

Parents and the modern age don't mix. They like things that come with cranking handles and uncomplicated colours. So don't be surprised when they work themselves into a tizzywhizz over anything to do with progress.

'Who needs a fluorescent pig? Who?' yelled WDT, throwing his arms into the air.

'What madness is this?' screamed HMB, stabbing at the picture in the paper with an accusatory finger.

'Woah there, tigers!' said I, holding up a calming hand. 'What's got your pretty heads in a muddle?'

'Some bored scientists in a laboratory in the back of beyond have come up with a pig that glows in the dark!' squealed WDT. 'Why? Why?'

It was true. I had a quick look at the paper that HMB was now shoving under my nose, and there was a pig that looked as if the local village youths had had a good go on it with a marker pen.

'Hmm,' said I. 'Prepare to brace, brace, brace, but I have to agree with you. Who needs a fluorescent pig?'

'Well, there was that time when those pigs ran away? Do you remember?' said HMB. 'Perhaps it's so they can find them in the dark?'

'But surely runaway pigs aren't a pandemic problem?' said I. 'They're not like foxes. You don't get random town pigs roaming round housing estates and turning over people's bins.'

'I've never seen one,' said WDT, shaking his head.

'Perhaps its so ramblers don't trip up over them in foggy conditions?' suggested HMB, who really meant that.

'Or for pig worriers,' added I. 'Who might want to enjoy their porkish treats at the midnight hour?'

'What does a pig worrier do?' asked HMB, looking perturbed.

'It's like a sheep worrier but for pigs.'

'Oh,' said she and stared at her feet.

'Perhaps it's to do with the security services?' suggested WDT, scratching at his wise man's beard. 'They could use the luminous pigs to assassinate people. Set the pig on them, and while they're all rolling around in the dark, the armed forces have enough light to shoot by?'

'Although the shock of being attacked by a luminous pig would probably kill them off in the first place,' noted HMB.

'Today a luminous pig,' I announced with a sense of foreboding, 'tomorrow it'll be us. Hmmm. Now I think about it – make children luminous and you could cut road accidents by a significant margin.'

'Oh yeah!' said WDT agreeing.

'Brilliant!' clapped HMB. 'Oh Tony, we're living in SUCH exciting times.'

THE SOLUTION

Do you see? They fear it. Yet they love it. I can remember the first time I saw a digital watch. I couldn't believe my bloody eyes. That's what every day is like for your parents. The world is a Wonka Wonderland as far as they're concerned. It's charming. So ride the breeze.

Buried alive

As your parents progress down the slip road of life, thoughts inevitably turn to their demise. Faffers are particularly preoccupied with their own deaths and will have been threatening to pop their clogs ever since you can remember so, as far as they are concerned, you can pretty much ignore everything they have to say. But the death of a parent is rubbish, all the more so because decisions have to be made about how they'd like to shuffle off. My advice here is to try and discuss the matter WAY in advance, preferably before either of them even get ill. Although giving them free rein to discuss anything is always going to be tricky.

'Would you like to be buried or cremated?' said I, suddenly.

'Oh!' cried HMB, clamping a hand to her forehead and slumping into the back of the sofa. 'Oh! What a question! Oh! Oh!'

'If I was an Ancient Egyptian ,' announced WDT, grabbing that baton and running with it, 'and I died, then your mother, you and the dog would have to be buried alive with me. That's what the pyramids were for. So everyone who got buried alive could wander round a bit. Before they died. So buried please. In a pyramid.'

'Don't start me on the Egyptians,' said HMB waving a hand into the air. 'I've always been very doubtful about the authenticity of the pyramids.'

'How else do you think they got there?' asked I, folding my arms.

'I'll tell you a story. We used to have two very good American friends. The husband was a brilliant engineer who designed wings for planes. And once, when we were on holiday with them, we got talking about the Egyptians. Turns out they had seen this huge stone that had been placed in a vault in one of the pyramids. It was sort of like a key stone.'

'A key stone?' said I, raising my eyebrows.

'Yes. A key stone. And no one could explain how it had got where it was. So the wife in all seriousness told me that aliens put it there. Now being sympathetic to the American predisposition to believing in aliens, I just gave a shrill laugh and said "Rubbish." But the husband was very quick to support his wife's theory, and he said it had to be aliens. No human could possibly have done this. And then I pointed out that he was an engineer who made wings for planes. And he said, "Yup but I'm copping out on this one." So there you go.'

'Sorry,' said I, twisting my lips. 'But is that it? What sort of story is that?'

'Well, I don't believe in aliens. That's the sort of story it is.'

'I do,' said WDT, holding his knees together. 'I believe in aliens.'

'So do I, I think,' said I. 'I met a man once who said he'd seen eight UFOs. He hadn't seen aliens though. So I asked him, if alien species were coming here all the time, why was it they weren't making contact, and he just said, "Because they can't be bothered." To which I had no response.'

'If I met an alien,' piped up WDT, who was grinning at the very thought, 'I would take them up the pub for a pint .'

'Hmm,' said I, looking at him. 'And what else would you offer them?'

'Pork scratchings,' said he, in a heartbeat. 'Not peanuts. Because they might have nut allergies. But mostly because pork rind is mankind's greatest delicacy.'

'Anyway,' added HMB, bored of all that. 'If anyone came round trying to bury me alive, I'd get someone to rustle up a new marriage certificate and pretend I'd had nothing to do with you. Even if I have been hanging round the house for the past 40 years.'

'Do you think a man would come round from the funeral parlour to get us?' wondered I. 'Do you think that's how it would work?'

'Yes,' nodded HMB, 'They'd be overwhelmed with demand to do that job. It's like traffic wardens. But worse.'

'Do you think the fact that I'm never quite sure of Dad's birthday would get me off the hook?' asked I.

'No,' said HMB. 'Tony, when you say "bury alive", are you speaking metaphorically?'

'No,' he replied, with a shake of his head. 'We'll all be buried alive. Except me. Because I will already be dead. It's what I would have wanted.'

'Hmm, because I still don't think it applies to me,' added I. 'I mean, I haven't been on holiday with you since 1984.'

'That doesn't affect anything,' said WDT.

'Does it not?'

'No.'

'Buried alive, eh?' said I. 'This is a bad business.'

'Mind you,' said HMB, with a sigh, 'there's no way you'd get planning permission for a pyramid. Not in Hitchin.'

Dad and Alien gone up the pub!

Thank God for that.

THE SOLUTION

You see. This is what happens when you let your parents make their own minds up about things. What I should have done was approach the subject with a little more cunning. I didn't and am now condemned to a living death in some sort of hellish sarcophagus. I only have myself to blame. Don't make the same mistake.

The wind of change

If you only take one lesson away from this book let it be this – don't fuck with the sausage. Dads, unless you've got a sensitive one who doesn't eat meat (WHAT?), are great fans of the sausage. I'd go so far as to say that for 99.9% of the adult male population, sausages are the bees' fricking knees. If they could, they would eat sausages morning, noon and night. They would smoke sausage cigars, have sausages grafted onto the end of their fingers and tape emergency sausages to their lips for those middle-of-the-night peckish sausage sweats. They bloody love sausages.

I had bought some organic pork and apple sausages.

'Blimey,' said I, biting into one, 'Aren't these sweet?'
WDT, who was round for supper, stared at the just
pierced sausage on the end of his fork. 'I don't think
its right,' said he, 'when people mess with things like that. This
sausage makes me livid. It's a sausage that's trying to be a pudding.'
WDT, it goes without saying, is a voracious sausage-eater.
'What are you having for breakfast?' I once asked him.
'A packet of sausages,' said he, throwing six sausages onto a grill pan.
'Can I have one?' said I.
'No,' said he.
'Do you remember that time you ate six sausages for breakfast?' said
I, feeling the urge to suddenly bring that matter up. 'Because I do. And

Possible world record??

it still leaves me breathless.'

'That's nothing,' chipped in HMB, who had entered stage left. 'I once had lunch with a woman who got into an argument with her partner because he insisted on having seven fish fingers. Which might seem manageable, but it meant everyone else could only have one each.'

'One fish finger is a measly portion,' agreed I.

'Fish fingers are a difficult portion to get right,' nodded WDT. 'I'm sticking my neck out, but I think it's two fish fingers if you want a light lunch, three if they're going in a sandwich (with tomato ketchup) and four if you're having them for supper and you're hungry.'

'Yes,' added I. 'Anything more than four and you're invading Greedy Town. But seven? Perhaps you could apply the magpie numbering system to fish fingers? *sings* One for a baby, Two for a light lunch, Three for a sandwich, Four for a substantial evening meal, Five for a large baguette that you're intending to share, Six for a low-grade, cheap alternative to a seafood salad that you can serve to some blind people, Seven for a greedy bastard who just wants to have seven fish fingers so that everyone else can only have one. And so on.' *singing ends*

'Hmm. So where does this leave Tony and the six sausages?' then asked HMB with devastating accuracy.

'Sausages don't count,' said he, shaking a hand. 'It's my duty as a man to eat as many sausages as possible. It's a man job. Like chopping wood.'

'Could you eat six of THESE sausages?' said I, holding up one of the pork and apple offenders. 'It's not quite savoury. And it's not quite sweet. It's the very definition of a Franken-furter.'

'Before I answer that,' said WDT with a sigh, 'I want you to know that whoever made those sausages is a twisted bastard.'

HMB placed a comforting hand on his arm.

'That said, I'll eat two and a half.'

'So brave,' whispered HMB, cracking open the mustard.

SHOPPING LIST

Eggs

Sausages

Bacon

Beans

THE SOLUTION

This is one of the rare times you'll see your father properly upset. NO ONE messes with mangled pork products and lives, as far as your Pa is concerned. It's all very well to have a go at the braver end of the sausage spectrum, but it's the plain, honest sausage that will keep the elder statesman in your family happy. Some might say that I am taunting my father with his weakness for the basic herb-flavoured sausage in this scenario. I couldn't possibly comment. All I know is that there's NO WAY I'm ever going to try him on the parmesan and sun-blushed tomato ones you can get in a certain high-street supermarket. Teasing is one thing, but crushing is out of bounds.

Uncommon
Ailments

Illness. It's rubbish. Bad enough if you're the one being ill although, during childhood, it is your duty to catch as many revolting diseases as you can and spread them. Measles, mumps and chickenpox, the holy triumvirate, are yours for the taking. And if you've got gastroenteritis, share it! It would be rude of you not to.

Being sick when little means you get to lie on the sofa all day and watch television. And in my youth, when there were only three channels and you were only allowed to watch two of them (ITV –More Dangerous Than Paedophiles, according to my mother), it meant an hour of programmes for schools in the morning, half an hour of a grumpy man doing woodwork and then forty-five minutes of ladies in headscarves drinking coffee. That was it. There was a brief respite at lunchtime when a scrag-end of a puppet called Hartley Hare would come on, but because he looked like an alcoholic tramp with myxomatosis, it didn't so much as entertain as just scare shitless. Still, it beat having to go to school. And that was the main thing.

It is your duty as a child to catch as many revolting diseases as you can and spread them

When a parent tumbles down the slide of ill health, it's chilling. In fact, there is nothing more alarming than a poorly parent. When you're a child, parental illnesses can be almost exclusively ignored because mothers (unless they're a Faffer) make things easy for you by constantly maintaining a façade of well-being. Even if they've sawn off half their lower leg with a lawnmower, they'll refuse to make a fuss, make sure you're on time for your violin lesson and insist on no one mentioning it to your father.

Dads, on the other hand, are the exact opposite. If they've got a hangover, you might find them vomiting noisily down at the bottom of the garden. If they've got a slight cold, the moaning will be heard three counties away. Even so, you're still not required to do anything. That is the law. But as soon as you've left home, all that changes.

As soon as you and your stuff have made the break for freedom, you can expect to be informed of every tiny physical complaint. My father thinks nothing of phoning me to update me on my mother's bowel movements – 'The poo was SOFT but not watery' – that's what I have to endure. Not only that, but as they get older, parents begin confusing you with a real doctor. This means bypassing all the medical formalities and just asking you outright whether 'the swelling on my eyelid is terminal'. If you have a parent like my mother, this will become a daily occurrence. My mum once went to her doctor wailing that she had 'neck cancer' because a small lump had come up. It was a blackhead. We've never let her forget that one. In these instances, my advice is this:

MAKE A NON-COMMITAL NOISE IN THE BACK OF YOUR THROAT, ONE THAT WON'T STAND UP IN A COURT OF LAW

Try that now. Good.

But there are some illnesses you CAN diagnose, and in this section of the book I want to help you identify them. On the next few pages, you will be able to use my quick-check flow charts as an aid to self-diagnosis. These are the illnesses that the medical profession refuse to recognise. But can you afford to ignore them? No. That's the answer. This isn't a trick question.

Are you in the car?	Yes ✓	No ☐
Are you driving?	Yes ✓	No ☐
Is your parent sitting in the car with you?	Yes ✓	No ☐
Are you driving any faster than 25 miles per hour?	Yes ✓	No ☐
Is your parent warning you every time they see a pedestrian crossing?	Yes ✓	No ☐
Is your parent screaming every time you overtake a parked bus?	Yes ✓	No ☐
Is your parent complaining of feeling sick every time you go through a light on amber?	Yes ✓	No ☐

Your parent has **CARTHRITIS**, a terrible affliction causing the sufferer to back-seat drive every time you give them a lift.

TREATMENT: Try putting a hessian sack over their head and putting them in the boot. That way, you can't hear them.

Are you in the house?	Yes ☑	No ☐
Are you a girl?	Yes ☑	No ☐
Have you got a friend with you?	Yes ☑	No ☐
Is that friend your new boyfriend?	Yes ☑	No ☐
Is your dad in the same room?	Yes ☑	No ☐
Is he saying very little?	Yes ☑	No ☐
Is his complexion livid?	Yes ☑	No ☐
Is he staring or even glaring?	Yes ☑	No ☐
Are his hands squeezed into fists?	Yes ☑	No ☐
Is he snarling uncontrollably?	Yes ☑	No ☐

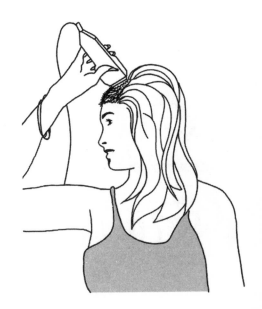

Your parent has **HIMMEROIDS** an irrational hatred of any boy you bring home.

TREATMENT: Consider becoming a lesbian.

Are you with a parent?　　　Yes ☑　No ☐

Is your parent complaining?　Yes ☑　No ☐

Is your parent complaining
that (*insert chocolate bar of
choice here*) used to be a lot
bigger in their day?　　　　Yes ☑　No ☐

Are they complaining that they
used to have proper winters
with proper snow?　　　　　Yes ☑　No ☐

Do they experience a crushing
sadness every time they have
to lock the front door and
see it as a living indictment
of the state of the world today?　Yes ☑　No ☐

Do they refuse to officially
recognise the metric system?　Yes ☑　No ☐

Your parent is suffering from **WISTYPOX,**
a constant longing for a more innocent
age where the world was all toffee lumps
and buttercups.

TREATMENT: Take away their car
and move the toilet to the garden.
This cure is instantaneous.

Are you in the house? Yes ☑ No ☐

Are you in the sitting room? Yes ☑ No ☐

Is the television on? Yes ☑ No ☐

Are you watching a programme you're interested in? Yes ☑ No ☐

Is your parent sitting with you? Yes ☑ No ☐

Are they asking a lot of questions about who is who and why someone's doing that? Yes ☑ No ☐

Are they talking non stop even though you have begged them to be quiet? Yes ☑ No ☐

Have they any intention of shutting up? Yes ☐ No ☑

Your parent has **VERBALAX** – the inability to keep their mouth shut during any series that you have been enjoying.

TREATMENT: Ask a friend to tape it and turn the television off. As if by magic, your parent will be silenced. In more extreme cases, you may need to smash in your television with a baseball bat

Are you planning on
going somewhere? Yes ☑ No ☐

Will your dad be driving? Yes ☑ No ☐

Is he worried about the parking? Yes ☑ No ☐

Is he worried about having
change for the parking? Yes ☑ No ☐

Is he worried about the
time restrictions imposed
while parking? Yes ☑ No ☐

Has he been talking about the
parking for at least a week
before the trip? Yes ☑ No ☐

Does he not want to go because
of the whole parking thing? Yes ☑ No ☐

Your father is suffering from **METERMONIA,** an overwhelming
fear that there will be nowhere to park.

TREATMENT: Go by train.

Doctors appointment!
Thursday 10.30am

Are you outside? Yes ☑ No ☐

Are you with your mother? Yes ☑ No ☐

Is she tutting a lot? Yes ☑ No ☐

Is she shaking her head and
looking disapproving? Yes ☑ No ☐

Is she shouting at strangers to
pick up litter? Yes ☑ No ☐

Is she advising people she doesn't
know on the best way to pack groceries? Yes ☑ No ☐

Is she telling random teenagers in
shopping malls not to smoke
and to do their homework? Yes ☑ No ☐

Your parent is suffering from **POCHINOSATICA**, the mistaken belief
that strangers' lives are enriched by her opinions.

TREATMENT: Very difficult to cure. Short of keeping your mother
in solitary confinement for the rest of her life, prognosis is futile. Ease
the pain by never going anywhere with her. What you don't know
can't harm you.

Jane & Steve – 8pm!

Spare Time plus Parents divided by You equals Armageddon unless you know how, where, what and why. Every moment your parent is unoccupied is a step deeper into a quagmire of troubles. Left unattended, your parent will take matters into their own hands and, before you know it, they'll have signed you up with a dating agency (irrespective of whether or not you are single) and given your details to every double-glazing firm within a ten-mile radius. Parents cannot help themselves. Anything to do with you and they want a piece. So distract them.

The trick to spending time with your parents is to stay on your toes and keep it simple. Like haemorrhoids, parents can flare up at a moment's notice so don't exacerbate the problem by making wild announcements. If you want to become a drug addict or a porn star, fine, but these things aren't going to go down well with a parent. So pipe down your cakehole! The less you can tell your parents about yourself the better. Even if you don't want to keep them in the total dark about your every day life, you should, at the very least, consider keeping them tethered in the twilight. It's going to come as a shocker, but if you want peace and a lot of quiet, then guess what?

 THEY DON'T NEED TO KNOW ANYTHING

That said, you are obliged to spend a certain amount of time with your parents. It's like flying hours but without the *joie de vivre*. With some parents, like the Wassername and the Blivyoid, it's going to be no better than having to do community service, but whatever your parent, you are going to be expected to chat, listen and engage. It's not going to be good enough to arrive home on a Sunday, make a beeline for the papers and hide behind them until it's time to go home again. No. For mothers with half-deaf husbands who only want to talk about fuel tax, they want and expect you to be congenial and convivial. You are their lifeline to the modern world.

Spending quality time with the Pezzers is a delicate balancing act between your needs and theirs. They need to worm their sticky tendrils into every aspect of your life. You need to feel the stiff breeze of freedom. Give parents boundaries and they should respond. And if you can teach yourself not to be quite so grumpy when in their presence and start thinking of them as friends, you'll be amazed at how your relationship with your parents will improve.

Enjoyment is yours for the taking. Observe.

GOING OUT FOR DINNER

Once you've got your own place, your parents are going to want to visit. When you visit your parents, you can sit back, put your feet up and relax. A trip back to the parental home is a metaphorical wiping away of the years. It's as if the intervening years between your leaving home and coming back have never happened. In short, the pressure is off and neither party has to make any sort of effort.

However, when your parents come and visit you, the rules are completely different. Your parents require entertaining. And that means cooking. It's a potential minefield. So my advice is – unless you're really good at making shepherd's pie, just GO OUT FOR DINNER. That way your parents can criticise someone else's cooking for once. But even restaurants can be like a man-trap for parental relations. Let's have a look and chat about it afterwards.

'What do you two want?' I had asked as we all sat staring at the menu.
'What do you want?' asked my mother.
'No,' said I, putting down my menu. 'I asked first. What do you want?'
'But what do you want?'
'I know what I'm having, and I'm not telling you.'
HMB fidgeted in her chair and stared at me with the sort of fright that only a very small mouse can muster.
'Tony,' she declared, 'pass me my glasses.'
She flipped open the menu and stared at it again. She then turned to WDT.
'What do you want?' she said.
He looked at her and said, 'What do you want?'
'Oh, for crying out loud,' said I, throwing my arms up into the air.
'Have the platter for two!'
They both looked at me. 'Is that what you want?'

ASK MUM FOR SHEPHERDS PIE RECIPE

'No! I'm having some edamame beans!'
'They sound nice. I'll have those,' said HMB, taking her glasses off and handing them to WDT.
'No,' said I, leaning into the table and putting a hand to my forehead. 'You're going to have the platter for two. You are not going to have what I have. The platter for two is very nice.'
'Is that what you want?' asked HMB, nodding.
I stared up at the ceiling and felt my nails dig into the table top.
'Just order the platter,' I said in a barely audible whisper.

Fifteen minutes later

'This chicken's lovely,' said WDT. He was all smiles.
'And aren't these prawns delicious?' said HMB.

I said nothing. My mouth was full of edamame beans.

'There's one lamb cutlet and one sausage left,' said WDT, fifteen minutes later. 'Which do you want?'
HMB looked at the depleted platter. 'What does Emma want?'
'I don't want anything.'
'I'll have whatever Emma doesn't want.'
'I don't want anything.'
'She doesn't want anything,' said WDT, staring at the cutlet.
'Yes, she does,' said HMB. 'You want the sausage.'
'I don't want the sausage.'
'There we are then, she wants the cutlet. Give Emma the cutlet.'
'I don't want the cutlet.'
'What do you want then?'

I looked at WDT with a face that had lost the will to live.

'She doesn't want anything,' WDT said, nudging HMB in the arm.

There was a pause.

'Yes, she does,' said HMB. 'Don't be so greedy, Tony.'

'I'm not being greedy; she doesn't want anything.'

'I don't want anything,' said I, my head falling lower and lower towards the table.

'Are you sure?' asked HMB with not a scrap of belief.

'I. Don't. Want. Anything. Any. Thing.'

'All right then,' said HMB. 'I'll have the cutlet.'

WDT's little face crumpled.

'I wanted that,' said he in his soft Welsh voice.

'Too bad,' said HMB, mouth full of lamb.

THE SOLUTION

Like St Elmo's Fire, parents not being able to make their minds up when they've got you to make it up for them is a naturally occurring phenomenon. There's very little you can do about it. When it happens, some people like to stand back and take pictures, but my advice in this situation is to make a decision and make it fast. Once indecision has taken grip of any parent, you're in trouble, so you'll be doing yourself the best of favours by taking this particular bull by its horns and wrestling it till it weeps.

SUNDAY LUNCH

The Alma Mater of parental get-togethers. It doesn't matter if it's beef, chicken or a giant-sized pumpkin, whatever it is it's got to be roasted and everyone's got to be sitting round a table. Think Christmas Dinner but without the trimmings. Or your granddad making inappropriate comments about breasts. Sunday lunch should always be regarded as an informal family gathering, but don't let that fool you into dropping your guard for even a nanosecond...

'I'll be there at one, Dad,' I had said early that morning.

But I was late. By ten minutes. I was coming off the A1 when my phone rang. It was WDT.

'Where are you, love?'
'I've just come off the A1. I'll be there in five minutes.'
'But it's ten past,' said he, his voice strangled with worry.

I made an indiscriminate noise and hung up.

On arrival, I was dragged in through the door and herded to the table where an accusing glass of wine was already sitting waiting for me.

'Drink that!' said HMB, pointing at it with an angry finger.
'But I haven't even taken my coat off yet,' I protested.
'Too late for that,' said HMB as pots and pans clattered in the kitchen.

A plate was thrown into the empty space in front of me.

'Beef, broccoli, potatoes and other vegetables' WDT shouted as he ran in with dish after dish.

Lunch was eaten at break-neck speed, and only then did WDT and HMB allow the eating to drop below Race Pace.

'What kind of person eats someone's last chocolate mousse?' asked HMB suddenly, in a tone that you would expect to be reserved for baby-killers.

We all looked up.

'I'll tell you who...,' said HMB, sitting back and dropping her cutlery. She then talked for twenty minutes without stopping and, as far as I could make out, not breathing either. I had terrible indigestion, and Poppy, My Most Excellent Beagle, had disappeared into the kitchen where she was attacking the bin with gusto.
'Why are you sitting there in your coat, Em?' said WDT, noticing me over the melted vegetables.

I chose not to answer. It is a Sunday after all.

THE SOLUTION

Difficult yet oh so very obvious. The Sunday lunch, in any family, ALWAYS starts at the same time every week. It doesn't have to be One O'Clock like it is at Kennedy Towers; perhaps your family do the two-er or the late three-er. Some families even push the hunger boat out and don't have their Sunday lunch till four.
The crackalacks. It doesn't matter.
But whatever time your family has their Sunday Lunch it will be AT THE SAME TIME FOREVER AND EVER AMEN AND MUST NEVER BE CHANGED NO NOT EVEN BY ONE MINUTE. I was late by ten minutes. They've got me banged to rights.
I lived. And I learned.

DO NOT FORGET TIME!

GETTING WITH THE KIDS' GRANDMA

So your parents are round at your place. This time there's no avoiding it. But like molluscs, once parents have got their toes over your threshold, it's quite hard to shift them. They'll stay for days if you let them. So don't. Make it quite clear that although welcome, their mere presence is a burden and a chore. Subtlety is the key here. You probably like your parents so there's nothing to be gained from being mean. Instead, try subliminal messaging. Parents are incapable of picking up on the obvious so change them by osmosis. Let's see what I mean. In the following scenario, the Pezzers had been at Kennedy Towers for two days, which, like dog years, actually feels like three months. Enough is enough. I need to start making it quite clear that it might be time for them to go home.

'You're treating this place like an hotel ,' said I to HMB and WDT, who were sitting on my sofa.
'It's A hotel, not AN hotel,' chided HMB.
'I know thaaaaat,' said I, belming (*To belm: verb: inserting the tongue into the lower lip and pushing it out while making an Err-err-err noise to convey stupidity*) 'I knoooow it's not AN hotel. I just like to say AN hotel. It's something I like to do.'
'Sometimes,' said WDT, looking at me, 'I think I'll never understand you.'
'You should be setting an example, Emma,' said HMB, nodding. 'I mean you went to Oxford AND you're on the telly. AN hotel. I mean, honestly.'
'It amuses me to say AN. Deal with it. I also like to not pronounce the H. AN Otel. AN. O-tel.'
'Anyway, Tony will have a coffee and I'll have a tea. Not too hot and quite weak.'
'And a biscuit if you've got one' piped up WDT.
'And a biscuit for me as well. And then we'd like our lunch in about twenty minutes. All right?'
'I refer you to my previous statement,' said I. 'AN. O. Tel.'

'I like hotels,' mused WDT. 'But they're not as nice as being at home, are they?'

'No,' said I, quick as a flash and then, with a glance at my watch, 'School run will start soon. And then the rush hour. And there's those roadworks... '

'Hmmm,' pondered WDT, going a little ashen. 'I think we should go now. Don't want to risk it.'

Victory.

THE SOLUTION

Yes. I am AN genius. Thanks for noticing. See how I drip-feed the word 'hotel' into the conversation a colossal six times. They don't know it, but they're being battered with a psychological jackhammer. Not only have I managed to induce feelings of longing for the familial home but I grab WDT by the jugular and prey on his greatest fear – being stuck in traffic. This is a basic yet effective manoeuvre, especially with a Practibot. The mere whiff of a vehicle snarl-up and they'll be out of the traps quicker than a greyhound. Traffic might not be your parents' *bête noire*, but whatever their worst case scenario the golden rule must be

MENTION IT EVER SO CASUALLY AND THEN RUN FOR THE HILLS

You can't fail.

WELCOME TO THE STEAM AGE

Like any half decent PLC, your family unit will occasionally need a group exercise to bind the ties and motivate you through the coming year. Unlike a half-decent PLC, you don't need to try rock-climbing or standing on poles while Mike from Resources vomits behind a bush because he drank too much at the hotel last night. No. You don't need anything so extreme. In fact, the simpler the better. Whether it's a rockery that needs creating or a life-size papier mâché horse that needs burning, nothing will bring you and your parents together quicker than an-all-hands-to-the-pump activity. It would be ludicrous to take HMB white-water rafting, so instead I tried another form of slightly wet entertainment – steam.

I had found myself sitting on my sofa, cup of peppermint tea in one hand and biscuit in the other. I was having my mid-afternoon break and I'd stuck the telly on to catch a bit of news but had ended up enjoying a shopping channel where a woman with bleached green hair had been extolling the essential virtues of home-made card kits. It was hypnotic. But that was nothing as to what was to come. On she came, a slightly overweight lady with a beaming smile who looked as if she couldn't believe her luck. She was demonstrating the magic properties of the steam cleaner, a household appliance of which I was ignorant.

'Look at this oven ,' she said, pointing into a hell mouth of crusted-on grime. 'Imagine the elbow work that you'd need to shift that!'
'I can imagine,' said I, taking a bite on my biscuit.
'Well, not if you're using this,' she proclaimed, holding aloft a small accessory that slotted onto the end of a hosepipe. 'You just steam and it's gone. Steam. And it's gone.'

I stopped my biscuit biting in its tracks. With one puff of the steam jet that baked on grease was gone. Gone!

'And it's just STEAM, Tracy!' said the presenter.

'I know!' said Tracy, for that was her name. 'With this, you will never have to buy another chemical product again.'

Needless to say, Tracy then ran through all the other things that just steam could clean: upholstery, windows, rugs, limescale, floors – you name it – the steam could clean it.

'And it's just STEAM, Tracy!' would say the presenter.
'I know!' would say she.

It was a Road To Damascus moment, and I swore then and there that I would get me a steam cleaner or die trying.

Cut to one week later. I'm in a large shopping mall with HMB.

'What do you want for your birthday?' said she, because that date was creeping up fast.
'A steam cleaner,' said I. 'I'm going to get a steam cleaner. You can give me a bit of money towards it, because I think the good ones are quite expensive.'
'Shall we go and look at some?' said she.

The steam cleaner – it's like Jesus is in a household appliance

And we did. And we got one. And we brought it home. And WDT read the instructions. And then we filled it with water. And nothing else. And then we turned it on. And then we started steam-cleaning.

'It's just STEAM!' I screamed, eyes a-poppin' as we watched it dissolve five years worth of crusted on condensation.
'I can't BELIEVE it!' yelled HMB, shaking her head.
'It's just STEAM!' shrieked I, as we watched it melt away spots on the front room rug that have never shifted for love nor even money.

'I've NEVER seen anything like it!' shouted WDT, holding his head with both his hands.

'Mum! Dad! Quick!' yelled I, as it made that ring of limescale that has made a mockery of a sham of every single chemical product I've tried on it since moving into Kennedy Towers vanish.

'I want a go on it!' screamed WDT as it cut a swathe through the oven grease.

'It's like Jesus is in a household appliance!' hystericalised HMB.

'It's just STEAM!' cried I.

Oh sweet God of household chores. It was bloody fantastic.

THE SOLUTION

So right now, you might be thinking 'So what?' Think it through people. Not only have I managed to bring my family unit together with a sense of communal wonder but look carefully – I got my Dad to clean my oven without having to ask. Result.

EMMA KENNEDY

SMELLS LIKE PRE-TEEN SPIRIT

Nostalgia. Everyone loves its sweet, dank smell. And no one loves it more than your parents. How they love to reminisce about the old days. Like that time you flooded the downstairs hallway because you wanted to make paper pulp in the toilet sink and you got bored and left the tap running. Happy days!

But nothing makes a parent happier than remembering the little things they used to do for you. Like the Saturday morning visit to Ali Bongo's Sweet Shop, where aniseed twists and Gold Rush bubblegum captured the mood and rotted your cavities. Tooty Minties! The Texan bar! They just don't make them like that any more. Mostly because they contained carcinogens and have been banned by the European Union, but that to one side – wasn't Space Dust brilliant?

My favourite childhood sweet was a Black Jack with a Fruit Salad chaser. In my day, they came loose in a big bucket and you could get four for half a penny. And you always had to have one with the other. Them was the rules. But nowadays, in our post-Jamie 'Killjoy' Oliver world, where children have to eat naught but couscous and raisins, buckets of congealed sugar are frowned upon. Unless you play your cards right...

Do they still sell penny sweets?

'Why is it,' said I, leaning back and folding my arms, 'that you can NEVER find a Black Jack or a Fruit Salad? I used to love them. They were my favourite. But you never see them any more. Not loose. Like they used to be.'
'I never liked Black Jacks,' said HMB, thinking about that. 'They make your tongue go black. But I did like Fruit Salads.'
'You can't eat one without the other,' chided I. 'That's very wrong. The Black Jack and the Fruit Salad exist in a symbiotic relationship. One does

not go without the other. Just like the donkey who loves to live with the pony. So are the Black Jack and the Fruit Salad. Constant companions.'

'Bit like me and your mother,' said WDT, with a sense of dreadful rue. 'But with no time off for good behaviour. Are you sure you can't get them anywhere? I bet I could find some.'

'Bet you can't,' said I. 'And just finding them in a plastic packet won't suffice. They have to come in a soft paper bag. That smells of pear drops.'

'Now THAT'S a sweet!' declared HMB, pointing a finger into the air. And we all nodded.

So let's leapfrog to the front room of Kennedy Towers one week later. I'm sitting. HMB is standing with her coat on. WDT is fiddling in his small man's handbag.

'Guess what I've got?' said he, eyes a-beaming.

'Herpes?' asked I.

'Noooooo! Black Jacks and Fruit Salads! In a bag! Made of paper!'

At this point, he held out a small, white paper bag. It felt weighty. I pulled it open and peered in. It was ramalangadingdong packed with Black Jacks and their best friend, the Fruit Salads.

'I found a specialist sweetie shop,' said WDT, feeling VERY pleased with himself. 'And I went in and I said, "Have you got any Black Jacks and Fruit Salads?", and the man in the shop gave me a wink and pulled out two containers from under the counter. They weren't even on display.'

'Well, they wouldn't be,' I nodded, 'they are only for special occasions.'

'I got you fifty. They were 1p each.'

'Blimey,' said HMB, 'you've pushed the boat out.'

WDT grinned and pointed into the bag.

'Black Jacks. And Fruit Salads.'

the black jack tongue

And then we ate them. Till our tongues went black.

THE SOLUTION

On the face of it, there doesn't seem to be a problem here. But I wanted to mention this incident to highlight a difficulty that can be easily overlooked. When your parents are retired, they are as bored as hell. So set them tasks. Not impossible ones like trying to get off with the Duke of Edinburgh, but simple, achievable goals that will increase their sense of self-worth and make them feel as if they are making a valuable contribution. WDT is like a bloodhound when it comes to tracking shit so it was inevitable that he would come good. But note how I play dumb on this matter. Result being – WDT feels great about himself and I get to stuff my face with sweets. Perfect.

Possible new tasks???

TEACHING YOUR PARENTS HOW TO PLAY POKER

Just the title of this problem should send chills through you. In retrospect, I don't know what I was thinking of. But at Christmas, there are only so many times you can play charades, and there was I thinking we'd make things a little bit more interesting...

'So!' declared I, shuffling the deck with a flourish. 'Texas no Limit Hold 'Em!'

'I thought we were learning poker?' said HMB, leaning forward and staring at the pack.

'That is poker. Texas No Limit Hold 'Em is poker.'

'Are you sure?'

'Shhh,' said WDT, giving her a nudge. 'Let's wait and see.'

'Wait and see for what?' asked I.

'Wait and see if you're wrong,' said WDT, as if that were obvious.

'So. In Texas No Limit Hold 'Em, you are dealt two cards. You don't show these to anyone.'

'Am I allowed to look at them?' asked WDT.

'Yes,' said I, whereupon they both picked up their cards.

'I've got a Queen and an eight,' said HMB. 'Have I won?'

'Noooo!' said I, taking back her cards. 'You're not supposed to say what you've got. That's the point. You keep those two cards covered. We'll start again. Right. Here. You're dealt two cards. I'm the dealer. Which means you're the Small Blind and you're the Big Blind.'

'Who's blind?' said HMB. 'Why are we blind? I thought we could see the cards?'

'No. It's just a word. It means that the two players to the left of the dealer HAVE to put some money into the pot before betting starts. It's to make sure there's always some money in the pot. So the Small Blind

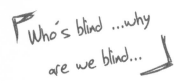

Who's blind ...why are we blind...

puts in twenty-five. And the Big Blind puts in fifty. So you put in twenty-five, Dad. And you put in fifty.'

'Why do I have to put in fifty?' protested HMB.

'Because you're the Big Blind,' said I.

'But that's not fair. Tony's only had to put in twenty-five.. So I'm only putting in twenty-five..'

'No. That's not how it works. You have to put in double the Small Blind. That's why you're called the Big Blind.'

'Well, I'm not doing it. This is a very unjust system.'

'All right! Swap places!' shouted I. 'Go on. Swap places with Dad. Now you're the Small Blind. So you put in twenty-five..'

'Yes,' nodded HMB. 'That's better.'

'OK,' said I, taking a deep breath. 'So now you've seen your cards and you decide whether you're going to bet. So we have a round of betting. I'm going to call. So I put in fifty.'

'But I've only put in twenty-five.,' said HMB, pointing at her chips.

'Yes. So now if you want to play then you have to put in another twenty-five.. If you don't, then you fold.'

'But I don't want to put in another twenty-five. I'm the Small Blind.'

'Yes. I know you're the Small Blind. But the Small Blind now has to match the Big Blind if the Small Blind wants to play. So if you want to play, you have to match his fifty. If you don't want to play then you fold.'

'So the Big Blind doesn't have to put any more money in?' asked HMB, staring.

'If no one raises, then no.'

'Well, I want to be the Big Blind. Come on Tony, swap places.'

And up they got again.

'Right,' declared HMB. 'So I'm the Big Blind and I'm not putting in any more money!'

'OK,' said I, head in hand. 'So no one has raised, so now we see the Flop, which is three cards that will be put down face up on the table. There are going to be five community cards, and the aim is to make the best five-card hand out of the seven cards available to you.'

BIG MONEY

'What?' said HMB.

'You've got two cards in your hand.'

'Yes.'

'And there will be five cards dealt onto the table.'

'Yes.'

'So that makes seven cards. But you only need a five-card hand. So if you've got a King and a Queen in your hand, and an ace, a Jack, a ten, a nine and an eight comes down on the table, then the best hand is your ace high straight. Do you get it?'

'No. I've got a seven and a three.'

'NOOOOO! Don't TELL us what you've got! Oh God! Right. Start again. Give me your cards.'

'Am I still the Big Blind?' asked HMB.

'Yes, you're still the Big Blind,' said I.

'Good,' said HMB, shooting WDT a smug smile.

'Right. There's your cards. I call. Do you call, Dad?'

'Yes, I call,' said he, pushing the fifty chips he'd already put in with his finger.

'Good. Now do you want to check or bet, Mum?'

'I'm the Big Blind,' declared HMB as if that imbued her with immunity.

'Well, let's just say you check, shall we? OK. So here's the Flop. That's the first three cards. And it's a King. A four. And a six. So – betting starts with you Dad. Do you want to check or bet?'

'Check what?' asked WDT.

'Check your cards,' said HMB, like suddenly she knows. 'You have to look at your cards and make sure you know what you've got.'

'No,' said I, fist clenching. 'To check does not mean to look at your cards. It means you want to stick. So if you don't want to make a bet, you check.'

Patience is wearing thin...

'I would like to check please,' said WDT.

'Check. Right. Now, Mum. What would you like to do?'

'So I can bet now, can I?' asked she, licking her lips slightly.

'Yes. And it's No Limit so you can bet as much as you like. You can put in fifty or you can go all in. It's up to you.'

'Oh well, all in then,' said she, smiling.

'Are you sure?' said I.

'Oh yes,' said she. 'All in, please. I've got a Jack and a Nine.'

'Noooooooooo!' wailed I. 'How many times? And anyway – what are you doing going all in when you've got nothing?'

'I have. I've got a Jack and a nine!' declared she.

'You've got nothing,' said I.

'Yes I have,' said she. 'Look. I've got a Jack and a King and a nine and a four and a six.'

'That's not how it works,' said I.

'Yes, it is,' said she. 'I should know. I'm the Big Blind.'

Never. Again.

THE SOLUTION

Let me say this – Sisyphus had it easy. Flying to the moon on cardboard wings would have been less of a struggle. My advice – stick to Snap.

FEELING PUZZLED

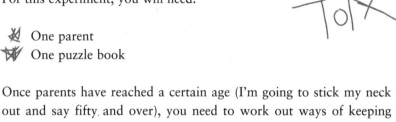

For this experiment, you will need:

 One parent
One puzzle book

Once parents have reached a certain age (I'm going to stick my neck out and say fifty and over), you need to work out ways of keeping them quiet. Parents will astonish you with their endless capacity for chat. It's like white noise. And sometimes you want that chat to stop. Puzzle books are brilliant for consuming every waking hour of an otherwise unfocused parent. Whether it's a Find The Word brainteaser or the number madness of a sudoku, try and get them hooked like a crack addict and then sit back and languor in the hours of golden silence. Disclaimer: Will not work on all parents.

It was a Tuesday, and HMB and WDT were lunching at Kennedy Towers. Having fended them off with a couple of egg bagels, I was sitting in my garden thinking about hanging baskets. WDT was enjoying a post-feast snooze in my hammock, and HMB was standing over him shouting, 'Be careful! You could crack your spine!' every time the wind blew.

In between the constant words of warning, my mother was chatting to me. In fact, she had been chatting without stopping for two hours and 35 minutes. Subjects had included encroachment on the Green Belt, why it was that no town ever wants to twin with anywhere in Columbia and the merits or otherwise of a built-up shoe. I had had enough.

'Oh!' said I, interrupting her mid flow. 'I've just remembered. I've been given a Big Book of Puzzles.'
'What's it called?' asked HMB, feigning interest.
'*The Big Book of Puzzles*,' said I, thinking that through. 'It's a big book. And it's full of puzzles. I might be going out on a limb here. But I think it might be a large book filled with puzzles.'

'I'm quite good at puzzles,' said HMB, throwing me a smile. 'Let's have a look at it.'

And so I went inside and fetched it out.

'Oooh, yes' squealed HMB. 'That IS a big book. Actually, I'm brilliant at puzzles. Try one on me.'

'So now you're brilliant at puzzles?' asked I, giving her a sideways glance. 'Because a moment ago you were only quite good at them.'

'No,' replied HMB in an imperious manner. 'I am brilliant at them. Go on. Pick any puzzle. Any puzzle you want. And test me on it.'

I opened the book. 'Alright,' said I. 'We'll start with an Easy Section puzzle. Here we are. Six coloured circles. You have to look at the six circles and name the famous fictional hero'

HMB peered over the page. 'Name the fictional hero? Just by looking at the circles?'

'Yes,' said I. 'Look at the colours of the circles. And they're in two rows. That may be significant.'

'Two rows?' muttered HMB, squinting. 'Different colours?'

'Look at them with your eyes,' advised I. 'On the top row there's a red circle, then an orange circle and then a blue circle. And then on the bottom there's a red circle and an orange circle and then a yellow circle. Think it through. Oh, who could that fictional hero be? Oh, the circles! Oh, for the colours!'

'Red. Orange. Blue,' mumbled HMB. 'And then Red, Orange, Yellow.'

'Correct. RRRRRed. OOOOOOrange. BBBBBlue. RRRRRed. OOOOOOrange. YYYYYYYellow. What could it mean?'

'Oh!' announced HMB, tapping the page with her finger. 'Got it! Darcy! It's Darcy! Red, Orange, Blue. Red, Orange, Yellow. Darcy! Obvious!'

PARENTS
the biggest puzzle
of all?

And with that, she walked back off down the garden wagging her finger at my father and screaming about slipped discs.

THE SOLUTION

For those of you momentarily caught short, the answer was, of course, Rob Roy, but let's not let the facts get in the way of a good debate. You may be feeling cheated right now. As if I promised a sure-fire method of occupying a parent with one fell swoop only to reveal that, at the most, the random parent was neutralised for no more than a matter of moments. Well, yes, you might think that. But what you don't know was that the same *Big Book of Puzzles* then kept WDT quiet for the next three hours. Plus, take note – HMB's incessant chatter was busted like a speakeasy during prohibition. Having said that, take on a puzzle with a Faffer at your peril. Nothing is more guaranteed to get you a one-way ticket to crazy town than working out puzzles with your mother. You may be biting off more than you can chew.

GATHERING WINTER FUEL *bah humbug*

Why anyone thinks Christmas is a magic time of year is a mystery. It's a prolonged build up of extravagance and till rage. Some people like Christmas shopping, but I don't. Especially if it's with you know who...

'Will she want this?' my mother screeched, holding up some shot glasses that screamed I AM DRUNK on the side. I was Christmas shopping, and on this particular day I was ticking off Friends and Work Colleagues. HMB wasn't helping.

'If there's something that sets my tolerance barometer to nought,' began I. 'It's when people suggest presents for people they don't know.'

'That's a good present!' said HMB, shaking the glasses at me. 'For someone who likes getting drunk. Does she like getting drunk? She might like them.'

'She doesn't want a set of shot glasses that say I AM DRUNK on them. I'm not getting them for her. Now or in any other lifetime. Put the shot glasses down. And walk away.'

'Hmm,' mumbled HMB, putting the glasses back where she found them. 'What about this? It's a funny thing. Would she like a funny thing?'

I stared at the object in my mother's hand.

'Do I think my make-up lady would like a plastic figurine of a drunk man whose trousers fall down and he pisses himself? Hang on. Let me think about that for a moment. Answer – no.'

'Someone might find that funny,' persisted HMB. 'Who on your list might find that funny?'

'Nobody on my list will find that funny. Nobody on anyone's list will find that funny. "Happy Christmas, darling! What have you got me? Oh! You've got me a plastic drunk man who urinates on himself! It's what I've always wanted! I love you!"'

'Well, someone must like it. Or they wouldn't make them,' said she trying to get a peek down his trousers.

'Just forget about the pissing man. We will not be purchasing him today.'

'She's your make-up lady, yes?' said HMB, moving to an adjacent aisle.

'Yes,' said I, looking at a display of foot products.

'Then would she like this?' asked she, holding aloft a packet of decorated chopsticks.

'They're chopsticks,' said I. 'Where's the sense of occasion?'

'Well, what about this?'

'No. She does not want a cushion for piles sufferers.'

'This? Look, it's a set of serial killer finger puppets.'

'OK!' said I, with a tight strain. 'That's enough of the, would she like this or this? You don't know her. You've never met her. I'll decide what she gets. Thank you.'

'I was only trying to help,' said HMB, with a small pout brewing on her upper lip.

'That's what they said when they invaded Iraq . So try and not be helpful. That would be good.'

'Who else is on your list?' asked HMB, tapping her fingers along a set of salad spoons.

'Nic, Phelps and Perks. They're the last ones,' said I, looking at a hand massager.

'Perks!' yelled HMB, with a beam. 'Oh, maybe she'd like…'

'No,' interrupted I, holding up a finger. 'Father Christmas is not interested in your opinions. He's got an excess of little helpers this year and doesn't need another one. Let's bring a sense of hush to the proceedings. Let's make like the carol and have a silent night. If I wanted a personal shopper, I'd lose three stone and move to Cheshire. What I'm saying is – thank you for your input but not one more peep. What are you doing now? What is that?'

'I'm just pointing. But not speaking,' said she, with a smug smile. And with that, off she wandered, jabbing her finger at things as she went.

top of my Xmas list (NOT)

I AM DRUNK

THE SOLUTION

Now, the more suspicious of you might think that HMB has deliberately tried to wind me up. You would be correct. Shopping with my mother is like having a woodpecker trying to pierce ants out of your eyeballs. But what you don't know is that HMB spends twelve months buying her Christmas presents. Every single gift has been pored over and chosen with the greatest of care. My Christmas presents are bought with 48 hours to go. HMB has smelt the panic and is trying to pour oil on troubled waters. I know it's impossible to conceive, but she's almost in the right. Almost. How irritating is that?

LAUGHING POLICE

Ho, ho

The chances of you having the same sense of humour as your parents are as slim as an anorexic. You like up-to-the minute humour and understand satire. They think that the links before the ad break in *Countdown* are cutting-edge comedy. This doesn't have to be problematic though; in fact, you can often turn it to your advantage. Thinking you have a better sense of humour than your parents can provide the warm glow of intellectual superiority. So please feel free to bask in it like a fat seal in the sun . But watch out, because parents are no fools. They can take you down faster than a speeding bullet.

'Something I've noticed about you,' observed HMB, 'is that you like laughing. A lot. You're always laughing. I'm not sure whether it's always appropriate.'

'Yes,' said I, thinking about that. 'I DO like laughing. I'd even go so far as to say that it might be one of my top hobbies.'

'Hmm, well,' began HMB. 'I think you might be laughing TOO much.'

'But that's not possible. In fact, they have proved that laughing can decrease your risk of heart disease and lower your cholesterol. So I should be laughing more. It's good for me.'

'That's as maybe. But have you ever thought that your laughing might not be good for OTHER people?'

'No.'

'Well, you should think about that. That's the responsible thing to do. You can't just go round laughing at everything.'

'But I don't laugh at EVERYTHING,' explained I. 'There's lots of things I wouldn't laugh at.'

'Such as?' said she, arching her eyebrows.

'OK. Well. I wouldn't laugh at an ugly teenager who had just found out he's failed all his exams and therefore the rest of his life is going to amount to nothing more than a broken egg.'

'No. That would be terrible.'

'Neither would I just laugh at an ugly teenager.'

'It's a difficult age.'

'I wouldn't dream of standing in a queue for over eight hours in order to pay my respects to the dead Queen Mother (or other member of the royal family) only to finally get there, point at the coffin and laugh.'

'You would probably be lynched.'

'Correct. I'm not an idiot. Similarly, I would never sit in a pub in Essex watching England play a crucial knock-out match in the World Cup and laugh every time one of them missed a penalty.'

'Madness.'

'Exactly. Just as it would be to laugh during any sort of three-minute silence just as the live televised coverage picks me out in the crowd. Waving would also be frowned upon in this instance.'

'Are you making fun of this, Emma? Because if you are, you need to rethink that sharpish.'

'No!' protested I. 'These are the genuine instances in which I freely acknowledge that laughing would be inappropriate!'

'Umm. Well, all right then.'

'You know, like laughing at a five-year old who's just been given a kitten for his birthday only to see it crushed to death under a Le Creuset casserole dish. Or laughing at a penis.'

'No, the penis thing's all right,' said HMB, 'but only in a controlled environment. I often laugh at your father's penis.'

'Don't want to know! La la la!' screamed I, sticking my fingers in my ears.

'Now THAT'S funny!' said HMB and off she trotted, laughing as she went.

THE SOLUTION  too much information!!

Do you see what she did there? The witch. There was I thinking I was being clever AND cheeky (a heady combination) when in she comes with a deftly placed mention of my father's genitals. Nay, nay and triple nay. I hate to say it but, in this instance, she's had the last laugh. This doesn't happen often so I suppose the best thing for all concerned is to bow and acknowledge her moment of triumph. You're not conceding defeat of course. The battle of child versus parent is an endless campaign. And you're signed up for life. So chin up, my brothers and sisters! Surrender is not an option. The day will be yours once more.

BORED GAMES

YAWN

Nothing can destroy the family unit quicker than a board game. From Monopoly to Yahtzee, Cluedo (Simpsons special edition) to Doh Nutters, you are dicing with familial death every time you pull a box out from a cupboard and say the fatal words 'Anyone fancy a game?' If it's the tail end of a long Christmas Day, you might as well be pulling a cracker filled with anthrax. There are many ways of approaching the board game but I can't say this enough – whatever the game, EXERCISE EXTREME CAUTION.

The first thing you need to do, before you do anything else, is to assess what sort of game player you're up against. Maybe you've got a Stickler who will insist on the letter of the law being applied at all times. This sort of parent will, for example, always require the first AND second name in a Trivial Pursuit

YOU ARE DICING WITH FAMILIAL DEATH EVERY TIME YOU PULL A BOARD GAME OUT OF THE CUPBOARD

answer (they may even ask for a correct spelling if it's for a piece of pie). Then you've got the Family Rules agitator who insists that the game rules as they appear in the box don't really need to be observed because they've made up their own version of the rules, which invariably makes it easier for them to win. If you're playing with two parents and one of them is a Stickler while the other wants Family Rules, nail down all furniture, lock up pets and remove all sharp objects from the room before you even sit down. Someone could lose an eye or an elbow in the inevitable battle that's going to follow. Protective clothing is also advisable in this instance. See left.

But the checklist doesn't end there. We now have to assess the competitive streak in every family member. The interesting thing to note here is that the Family Rule representative is more often than not the person most likely to cheat. If you're playing Monopoly, for example, don't let them be the banker. They'll be half-inching hundreds every time you pass Go. On top of that, the Stickler will be so desperate to win that if he or she doesn't, that's the day over right there. The winner's going to be disinherited, your dinner's going to be up the wall and everyone can piss off home. So the golden rule when it comes to board games is:

 ### ASSUME THE WORST. THEY'RE ALL C**TS

'I'd like to buy a hotel, please,' announced HMB.
'You can't,' explained WDT. 'You haven't got any houses there.'
'But I don't want houses,' answered HMB. 'I want a hotel.'
'Number One,' said WDT, holding up a finger, 'you have to have all the properties for that colour. Which you haven't. Number Two, you have to have houses first. THEN you can have a hotel .'
'No!' declared she, with a waft of the hand. 'I can have a hotel now. If I was a developer and I bought a plot of land, I wouldn't say "Ooh, I want to build a hotel but I'd better have houses first" would I?'
'No, but that's beside the point. You have to have ALL the properties for that colour. AND you have to have houses! Plus, this is a game. Not real life.'

At this point HMB leant across the board and took three hotels out of the designated compartment in the box. With a defiant flourish, she then placed them on her property.

WHERE'S THE RULE
BOOK GONE??!!

'There! Now, how much will that cost please?'
'No! You CAN'T have the hotels. And even if you did, you can't have three at once!'
'Why not?'
'Because you CAN'T!'

'That will cost £30 000,' said I, looking at the back of her card.

'Don't be ridiculous,' snapped she. 'Of course it isn't £30 000. I'll give you five-hundred. That's reasonable.'

'NO!' screamed WDT, holding his head. 'That's NOT how it works. You can't just make up a price. If you want a hotel, you have to pay the proper rate!'

'So I can have the hotels now, can I?'

'NO!' answered WDT, picking up the three hotels and putting them back in the box. 'You can't even have a house! You haven't got all the properties for that colour!'

'Well, how many properties do I need before I can have them?'

'Three,' said I, 'And you've got one. So you need to buy the other two, which you can't. Because Dad's got them.'

'Well, then he can give them to me,' announced HMB, taking the cards from WDT's pile.

'Give those back!' said he, making a grab for them.

There then followed a small, undignified scrabble.

'Right!' shouted HMB. 'That's it! Just give me a hotel! And then we can carry on!'

'Don't you dare give her a hotel!' yelled WDT, pointing at me.

'All right!' said I, holding up a calming hand. 'How's about if I let you BOTH have a hotel, just one, and then we'll call it quits?'

'No! Tony can't have a hotel!' said HMB, shaking her head. 'He hasn't got all the properties in that colour!'

'Well, neither have you!' squealed WDT. 'You've only got one!'

'OK!' said I, taking control. 'You're both getting a hotel. And that's that.'

'You see?' said HMB with a sense of triumph. 'Games are MUCH better when you're creative aren't they?'

THE SOLUTION

My mother's modus operandi when it comes to games is only playing the ones where there are plenty of opportunities for cheating. If she's not stealing money, she's demanding a recount. If she's not manipulating dice, then she's quietly moving pieces. This is the woman who thinks there should be four shooters on a netball team and whose catch-phrase, as soon as she's given up all hope of winning, is 'I'm not playing any more'.

So what can you do? To be honest, I wouldn't get the game out in the first place. You know it's going to end up like the mashed-in face of a bare-knuckle boxer so do yourself a favour and call the whole thing off. If you absolutely, positively, have to play a board game, then take my lead, remain as neutral as a UN peace-keeping force and prepare to cave in to every demand. You'll lose, but at least you'll keep your teeth.

LIMPIC SPIRIT

By now you should be enjoying your life as a family member so let's take things to the next level. Bonding is an advanced technique and can be difficult to achieve. Health and Safety laws require me to warn you that, while bonding with your parents, it's not impossible for both parties to find themselves thinking the same thing at the same time. Terrifying, but don't panic. A fear of being on the same wavelength as your Pezzers is a normal phobia and not a permanent condition. The benefits of bonding far outweigh the debilitating mental risks you run by allowing any thought, however fleeting, to be the same as anything that's rattling round your mother's cavernous brain. The advantages of bonding are as follows:

- Your parents will enter into a state of bliss
- While in this state, they will be easier to influence
- You may look at them and think things like, 'They're not so bad really. In fact, I might love them loads.'
- It'll give you something to talk about at Christmas.

'I'm so excited that London has got the Limpics!' said I.
'Me too!' nodded WDT. 'I love the Olympics!'
'Limpics,' I corrected. 'Call it by its proper name.'
'And me!' piped up HMB. 'I'm excited too!'
'I'm going to go every day!' said I.
'And I am!' agreed WDT.

LONDON 2012

'I want to do that too!' enthused HMB. 'We could all go together!'
'You know what we could do?' said I, having a sudden brainwave. 'We could sign up as volunteers! That way we could be at the Limpics every day for free!'
'How exciting!' clapped HMB.
'Do you think we'd get uniforms?' whispered WDT, in a reverential hush.
'I would be astonished if we didn't!' said I.
'And we'd get free parking, wouldn't we?' continued WDT. 'I mean, they'd have to lay on parking.'

'Goes without saying!' nodded HMB.

'Hooray!' shouted I. 'Let's do it! Let's sign up! Let's do it now!'

And so we did. As we basked in the warm glow of a post Internet log-on, HMB folded her arms and sighed.

'You know what I love the most?' said she. 'The bit in the opening ceremony when everyone runs on in a coloured cagoule and arranges themselves into a spectacular shape that can only be seen from a helicopter.'

'Like when the Italians arranged themselves into the shape of a ski jumper?' noted I.

'Yes! That was amazing, wasn't it?' nodded HMB. 'I wonder what shape the people at the London opening ceremony will arrange themselves into.'

'Plate of fish and chips ?' suggested WDT.

'Hmm,' pondered I. 'It's tricky isn't it? Because opening ceremonies are all about the culture of the host nation. We've got lots of historical culture but we haven't got much modern culture. Well, I suppose we've got binge-drinking but no one's going to want to watch a thousand volunteers running on and making the shape of a scantily dressed drunk girl. Who then vomits.'

'No,' said WDT, shaking his head.

'I expect we'll have Morris Men ,' mused HMB. 'And something to do with Shakespeare.'

'That's a given,' said WDT. 'But there's only two things we're obsessed with in this country. The 1966 World Cup and the Second World War. Because they are the only things we've ever won.'

'We won the Eurovision Song Contest a couple of times,' thought I.

'But none of those things would be suitable for an opening ceremony.'

'Especially the Second World War thing,' opined HMB. 'That would upset the Germans.'

'Hmm,' we all nodded and thought about that for a minute.

'I won't be happy if I don't see some women in Welsh national costume,' announced WDT, pointing a finger. 'I just want to say that now. But not dressed like leeks. That would make me cross.'

'Would you accept a daffodil?' asked I, because it's good to know

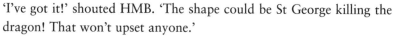

these things.

WDT looked up to the ceiling, froze and then said, 'No.'

'I've got it!' shouted HMB. 'The shape could be St George killing the dragon! That won't upset anyone.'

'No,' said I. 'Except the Scots and the Irish and the Welsh. And animal lovers.'

'This is a minefield!' declared HMB, shaking her head.

'Well!' said I, throwing my hands into the air. 'It doesn't matter what it is if we're all doing it together, does it?'

'No,' nodded WDT. 'It'll be magic.'

'But I don't want to be the vomit bit,' piped up HMB.

'Nor me,' said WDT.

'Hooray!' yelled I. 'We've got the Limpic Spirit all right! Gee whiz! I love you guys!'

'I'm so happy,' said Ma.

'And me,' said Pa.

'Oh and by the way, can you have the dog for a month? I'm going to Edinburgh.'

'Of course we can!' said they. Hugs all round!

THE SOLUTION

Masterly handling, even if I say so myself. You're never going to see a more effective bout of bonding. I start safely enough, picking an easy subject to get us out of the blocks, but note the bold, maestro stroke of suggesting we sign up for the Limpics together. It's the last thing your parents are going to expect – the fact that you actually want to spend three whole weeks with them. It's Christmas come early as far as they're concerned, and from that moment on, they're putty in my hands. Be careful not to jump the gun though. If I had mentioned the fact that I need a dog-sitter for four weeks while I gad about at an International Arts Festival getting drunk and kissing before the moment of critical bliss, I might have had a knock back. So tread carefully.

MATERNAL INSTINCTS

So let's put this rumour to bed once and for very all. Is it true that my mother has never made me a meal? Yes. It is. Not even toast. She did try once in the early '80s because WDT had gone into hospital to have a piece of Teflon put in his ear. 'This is your big chance with me,' I had said to her, aged eleven, PE kit slung over one shoulder. She had stared at me and nodded, and a moment of profound understanding passed between us. I returned home eight hours later to be greeted with a pot of cockles (which we couldn't get the lid off) and the breathtaking announcement that dinner was going to be 'Rice and garlic!' To conclude – I made myself a sandwich.

I, Emma Kennedy, do solemnly declare that my mother has NEVER made me a meal

All that week, as we stood staring at the fridge and not knowing quite how to make the stuff inside it turn into meals, HMB would get me to ring round friends of the family and plead starvation. Net result – they would ask if I wanted to come for dinner. I would say, 'Yes, and can my mum come too?' We were like the Bonnie and Clyde of suppers. I would be in a constant state of mortification and, at the conclusion of every wrangled meal, would insist on washing up. HMB, on the other hand, would just sit laughing her head off because she couldn't believe the cunning wheeze we'd tapped into, and whenever I would turn to her and ask if she was going to help me clean up, she would utter the now immortal phrase, 'Emma – I can't lift a pan. My womb will drop out.'

So what can we conclude from this? HMB is the most slippery of characters. Observe.

'Come over to dinner,' had said HMB. 'Your father's got to go somewhere or other and get something for the car. It'll just be us.'

BURNT TOAST

And so twenty-four hours later I turned up. Would this, I wondered, be the day that my mother finally put that no meal demon to bed? I was expectant and determined.

'What are you making me?' asked I, bold as brass, on arrival.

'Hmmm,' said HMB, looking furtive. 'I don't know if it works like that. Couldn't you just cook it for me?'

'Hold up,' said I. 'You do realise that by inviting ME over to dinner it means YOU have to cook it.'

'Does it really though?' said HMB, who was shifting (some would say) uncomfortably.

'Well, let's examine the Rulebook of Inviting People Over To Dinner, shall we?' said I, flipping open an imaginary book and thumbing through its pages. 'Oh look, Rule Number One – When you invite anyone over for dinner. Anyone. I should stress that. Then YOU have to cook THEM dinner. That's what it says. It's quite specific. It's unequivocal. That's how it works. That is the very essence of the definition of being invited over for dinner. The crucial bit is the invitation. It means you are automatically elevated into a special category not unlike a VIP or a holy figure chanced upon by pilgrims. For the duration of the visit, the invited person does nothing. Maybe, just maybe, you might be expected to pass the salt, or help yourself to a glass of wine. But that's it. You're the guest. Therefore you do nothing. NOTHING. That's what it says here in Rule Number One of the So You've Invited Someone Over To Dinner Manual.'

'The name of your book seems to have changed.'

'That doesn't matter. The point I am making is this. YOU invited me to dinner. That means YOU do the cooking.'

'So are you going to make the dinner?' said HMB, looking up at me. Small silence.

'No,' said I, unblinking.

'Do you remember that time I thought I was boiling broccoli and it turned out to be a bag of parsley?' said HMB, parrying back.

'All right,' said I. 'What's in the fridge?'

cook
∧ dinner at mum's

I made oriental pork noodle soup.

And I washed up.

I can't help feeling that something somewhere isn't right.

THE SOLUTION

Never underestimate the level of cunning that bubbles under the surface of any parent. To the untrained eye, it might look as if I've rolled over and died like a depressed cocker spaniel. I haven't. I've assessed the situation and quickly reached the conclusion that if my mother ever did cook me a meal, it would be shit. So what's the point? I could have something edible or something a starved cat would turn its nose up at. Where's the choice? Use your noggins, people.

TIPPOO'S TIGER

Balloon Lips, Magic Tricks and Devil Me Maiden. Parlour games have been at the bedrock of the family get-together since time immemorial. Perhaps your dad, like mine, mimes the same TV programme during every Christmas charades session? Without fail, he gets up, makes the shape of a square, holds up two fingers, then pretends to be cold for the first word, and then slam dunks the second by just pointing at his penis. Answer – yes! It's *Blue Peter*! What would we do without him? But some parlour games are even more sinister than your father gesturing towards his crotch. I know that's almost impossible to imagine. But it's true.

It all started when Adam Christmas, the man with the best name in the universe, sent me a link to the Tippoo's Tiger page on the V&A website. If you want to play along, you can go and have a look at it now at *and so the story began...* www.vam.ac.uk. Once you're there, just type in 'Tippoo's Tiger' and let the fun commence. On the website is a picture of Tippoo's Tiger, an infamous knick-knack cum parlour game of a tiger mauling a poor man to death.

'What sort of parlour game psychopath thought that up?' asked HMB, who is so fascinated by anything to do with my computer that every time it's on, she stands behind my shoulder and makes 'Oooooh!' noises. 'Look,' said I, with my Pooty Know-How, 'if I click here, you can hear the noise it makes. Can you see? – there's a little handle there, and if I click on it then... .'

'Weeeeeeeeeeeeeeeeeeeeeeaaaaaaaaaaaaaaaaaaaaaahhhhhhhh!' wailed the computer.

'Oh, that's awful' said HMB, recoiling a little. 'Do you think that's the exact noise of a man being mauled by a tiger?'

'Well, it is a terrifying and haunting scream, so I'm guessing yes. Oh and look – if I click here, on the tiger's belly, then it opens up to reveal a keyboard. And if I click on THAT then... '

And thus poured forth the tinkles.

'So let's get this straight,' recapped I. 'It's a parlour game. Of a man being eaten to death by a tiger who screams while you play tunes on the tiger's organ. Ah ha. Tiger's organ. I am funny.'

'Perhaps Tippoo's Tiger was not a one off?' pondered HMB. 'Perhaps musical instruments based on ghoulish killings by ferocious animals were all the rage in the Victorian age.'

'Interesting,' mused I, nodding. 'Something like a small boy being crushed by a python treble recorder ?'

'Yes,' said HMB. 'Or a woman half eaten by a crocodile violin?'

'Or even, and I think this would be my personal favourite, a blind man with no legs being arse-raped by a gorilla bassoon?'

'Oh, you've gone too far,' chastised HMB. 'There would be an outcry.' We both thought about that.

'I'd quite like to see a Rod Stewart being chewed by a pack-of-lions electric guitar,' added she, relishing the thought.

'What's the matter with him?' wondered I, surprised at the outburst.

'Well,' shrugged HMB. 'He's been mauling music for years. Think of it as payback.'

THE SOLUTION

OK. So I've used a Victorian parlour trinket as a tenuous excuse to write the words 'arse-raped by a gorilla bassoon' in a book. I have. So sue me. I defy you to find that combination of words anywhere in any book ever written in any language. I like to think of that as some sort of achievement. Anyway, the point here is that there is no point. I just got to write 'arse-raped by a gorilla bassoon'. Joy.

TOP O' THE BILL

Nothing annoys your parents more than television. NOTHING. That doesn't stop them watching it, of course. In fact, the more they hate something, the more they love it. Bad mass entertainment spectacles are honey to the bee for parents, and the nadir of their annual viewing is the *Royal Variety Performance*, which, every year without fail, acts as the rallying point for all televisual niggles that have bubbled up over any twelve-month period. It makes them LIVID. My advice from the off is just not to be in the house when it's on. But even that isn't going to guarantee your safety. When they're in Moan Mode, they will track you down like bloodhounds, like that time my mother had me paged in New York just so she could tell me how angry she was that a hairdresser had got water in her ear.

'Why are we watching this?' cried out HMB, as Jimmy Carr stepped out from behind a velvet curtain. 'Why?'
'What I'd like to see,' chipped in WDT, 'is a Royal Variety Show where the celebrities are in the audience and the Royals are doing the entertaining!'
'Prince Phillip tap dancing!' yelled HMB, nodding wildly.
'Or Prince Edward singing a medley of James Brown songs,' agreed WDT, pounding a finger down on the sofa. 'But no! Instead we get the same old rubbish. Year in, year out! Half-witted, smug comedians and so-called personalities! Why is Cliff Richard the headline act? Why?'
'Because he's got that house in the Bahamas!' screamed HMB. 'He lets them all go there if he's the last man standing. It's a massive conspiracy!'
'But he can always be relied on,' said I, leaping to the wrinkled pixie's defence. 'I once bumped into Cliff Richard. I was at Schiphol airport. He was looking at the Gouda . Anyone who likes cheese can't be all bad.'
'And what's he going to sing?' wailed WDT, incensed. 'Summer bloody Holiday? Mistletoe and shitting Wine?'
'Perhaps he'll sing that song from *Heathcliff* the musical?' mused I. 'The one where he went all dangerous by not shaving. Anyway. Let's give the man a chance.'

ROYAL VARIETY
PERFORMANCE
8PM SAT

At this point, thinking that Sir Cliff would wheel out one of his show-stopping favourites, I settled back into the sofa and folded my arms. Perhaps he would rock the house with a spirited rendition of 'Devil Woman' or kick the stalls into a frenzy with 'Living Doll'? Or, because Christmas wasn't a million miles around the corner, perhaps the Peter Pan of Pop would remind us all of the true meaning of Christmas with his Jesus Jolly, 'Saviour's Day'? Perhaps, nay SURELY, he would sing one of those. Because that would slightly justify putting him at the top of the bill ahead of Elton John or Liza Minelli. But instead of all or any of those things, Sir Cliff, for reasons best known to himself, began to sing something unrecognisable that was so thumpingly dull that the word 'turgid' wouldn't have been out of place.

'What's he doing?' wailed WDT, gesturing towards the television. 'Now's not the time to try out new material. He's Sir Bloody Cliff! He's got responsibilities!'
'Do you know?' added HMB shaking her head, 'if Prince Charles took out a shotgun now and killed Cliff Richard in the mouth or face, no one would be angry.'
'There's not a court in the land that would convict him,' said WDT. 'Not on this evidence.'
'No,' said HMB. 'And anyway, it would be self-defence.'

At that point, Sir Cliff did a 'dance move' which, putting his words to his pictures, seemed to be a mime of a butterfly but, looking at it, if we'd been playing charades, I would have guessed the words 'constipated albatross'. But sadly, Sir Cliff was not acting out the book *Jonathan Livingston Seagull;* instead he was banging the nails into the coffin that was the *Royal Variety Performance.*

There was a brief moment of hope when Sir Cliff, holding his mic with two hands and gurning through his front teeth, brought on Olivia

Newton-John. Would they perhaps perform a song from *Grease*? Would Olivia take to the floor and belt out 'Xanadu'? Or would they sing that song that they did sing together all those moons ago? That would be nice for old time's sake. But no. They sang another song no one had ever heard of that was just as slow and dull as the first.

'Whatever happened to the big ending?' asked WDT, holding his hands up to the heavens.

But the big ending was, of course, nothing to do with anyone who was performing. The Big End to the *Royal Variety Performance*, as any fool knows, is when Prince Charles goes backstage to meet the cast. Strangely, the Big End was cut very short this year. He got as far as Liza, the credits ran like Billy Whizz and the whole thing ground to a halt.

'What?' said I, 'no full Prince Charles Meet 'N Greet?'
'I expect they had to cut it,' said HMB. 'I bet he got to Cliff and punched him.'

Now that would have boosted the ratings.

THE SOLUTION

It is always something of a mystery to me that an innocuous variety show can bring out the worst in people. But the *Royal Variety Performance* is the treasure chest of outrage as far as my parents are concerned. There's nothing to be done about this, of course, unless you are the controller of television and are in a position to drive round to my parents' house, have a nervous breakdown and ask them to be in charge of it next year if they think they can do any better. As I was writing this, I turned to my mother and asked who she would have as the headlining act if she were in charge. Without a second of hesitation, she came out with it: 'Germaine Greer. Singing "Hit me with your Rhythm Stick"'. Now THAT I'd watch.' Amens all round.

Mom, Dad, I'm
moving out...

What's that noise? It's like a dread wailing spliced with the slow death rattle of an elephant. Oh yes. It's your parents two seconds after you've told them you're leaving home for ever. The paradox here, of course, is that by the time you're in a position to leave home, your parents can't wait to get rid of you, but when that moment comes, all grief-stricken hell is going to break loose.

If you're in a family that has lots of siblings, you can count yourself lucky. The pain is spread so thin that by the time the youngest of you leaves you'll be struggling to get even a grunt of a goodbye. That's how disinterested they will be. But when you're an only child, like me, you need to prepare yourself for the slaughterhouse floor of muck that you're going to be knee deep in.

Like pulling a plaster, don't prolong the agony. The more sensible of you will have pre-packed and have the taxi waiting before you tell them. Just walk away and let the St John's Ambulance volunteers pick up the pieces. The transitory period will be painful for both parties. Your parents may need transplants after crying their eyeballs out of their sockets, while you may find yourself staring at your dirty washing and wondering if it can magic itself clean. It can't.

So the next step is to settle into the new phase of your lives. You may be gone but you're not forgotten. Parents may find themselves prostrate on an upstairs carpet feeling distraught. That's quite normal. As are uncontrollable urges to redecorate your old room immediately. While this may induce livid outbursts from you when you discover that all the stuff you've left behind has been consigned to the netherworld of the attic, it is important for you to recognise that losing your official space in the familial home is an important step towards your parents' recovery. They may even need to pretend you're dead. That is literally their only way of coping.

But the real trouble is only just beginning. Parents are tenacious. Your new home is their sheer rock face. They've got the crampons and the will-power, and they're going to cling on for dear life. So saddle up your beasts of burden and let's explore the mountain ranges of your parents' minds.

HOME SWEET HOME

The Ancient Greek philosopher Plataflax once wrote, 'All a parent wants is for their child to leave home. But when they do, all a parent wants is for the child to come back.' Stay alert, anyone who has a parent, because this one can creep up on you.

Let's examine an incident that happened not that long ago. It was the sort of moment that was so chilling that clocks stop, birds freeze in mid air and small mammals spontaneously combust. Prepare yourselves.

'So, I've been thinking,' said HMB, who was resting under a blanket.
'Dangerous,' said I, flicking through the *Guardian Guide*.
'If I sold my house. And you sold your house. We could buy one big house. And all live in it.'

mouse in hedge outside sitting room window goes up in flames

'Pardon,' said I, fingers frozen.
'We could all live together. In the one house. Like *The Waltons*. Except there's only three of us. And Poppy.'
'Hang on,' said I, turning to look at her. 'Are you saying, in a round about way, that you want me to move BACK home?'

HMB twiddled with the edge of her blanket.

'I think it would be lovely.'
'What would be lovely?' asked WDT, who had just walked in with a cup of tea so weak it needed crutches.

'If Emma moved back home.'

'Oh yes,' nodded WDT, handing me the tea. 'I'd love that. I hate it when you go home.'

'I don't even call your house your home,' confessed HMB. 'I refuse to officially recognise it.'

'Dad,' said I, slightly reeling from this mass confessional, 'I'm looking at this tea and I'm wondering whether you just put hot water in a cup, added the milk and just showed it to a tea bag.'

All a parent wants is for their child to leave home. But when they do, all a parent wants is for their child to come back

'Ha ha,' said WDT.

'That to one side,' said I, gripping myself about the neck. 'Are you saying that you actually just want me to move back home?'

'Yes,' said HMB, putting on her best Princess Diana on *Panorama* face. 'Because I deserve it.'

'Hmm,' said WDT. 'My watch has stopped.'

THE SOLUTION

Chilled. To. The. Bone.

FAMILY FORTUNES

Thanks to various television programmes specialising in antiques and memorabilia, all offspring live in perpetual hope that their parents just might have a knick-knack tucked away in a cupboard so valuable that everyone can retire to the island of Mustique and live off pan-fried swan for the rest of their days. HMB spent years trying to convince me that a photograph of some Samurai swordsmen that hung in a frame in the upstairs hallway was 'priceless' and that I was never to let any-one 'touch it'. But then one day someone did touch it, and it fell off the wall and smashed only to reveal that the 'priceless' photograph of ancient warriors was actually a souvenir postcard from Bournemouth. Value – approximately ten of the Queen's own pence. Despite various setbacks, parents should always be encouraged to root around for fam-ily treasures. You never know, that revolting pot you've been putting your car keys in for years might be a priceless heirloom, and if it is you can put your feet up til the end of time. So crack on Pezzers! And find the bacon!

'The man at Bonhams,' whispered HMB. 'thinks it might be a Pissaro.'
'Are you sure you heard that right?' said I, looking up at the painting of a hill that, while very nice, did not inspire me with visions of the Impressionists.
'But I sent him a photo,' said HMB, nudging me in the arm.
'A photo of this painting?' said I, lifting a finger. 'Or did you cut a picture out of a book and send him that?'
'NO!' yelled HMB, aghast that I was not comprehending the enormity of the moment. 'Don't you understand? The man from Bonhams... BONHAMS... thinks THIS painting might be a PISSARO.'
HMB then frantically gestured towards the painting on the wall.
'Has it been signed by Mr Pissaro?' said I.
'No,' said HMB, returning to a whisper, and then casting a sly look over her shoulder, 'but that might not be a problem.'
She then nudged me again and then, for reasons best known to herself, started cackling. I just stood and stared at her.

'What are you staring at?' asked HMB, when she'd finished.
'Nothing. I'm just waiting for you to say, "And I'll get you and your little dog too."'
'A PISSARO, Emma! Imagine that!'

The picture in question is one that has been hanging on the wall in my parent's house ever since I can remember. I think they might even have bought it before I was born. It's pleasant enough. It's a squidgy seascape with a hill in the background. A bit like St Michael on the Mount. In fact, it may even be St Michael on the Mount. You get the idea. So, having stared at this picture day in day out for over thirty-eight years, HMB suddenly decided to send a picture of it to a man at Bonhams. Apparently (and I'm twisting my lips into an aniseed of scepticism), the man from Bonhams rang my mother and told her it might be by a very famous impressionist painter, which would have made it practically priceless. Hence the whipped-up frenzy that we were currently enduring. But let's cut to one week later. In the intervening time, HMB, convinced that any Tom, Dick or Harry could creep in and steal her newly found fortune, had insisted on complete telephonic silence on the matter.

'You never know,' she had whispered, 'who might be listening.'

So it was something of a surprise when the phone rang and it was the woman herself. She was in something of a state.

'Can you believe it?' she squealed. 'All the way to Bonhams. He takes one look at it, puts it down and says, "Nothing special. Probably worth £100." I mean, honestly!'
'So it's not a Pissaro?' asked I, laughing.
'No, it's not a bloody Pissaro!' answered HMB. 'Oh well. I'll just have to become a plumber or something.'

Now THAT would be priceless.

THE SOLUTION

Television programmes will give your parents ideas. They're more susceptible to suggestion than newborns in that respect. So the lesson to learn here is that, although it's great that your mother or father wants to see if anything in the familial home is worth flogging, the reality is that pretty much everything in your parents' house is worthless tat and, as a result, you're never going to bounce down Easy Street wearing golden frills and hats made from caviar. Disappointing. Having said that, I was impressed by HMB's tenacity in this instance. When she's got an idea, she excels at seeing it through to its tedious conclusion. Throw her a bone and she's like a ferret with a presenter's finger, and for that she should be applauded.

LESS OF A HELPING HAND

We come to a tricky area now – the times when your parents want to do something nice for you and it all turns out wrong. You're immediately on unsteady ground. On the one hand, their intentions have been good. On the other, they've made a bleeding arse of things. What do you do?

'Now don't be angry,' said HMB as she met me at the door. She and WDT had been *chez nous* all day tending to the every waking whim of Poppy, My Most Excellent Beagle.

Whenever HMB is calm, I know something very, very bad has happened. HMB is only ever hysterical when nothing of any significance has taken place. In true crises, she excels. With this in mind, a cold chill swept over me. I could see Poppy (she was up on her hind legs and pawing at me for a cuddle), and I could see WDT skulking behind HMB, so whatever it was, it wasn't to do with them. But then I looked at WDT again. He was definitely skulking. If I were a top-flight detective, WDT would be 2–1 odds on favourite for him what done it.

'What's happened?' said I, shrugging my wet duffle coat onto the floor and bending down to scratch My Most Excellent Beagle.
'I don't know how it happened,' said WDT, looking guiltier by the minute. 'It was only a bit of pencil.'
The plot was thickening. 'A bit of pencil?'
I wondered. How could a 'bit of pencil' have turned HMB into a paragon of capability and WDT into a quivering wreck?

SHOCK HORROR

And then I saw it.

I had recently won a rowing competition and, as is the way with these things, you get given a decorative blade, which is a massive thing that needs hanging on a wall. WDT had taken it upon himself to put the blade on the wall in my absence. He's good like that, handy, like real men are supposed to be. During the course of his hanging my blade true and high, WDT had accidentally made a long, thin pencil mark along the wall as he was getting down from his stepladder. Nothing wrong with that, we all cry. It's only a 'bit of pencil'.

But WDT, seeing he had made a long, thin bit of pencil mark on my cream wall, went and got a wet, wire-wool scrubbing pad from my sink. The stain experts among you may well already be throwing up your arms in horror at this point, and if truth be known, I too, when informed of said manoeuvre, couldn't help but scrunch my face into the shape of a decision badly made. Who uses a wet, wire-wool scrubbing pad – a wet, wire-wool scrubbing pad that is used to clean the cooker – as the tool of choice for tackling a bit of pencil on a cream wall? Who? All right, let's hear the man out.

'You used a wet, wire-wool scrubbing pad?' said I, 'The one I use to clean the oven? On a bit of pencil? What's wrong with a rubber?'
'You can't use a rubber on a wall,' said WDT.
'But it was a bit of pencil,' said I. 'And you used to be an art teacher. I would have thought that you, of all people, would know how to remove a small, thin line of pencil from a cream wall. I don't think I'm being unreasonable when I say that your knowledge of removing pencil marks from anything should have been better than this.'
'Hmm,' said WDT and shuffled on the spot a bit.

But, of course, he didn't use a rubber. He used the wet, wire-wool scrubbing pad that I use to clean the cooker. Next thing he knows and the long, thin, barely visible bit of pencil has turned into a two-foot wide circle of brown oven grease. The more he scrubbed it, the worse it got. I can only imagine the scenes of panic.

I stared at the large brown swirly mess on my creamy walls and thought about what I would say.

'Blade looks good,' said I.
'Doesn't it?' said HMB.

Oh well. It's only a cream wall. Perhaps I can pass it off as a Damien Hirst.

THE SOLUTION

Couple of interesting things here. Note how HMB keeps very, very quiet during this encounter. That's not like her. We all know that. But she's not stupid. She had nothing to do with the wet, wire-wool scrubbing pad incident, and she wants to keep her copybook clean. Instead, she assumes the role of the gentle appeaser. She's warned me the moment I step through the door that something revolting has happened. By doing so, she removes the element of surprise. Cunning. But then watch how she vanishes into the background only to leap in at the end with a diversionary affirmation. She's good. I'll give her that.

WDT, of course, is in bits and has almost certainly been yelled at for upwards of an hour before my return. There is, therefore, nothing to be gained by making his life any more of a misery. He's suffering. In these circumstances, you're allowed one, short, sharp sarcastic comment (see above) and that's it. Shake hands and move on.

THE EVER-
INCREASING
STAIN

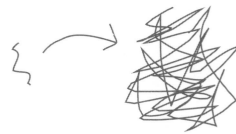

THIS LITTLE PIGGY

It's good for a man to have a hobby. That's as true as the tides. Some gents love a fishing rod; others adore nothing more than to stand on dead patches of grass and take photographs of aeroplanes. Nothing wrong with that. But when that hobby is phoning you very early in the morning – on a SUNDAY – then it's easy to see how difficulties will arise. I've been having a problem with WDT on a week-by-week basis. Every Sunday at 8 am, the phone would ring. It would be WDT and he'd be shitting rubbish out his cakehole. So what, oh what to do? Examine the evidence please. And file your report with the correct authorities.

The answer machine clicked into action.

'Hiya, Em,' said the all-too-familiar voice of WDT. 'It's Dad.'

Thank God he told me. Because I might not have been able to work out who was phoning me at 8 am on a Sunday morning. Again.

'Just wanted to know,' he continued, 'whether you like pork? I can get a duck. Or a chicken. Or a bit of beef. So, you know, give us a call.'

I stared up at the ceiling. My father has known me since the day I was born and he still doesn't know whether I like pork? This from the man who used to give me Breakfast Slices, the porky precursor of the Turkey Twizzler in which every pig toe, testicle and tendon was mashed into a suspicious pink strip. This from the fellah who would bring me home not one but TWO packets of pork scratchings whenever he went to the pub. And he's wondering only NOW whether or not I like pork?

Let me state it for the record. I am a great eater of pork. I like the loin, the chop, the neck, the leg and the belly. I am an avid supporter of the boiled ham, the roasted gammon, the pâté in all its forms. I draw the line at the ear or the tongue, but I have always been on call to embrace the sausage in all its reincarnations, and there are not words enough that can express my adoration of the bacon sandwich. I like wafer-thin ham, the hot dog, a slice of just-cut saucisson. I like the minced, the fricaseed, the shredded and the barbecued. I like a rack of ribs, a spare rib and a sweet and soured ball. I like the crackling. In fact I LOVE the crackling.

To conclude, I like pork. And I was affronted that my allegiance to it should be called into question.

IT'S THOSE SAUSAGES AGAIN

So I didn't return WDT's call. If he didn't know I liked pork by now, he could go hang. Plus it was 8 am. On a Sunday morning. So I'd like the hanging offence to be mostly for that.

Five hours later and I'm three minutes late for lunch. The more astute of you will now know that that meant there was no time for pleasantries.

'I haven't had pork in ages,' I said as I sat down at the table. If truth be told, I was looking forward to it: the juicy roasted meat, the jaw cracking rind and apple sauce a-plenty. Mmmm-mmmm!

WDT looked at me.

'We're having lamb,' said he.
'But you rang me this morning,' said I, taken aback, 'to tell me we were having pork.'
'No,' replied WDT. 'I rang to ask if you LIKED pork. You didn't ring back. I couldn't take the chance.'
'How can you not know if I like pork? I have eaten pork all my life. Have I gone Jewish? No. Is it Ramadan? No it's not. Am I a vegetarian? Heaven forbid. Clearly, I eat pork. That to one side – let's not beat about the bush – do you REALLY need to phone me at 8 o'clock on a Sunday to ask me?'

'Your mother made me do it,' said WDT, quick as you like.

'Did NOT!' protested HMB. 'I wasn't even awake.'

'Come clean,' said I, pointing a finger. 'You ring me EVERY Sunday morning. You DO! It's just a spurious wheeze on your part. Don't think I don't know your tricks!'

'SO busted,' said HMB, shaking her head.

'But the thing is,' began WDT, in something approaching a whine, 'I was up and I was thinking...'

'Your first mistake... ,' I interrupted.

'And I was thinking, and I thought about doing pork for lunch, and then I thought I'd just check with you because I wouldn't want you to turn up and not want it. And I'd had my breakfast. And Mum was asleep so I couldn't ask her. And so I thought I know! I'll just leave Em a message. And that was how it was.'

'OK,' said I nodding. 'Your motives were noble. We all accept that. But let's come to an agreement. If you're up early on a Sunday ever again and you find yourself in the perilous state of having some thoughts that require answers – write them down! Just jot them down on a piece of paper . And we'll all deal with them a bit later in the day. How's that?'

'All right then,' said WDT, nodding. 'So. You like pork then, do you?'

Pfffffffffffff.

THE SOLUTION

The Practibot's need for checking and double-checking is as unavoidable as the dawn. Some men like to play football on a Sunday. WDT likes to phone me. This is the way of the world. Phoning me is fine. But not when I am having my one and only proper lie in. Note the firm tone I assume. Practibots respond well to a low, authoritative voice, so practise that now. Clenching your buttocks, project from the diaphragm and try saying 'Fuck off. I'm sleeping!' Your voice should be so deep that it'll make a small child feel nauseous. Practise near some toddlers and see if any of them vomit. As soon as they do, you should achieve immediate results.

HIM WHO'LL FIX IT

About five years ago I had a new kitchen fitted.
A pair of lads with moody lips and angry eyebrows did it. At the time, I remember thinking, 'I do hope they know what they're
doing'. Anyway, it turned out they didn't,
and ever since I have been sporadically
discovering flooded washing machines,
live electrical cables hanging behind
cupboards and holes in walls through
which a thousand flying ants launched
an invasion. These are the moments
your father dreams of. Because dads, whatever their breed, will always claim to know
someone who knows someone else who can fix things.

'Leave this with me,' said WDT, with a sweep of his hand. 'I know
someone who knows someone who can sort this out.'
'Yeah, but I want it done properly,' said I, frowning.
'Ssssh,' said WDT, putting a finger to his lips. 'Leave. This. To. Me.'

And so I did.

'I've never seen anything like it,' said someone who someone my dad
knew. He was on his hands and knees staring into the black abyss
beneath my kitchen sink. 'Who did this?'
'Don't ask,' said I, holding my forehead in my hand.
'Some blokes,' explained WDT, with his arms crossed. He then shook
his head for a respectable length of time.
'It's the worst bit of plumbing I've seen in fifteen years,' announced he,
before joining in with the shaking head thing.
'Hmmm,' said I, because I could believe him. And then I joined in with
the shaking head thing. It felt appropriate in the circumstances.
'I mean, it's just awful,' added he, who then began an extended riff of

'Ooohs' and 'Tutts' as he grappled with said shoddy workmanship.

As I stood, watching him, I remembered the faces of those blokes who'd spent three days in my house ruining it while I paid them to do so, and I allowed myself a small fantasy about punching them in the bollocks. Just the once. I'm not a mental.

'I used to have my own business,' said the fellow, staring down at his hands. 'I had a van and everything. It was brilliant. It had the rose off the English Rugby shirt on the side.'
'That's nice,' said I, nodding.
'I loved that van,' said he, in the saddest of voices.
'Oh,' said I. 'Did something happen to it?'
'Well, I had to give it up, didn't I?' said he,
standing up. 'I fitted a power shower wrong.
Electrocuted a mother and her daughter.'
'Oh well,' said WDT quickly and shook his head
as if his life depended on it.

Oh well, indeed.

THE SOLUTION

The point is this. Your dad is always going to try and make out that he can get anything sorted. He can't. And that's the end of that lesson.

GREEN FINGERS

Let's take some tentative steps
onto the trampoline of trouble.
Prepare yourself for the following statement:

 **SOMETIMES YOUR DAD KNOWS STUFF
THAT YOU DON'T**

Wowzees. I'm feeling the burn. While the above IS true, it's mostly about stuff that there's no point in you knowing, so try not to feel too bad. It's a 'he knows it so you don't have to' scenario. Like U-bends. And guttering. And relax. Let's examine.

'Can someone please explain to me how it is that I can grow THE most enormous courgette plants this year and have not one courgette on them?' cried I, standing over my vegetable patch and pointing. 'It's because all your courgettes are male courgettes' said WDT, hands behind back.

*Courgette!
Vegetable or fruit??*

'Don't be ridiculous,' said I. 'There's no such thing as male courgettes. A courgette is a vegetable. It does not have a penis. It might look like one, but it is not one. It has nothing to fear from the female species. Apart from maybe Kinga from off of Big Brother 6. The courgette is right to be a-feared of her.'
'Who is Kinga off of Big Brother 6?' asked WDT. 'I have not watched any of it.'
'She was a housemate. In the Big Brother house. She was a bit like a car crash,' said I. 'Awful, but you couldn't help staring. I won't beat about the bush. She did some masturbating with a wine bottle. It gave a whole new meaning to the word corkscrew.'
'I beg your pardon?' said WDT, hands dropping to his side. 'Why would you do something like that? In front of everyone?'

I shrugged. Somehow, by watching Kinga from off of Big Brother 6 I have become permanently besmirched. I will never be clean again. But let's get back to the courgettes.

'I'm telling you,' said WDT, 'courgettes are male and female. Only the female ones bear the fruit.'
'A courgette is not a fruit. It is a vegetable.'
'You know what I mean,' said WDT, giving me a special stare.
'Number one,' I began, 'I don't believe you. I have never heard of a courgette being either a male or a female. Number two – Even if that was true, which it is not, what are the chances of every single courgette plant I have planted this year being male?'
'Look. Courgettes are male/female and normally they cross-pollinate to make the courgettes. They don't do it on their own.'
'So courgettes can't wank?' I asked.
'No,' said WDT.

Which is ironic. If you think about it.

THE SOLUTION

It's in the official Dad Job Description that, every now and again, it's their duty to come to you and say things like, 'Have you ever seen a worm ball?' and then drag you off down to a compost heap and show you one. This is what they do. I'm not saying that episodes like these should be treated with suspicion, but you're just going to have to accept that dads' brains only store the weird shit. Use this to your advantage. I know it's incredible to comprehend, but they actually know how to use an Allen key. And the worm ball WAS good so, you know.

12 again...

ETERNAL YOUTH

Your mother will never accept that you have grown up. NEVER. You could be a high court judge and she'll still try and wash your face with her own spit. Why do they do that? Why? Some mothers (mentioning no names but let's just say I'm looking at her) are so determined to keep you infantile that they will actually refuse to officially recognise any birthday past the age of twelve. They'll still give you presents, but it's the SORT of present that gives the game away. Observe.

'I hope you like it,' said HMB, beaming. 'It arrived at last. It's your birthday present. Remember?'

We were sitting in the front room of Kennedy Towers. It was December. My birthday is in May.

'Hang on,' said I, 'that's not my birthday present is it?'
'Yes,' said HMB. 'It is. I haven't wrapped it.'
'So let me get this straight. The present you ordered for me over the Internet and have been going on and on about since the end of May has finally arrived. And you haven't wrapped it?'
'Correct' said HMB.
'Card?'
'Don't be ridiculous.'

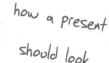

how a present should look

HMB then bent down and pulled up what looked like a very thin blue plastic bag. There was an unwieldy looking box inside it.

'Looks big,' said I, eying my long-awaited birthday present.
'Hmm,' said HMB, allowing a fleeting expression of worry to pass across her brow. 'The long wait may have diminished its allure. Anyway. Here you are. Happy Birthday.'

I took the plastic bag and looked inside. The words 'Star Wars Mr Potato Head' screamed up at me. I pulled out the box. HMB had got me a Darth Tater Mr Potato Head. I looked at her. She was sniggering and looking very pleased with herself.

'Oh, that's nice,' said I, pointing to the box. '"Ages 2 plus." So that's good. Ooh. Look at that,' I added, flipping the box to look at the back. '"Use your imagination to create all sorts of wacky looks." That's what it advises. And look at that. There's Mr Darth Tater (I see what they've done there), and he's saying "Together we shall rule as father and spud." I mean, that's OK, but son doesn't really rhyme with spud so the allusion is flimsy at best. And look here. It says "As a Dark Lord of the Sith, Darth Tater was once a promising young Jedi who lost his roots." Yes. That's because potatoes have literal roots. They've been very clever. It works on so many levels, doesn't it?'

HMB was now doubled over with delight. 'And look at that,' she said, tapping at the side of the box. 'Storage compartment for your parts. You can keep all the eyes and lips and mouths in the backside of the potato.' 'Great,' said I, staring at her. 'That's just great.'

There then followed a short period of silence in which we both stared at the Star Wars Mr Potato Head that my mother had ordered off the Internet and had to wait six months for.

'I ordered it after Tony made those baked potatoes,' said HMB, in a soft, almost sad voice, and then stared off into the middle distance. I am thirty-nine years old.

THE SOLUTION

There are two ways of looking at this. The fact you're still getting children's toys for your birthday maintains a sense of innocent joy and bonhomie. On the other hand, you've been given a plastic potato in the shape of a character from a science fiction film. You loser. Having said that, what's worse? Being given a plastic potato or being given a set of screwdriver bits and socks that smell of lavender? Suddenly the potato don't seem so bad...

It's
a Dogs Life

So I went and got myself a dog. Nice, you might be thinking. Hmm. You might want to reserve judgement. As soon as you've grown up, parents are in a constant state of alert for anyone or anything that's going to plaster up the gap in their hearts. The more organised of you can achieve this by giving them grandchildren. For the rest of you who plain couldn't be bothered, you're running an emotional gauntlet so dangerous that your chances of survival are on a par with a mayfly. Think of your parents as a leaking levee. You need to plug the hole or you're all doomed.

Enter stage left, one perfectly formed hound. Now, on the face of it, a small, cheeky-looking beagle doesn't look like the answer to all your problems but, hang on – what's this? Your parents start phoning to 'speak to the dog', soft, squeaking toys are piling up in your sitting room at an alarming rate, and your mother's been at your house for half an hour and she still hasn't spoken to you. Blow me, but that dog's working! There is no doubt that introducing a small, doe-eyed creature into the family mix will retract the parental beams off your back quicker than the speed of light. Have we, by sheer dumb luck, chanced upon the perfect antidote to all things parental?

No. Of course we haven't, because it's just not that easy. According to the laws of the universe, every action must have a reaction, and the smaller and cuter the dog, the more your parent's brain will turn to the consistency of mashed swede. This isn't a good thing. Not only that, but you're going to find yourself a permanent fixture on the family subs bench. You were once the master of all you surveyed. Not any more. Your relegation to the bottom of the family pile will be swift and ruthless. You can't compete. That dog's got soft, floppy ears. She's not playing fair. It's time to face facts. Your dog is actually your nemesis.

GIVE THE DOG A WANK

I'm sorry???

So you've got a dog. And hey presto, your parents are obsessed with it. They've got to be because they've given up all hope of you ever giving them grandchildren. But be warned. Parents will latch onto anything that shows them even a scrap of fondness. They're a bit like battered donkeys in that respect.

'I've bought Poppy a ferret,' said HMB, screaming with the excitement. 'Not a real one! A toy one! Ha ha ha ha ha ha ha ha ha ha ha ha ha ha hahahahahahahaahhahahhaahhhaaaah!'

She then pulled a large stuffed ferret out of a bag and ran round the house with it hooting with laughter as Poppy, My Most Excellent (and indulged) Beagle, wagged her tail and scampered round after her. Ten minutes later and they were both exhausted. Poppy leapt up and sat next to me while HMB slumped herself into a chair opposite. At no point did HMB look at anything other than Poppy.

'I can't believe you got Poppy spayed,' said HMB eventually, with something of a choke in the throat. 'It makes me so sad.'
'Why does it make you sad?' asked I, giving said beagle a quick stroke. 'It's the responsible thing to do.'
'But Poppy won't be able to have babies now,' wailed HMB, 'And even worse, she'll never have a satisfying love life. It makes me feel devastated.'
'Hmm,' said I. 'She's just a dog, Mum. I don't know if dogs do have satisfying love lives.'
'She's not a dog!' insisted HMB. 'She's a human!'

Wet nose ✓
Tail, waggable ✓
Floppy ears ✓

'Let's examine that statement. What do dogs have? Four legs. Check. Wet nose. Check. Tail, waggable. Check. Floppy ears. Check. Stinky breath. Check. Obsession with anus. Check, check and triple check. I hate to tell you this, but the evidence is irrefutable. Poppy is a dog.'

'No,' whispered HMB, almost in tears. 'She's a human. Trapped in a dog's body. A human who is now condemned to die a virgin.'

'It worked for the Pope,' suggested I.

'Don't be awful. She's a little person, aren't you? Yes! A little person!'

'Mum,' I interjected. 'It's not good to treat dogs like children. It makes them feel confused. All these cuddly toys you keep buying her. It's a bit crazy-making.'

'But she loves the cuddly toys. Don't you? Yes! She says yes!'

'The place is awash with them. It's like I'm living in a retirement home for mauled toys. All of them have got their eyes chewed off. It's chilling. Try being here after dark.'

It was at this point that in walked WDT.

'Here it is!' he said holding yet another fur-covered proffering. 'I left it in the car!'

It was a hot-water bottle cover. In the shape of a very fat cat.

'Here you are, Poppy!' mustered WDT, throwing the thing in the dog's direction. 'Yes! Poppy! Oh she loves that! Yes! She loves that!'

And we all sat and watched as Poppy took it by the throat, shook it, shook it again, ran out of the room with it, ran back again, chewed its face and then suddenly, and without warning, mounted it from behind and humped it with a sense of frantic fury. Everyone was stunned into silence.

Moments later, and my dog's very first masturbation had reached its startling conclusion. She dismounted, kicked her back legs out with a sense of gay abandon and ran in a circle to celebrate.

'I take it back,' said I, folding my arms. 'That dog is satisfied.'

THE SOLUTION

There's very little you can do here other than just get pregnant. But in the absence of children of your own, any pet is going to bear fruit. Bear in mind that just because YOU'RE so over them, it doesn't mean that small things with lumps of mud for brains aren't. That dog adores my parents. So, in many ways, the pressure is off. Just shut your eyes and pretend it's not happening

GIVE THE DOG A BONE

Once you've established that your parents are more interested in your dog than they are in you, you will need to be on a constant vigil. Turn your back for one second and they'll be in there with all manner of soft, squeaky toys and stinking chews. Add into the mix a dog who specialises in doe-eyed manipulation and you've got a recipe for disaster. So how do you maintain the discipline?

HMB and WDT had been to the matinée of a play that had a friend of mine in it. And HMB (who has never met her) arrived back, swanned into my office and declared, 'She looked straight at us, of course.'
'She doesn't know what you look like' said I.
'She must have fancied me then,' said WDT, because he is easily convinced.
'I thought she was wonderful,' said HMB and then launched into a five-minute monologue on why that was, and how when she was in a student production of the same play back in the day, she had used a walking stick as a character prop.
'I wish the lead actress had used a walking stick,' she added with a sense of misty-eyed regret.
'Anyway,' she continued, because she was not finished, not even by one of the longest of chalks, 'your friend really was wonderful.'
'I looked away when she took her clothes off,' interjected WDT. 'You know, because she's a friend of yours.'
'Good,' said I, nodding because actress or no actress, my father doesn't need to see anyone I know in the nudsy.
'I didn't look away,' said HMB.

We all thought about that for a minute. *MOMENT'S PAUSE*

'Anyway,' sighed HMB, clapping her hands on her knees as she sat down, 'I hope she makes a name for herself.'
'So do I,' said WDT.
'What's for supper?' asked HMB, patting her tummy.

'Shepherd's pie,' said I. 'I made it while you were out. It'll be ready in twenty minutes.'

'Twenty minutes?' asked HMB. 'Good. That gives me time enough to tell you about my battle with BT.'

'And Powergen' added WDT.

'Yes. And Powergen. Oh, and the Council Tax people.'

'And the Inland Revenue.'

'Yes. And the Inland Revenue.'

'Never mind that. I've got a bone to pick with you. Why is Poppy's treat jar empty?' I asked, picking up said offending item and then pointing at Poppy My Most Excellent Beagle's bloated dimensions. A sudden, dread hush fell, which in the circumstances was no bad thing. But that to one side, the fact that both WDT and HMB were now staring at their shoes and SAYING NOTHING told me everything I needed to know.

'I put it to you,' began I, tapping said jar with a finger, 'that when you were left alone with the dog this morning, you gave her all the treats from this jar. Can you deny it?'

CAN DOGS DIET?

'I may have given her one. Or two,' whispered HMB. 'Because she looked very hungry.'

'She's always hungry!' said I. 'She's a beagle! She'd eat till she burst. This is the dog I found lying in the street once because she'd gorged herself on the contents of the neighbour's bin! This dog is a food hoover! She's a walking compost heap!'

'But she's so pretty,' whined HMB. 'Look at that face! It says, give me treats! Yes it does! It does!'

'No. Don't do the dog voice,' warned I. 'Now, either you gave the treats in this jar to the dog or you both ate them yourselves. Now which is it?'

'Mum was quite hungry this morning,' began WDT, giving her a sideways glance. 'And there wasn't any cheese in the fridge...'

'I'm not THAT bad!' declared HMB, giving WDT a sharp nudge. 'Although the chicken ones do smell quite nice.'

'All right,' said I, with a sweep of the hand. 'I shall dismiss the thought as unworthy. But did you or did you not give this dog a load of biscuits?'

'But can't I tell you about the Inland Revenue?' tried HMB.

'No. Not the Inland Revenue. Dog biscuits. Yes? Or no?'

'Yes, we gave the dog some biscuits,' confessed WDT in a small mutter.

'SOME biscuits?' asked I.

'All the biscuits,' said he.

'Right. Good. So that's that mystery solved. And how do we feel now about the biscuit thing?'

'We're sorry about the biscuit thing,' mumbled WDT.

'I'm not,' said HMB, with a sense of defiance. Whereupon Poppy got up from where she was sitting and vomited a neat pile of barely digested biscuits.

'Oh, Poppy,' said HMB, clutching at her chest. 'You didn't have to give them back!'

Slapped wrists all round.

THE SOLUTION

Parents need to be taught that, in your house, there are boundaries. It's not their house. It's your house. So treat them with the disdain that deserves. Sometimes public dressing downs are the only way forward, but note here how I catch them unawares. Stealth is everything when it comes to pinning down your parents. I've let them rattle on about that play for a good ten minutes before stepping in and clubbing them like the pretty pups they are. They fessed up. I have the upper hand. Thank you very much.

LEAD AND THEY WILL FOLLOW

Poppy, as we all know, is a Most Excellent Beagle, but I'm going to come clean – I don't understand her one jot. My dog is lazy, we all know that, but matters aren't helped when you've got Pezzers who are wilfully blind to all her shortcomings. Again, this is entirely my fault for not springing sprogs out my clacker. But you know you've got a problem when they think the dog can do no wrong.

'I think Poppy's buried it somewhere in the garden,' said HMB. 'I can't find it anywhere.'
'Don't be ridiculous,' said I, squinting in disbelief. 'A dog doesn't bury its own lead.'
'Well, it's vanished,' said HMB. 'We took her for a walk. I hung the lead up on that peg and it's gone. She's taken it. And your father can't find it anywhere.'
'I can't find it anywhere,' said WDT, holding his palms to the heavens.
'So let me get this straight,' said I, squeezing the bridge of my nose betwixt two fingers. 'My dog has buried her own lead?'
I turned and looked at Poppy who was sitting, cross-pawed, on a chair and looking the picture of perfect innocence.
'Clever girl,' I said, through slit eyes. 'But not quite clever enough.'

Poppy's ears raised ever so slightly.

'Not quite clever enough!' I repeated, so that my genius dog would understand that she would never beat me. NEVER. 'Because I have ANOTHER lead!'

Poppy stared at me.

Puppy dog eyes

'Oh yes, my friend,' said I, wagging a finger.
'You may have won the war, but you haven't won the battle.'
'Don't be mean,' said HMB, suddenly. 'She's just exhausted.'
'Exhausted?' exclaimed I. 'She's a beagle! A breed renowned for their

ability to go all day. In the canine world, they're the 24-hour battery. This dog is lazy. Plain and true.'

'She's not lazy!' protested HMB. 'She's just being resourceful. Leave her alone. If Poppy wants to bury her lead, she can bury her lead. Can't you? Yes! You wanted to bury your lead! Yes, you did!'

'I can't help but notice,' began I, folding my arms, 'that you seem to be very fond of taking the dog's side over mine.'

'Yes,' nodded HMB. 'That's Granny's job.'

'Unless your real name is Baynard Mandy Foxtrot Parsley Paws, you might want to rethink that statement,' said I, giving her a stare.

'But it's my job to protect the little ones,' whined she. 'I'm like Jesus in that respect.'

'So Jesus,' began I, 'used to stand up for small, slightly naughty dogs, did he?'

'Well,' shrugged HMB. 'It's NOT in the Bible, but reading between the lines… I expect he did. Yes.'

'And what about "Respect your Mother and Father"?' asked I. 'Are dogs supposed to do that?'

'Sssssssh,' whispered HMB with a sense of terrible urgency. 'Poppy's *adopted*!'

POPPY'S ADOPTED!

At which Poppy looked away, yawned and started snoring.

THE SOLUTION

Gobsmacked. Do you see what I'm up against? It's a maelstrom of madness. Maternal theories should always be discredited as soon as they arise. This won't stop them, of course, but at least it gives you a foothold on the slidey face of Insanity Mountain. The point to make here is that whether the small thing in your control is a dog, a child or a fish, your mother will ALWAYS line up behind it. Her colours are pegged to the mast. So buy yourself a cutlass.

ONCE AND FOR ALL

Let's get one thing clear right now. YOU are the centre of the known universe when it comes to your parents. You are the sun that never sets, the star that never stops burning. Only one thing can challenge that. And that's a dog. When I first got Poppy, My Most Excellent Beagle, I did so in the knowledge that HMB hates dogs. HATES them. In many respects, it was a back-door excuse me that might mean my mother would never come to Kennedy Towers again. And then something a little bit Frankenstein happened because my mother transmogrified into a dog-doting idiot. And that's when the trouble started...

'OK,' said I, with a sense of purpose. 'There's something that's been bothering me. Do you or do you not like me more than the dog?'
'Of course I do!' exclaimed HMB who then thought that through.
'Although it is a VERY close-run thing. Because there was that time when Poppy was ill . And I probably DID love her a bit more than you during that. I'm just being honest. There. I've said it. Let's never talk of it again.'

Do you or do you not like me more than the dog?

'Do you remember when you hated dogs?' asked I. 'Can you even believe that?'
'Don't,' whispered HMB. 'Poppy might hear. It would make her feel confused.'
'Poppy can't understand complex moral issues,' said I. 'Just treats and tummy rubs. That's her world in a nutshell. And finding stinky things. Anything that stinks. The stinkier, the better.'
'Do you remember when she was ill though?' gasped HMB, grabbing herself around the throat. 'Oh! It was terrible! And that bit when we handed over her lead to the vet. And she got taken out through the back door. And the vet looked at me and said, "It's all right, she'll be fine", and I didn't believe him because he had unnaturally wet lips.'
'Yes. That was quite sad. But not as sad as that time we watched *Casper the Friendly Ghost* and Casper came back from the dead and was a boy again, and his dead mum was there, and then she wasn't and

he realised he was all alone in the world without even one friend. It wasn't as sad as that.'

'Oh, that WAS sad,' nodded HMB. 'But poor Poppy. That was just awful.'

'Was it less awful or more awful than when I had glandular fever?' asked I, probing deeper.

'Loads more awful,' snapped HMB, as if that was obvious.

'I was ill for a YEAR with that!' protested I.

'I don't care. I couldn't visualise where she was. There could have been anything through that door! They could have tied her to a pole in a concrete garden and left her to the mercy of a bunch of cats! '

'What would they have done?' quizzed I.

'I don't know! Pointed at her and laughed. Or something even worse. Poor Poppy.'

'Poor, poor Poppy!'

'Don't mock. And do you remember, when she came home and she wet herself on the sofa? And we didn't know she'd done it. And so she struggled off the sofa, came and found you, took you back to the sofa and pulled off the blanket so you could see. Oh! If she isn't the bestest, bravest dog there ever was, I'll eat my own gall bladder!'

'What would you do if I wet myself on your sofa?' asked I.

And without a moment's hesitation she turned, looked at me and said 'Have you adopted.'

I think it's good to know where you stand. Don't you?

THE SOLUTION

Some of you might want to neutralise the opposition. In which case, get your dog a pet passport, fly to Peru, enter into the jungle, get kidnapped by some natives, wait till they're off their tits on some random hallucinogen, leg it with dog in toe and then, three weeks later, when you are lost, mad and desperate, eat it. If your mother has a go at you about the fact you've roasted your own pet, you can, with proper conviction, tell her it was you or the dog. Job done.

SERIOUS RED-FACED MOMENT

Where to begin? When it comes to relating moments of intense embarrassment caused by my parents, I'm spoilt for choice. Most of the more horrific incidents are going to happen in front of your friends at school. That's a given. Like the time it snowed and everyone at my school was gathered in the main hall for the announcements on who was allowed to go home early. Out of the blue, the deputy headmistress, who was a compact vision in grey, walked up the aisle, tiptoed onto the stage and shouted 'Emma Kennedy! Put your hand up!' Thinking I was finally being given a prize for something tremendous, up shot my arm; the deputy headmistress looked at me and said, with withering scorn, 'Your mother is at the back of the hall. She has brought your wellingtons.' At which point, every girl in the school turned to look over her shoulder at the woman standing in the rear doorway who was holding a pair of yellow rubber boots aloft, waving and squealing 'Coo-eee!'

That might not seem so bad now. But when you are thirteen years old, that's worse than having your legs chewed off by a crocodile. And then there was the time my mother was learning to drive. And she persuaded her driving instructor to let her drive past my school gates at home time. There I was, with all my friends and some boys I liked, when she stopped the car, waved at me, laughed and then reversed into a tree.

These are the things that hang round our necks like the medallions of shame that they are. Think of them as badges of dishonour. They're the battle scars of life. It's your parents' job to make your teenage years a squirming hell. But Embarrassment Avenue isn't a one-way street. Sometimes you can strike back.

One of the most mortifying experiences of my life was entirely self-induced. My parents had arranged for two German exchange students to come to supper. It was around the time that the infamous 'Don't mention the war' episode of *Fawlty Towers* had been on television. My dad, who was always looking for an excuse to tease me, casually took me to one side, said, 'Now you must make sure you DON'T mention the war. DON'T. MENTION. THE. WAR!' and then skipped off giggling. I, on the other hand, being in the midst of my more intense teenage years, took this to heart and became obsessed that somehow, I was in dire danger of bringing up the atrocities of the Second World War during a casual dinner with some Germans. I worried about it SO much that I decided that the ONLY topic of conversation I could safely enter into was the Eurovision Song Contest. That was it. There could be nothing else discussed. If I stuck to that, nothing could possibly go wrong.

The evening of the supper arrived. There was I. There were the two thirteen-year-old German girls. I was determined that I would not mention the war. So, taking the bull by the horns, I cracked off the conversation with my safe-as-houses opener, 'So. Did you see the Eurovision Song Contest?' The two girls nodded. One of them smiled and said 'I think that Switzerland came first.' The other agreed and said 'And I think that France came second.' And then it was like my mouth was separate from the rest of my body because all I heard coming out of it were the bombshell words 'Yeah! And Hitler came third!'

I spent the rest of the evening face down on the kitchen floor.

Anyway. It's all about being embarrassed. And then there's the sex thing.

shakes head and wanders off to lie down

DO NOT MENTION THE WAR

REPEAT: DO NOT MENTION THE WAR

MUM, DAD, I'D LIKE YOU TO MEET...

This one's enormous. There are never going to be more defining moments in your family's history than the times when you bring anyone home to meet the Pezzers. There are no shades of grey with this one. It will either go very, very well or it will go very, very wrong. It's a bit like getting on an aeroplane in that respect. I suppose there's little if no point in relating any of the times when the first meet-and-greet has gone well. So let's concentrate on the pant-ripping disasters.

Be scared...

VERY scared

I'm fifteen. Jonathan is two years older than me. We've met at an athletics match where he asks me out on a date after watching me throw the discus. He looks like Phil Oakey, the lead singer of the *Human League* but without the high heels. So I say yes. Cut to three days later and Jonathan makes his one mistake. He turns up at my house in his dad's borrowed car. It is the first time that anyone other than a responsible adult with a mortgage has been about to give me a lift anywhere.

WDT says nothing. But instead, he goes outside and walks very, very slowly round Jonathan's dad's car. He comes back in. He says nothing. But, I notice, he's doing a lot of hard staring. HMB, meanwhile, has somehow managed to magic a cake onto a plate. This is the first time I have EVER seen her present anyone with food. It makes me feel nervous.

We sit down. A deathly silence descends as we sit, eating the cake. It's a bit stale and is something of a struggle to get down. WDT is still staring.

'My mother,' began HMB, without warning, 'used to have a budgie. It was called George. She loved that bird. Used to let it fly everywhere. It was never in its cage.'

Jonathan stopped eating his cake. I suspect he was glad of the chance to do so.

'The first time I brought a boy home my mother gave us cake. In fact, she laid on a proper high tea. Sandwiches. The lot. And we sat and ate it in front of the fire. The boy I had taken home to meet my mother was very nervous. He had crossed his legs and kept bouncing his top leg up and down. Up and down. Because of the nerves. So just as he was bouncing his leg up, George came flying down. Hit the end of the boy's boot and went careering into the open fire. Where he burnt to death. In front of my mother.'

'Any arsehole can put their foot on the accelerator,' muttered my father, suddenly.

I never went on a date with Jonathan again.

THE SOLUTION

When it comes to quiet menace, nothing is more terrifying than a parent who is trying to be nice because they know they have to be. Everything about the above encounter is horrible. The only thing that didn't happen was that my father managed to not tell the story about how he once had to snap a bright yellow shit out of my anus with his bare hands. A fact he would happily reel out to anyone in possession of ears. So, you know, it could have been worse. In these situations, you just have to grin and bear it.

In your teenage years, you can safely assume that your parents will detest pretty much everyone you're interested in kissing. That's just the way it is. So roll with it. Add into the mix a car and a newly acquired driving licence, and you'd be better off taking home Osama bin Laden. He might mastermind international atrocities, but at least he's not going to get drunk and drive your soft head into a lamp-post. My advice then is, don't bring anyone home unless you absolutely have to. You know, like until you're telling your parents you're getting married. And even then, do you really need to take your Otherarf home? What's wrong with just introducing them at the wedding? Nothing.

GETTING YOUR OWN BACK   HAHA!

You're NEVER too young to start trying to embarrass your parents. Think of it this way – they're going to embarrass you to hell and back when you're older so take your chances to get even wherever and whenever you can.

When I was three years old, I had two vinyl records. One was a recording of *Alice Through The Looking Glass*, and the other was the original cast recording of *Hair* the musical. Because I hadn't yet discovered the joys of Elvis or *The Osmonds*, I listened to those two records again and again. Nothing untoward there, you might think, but I was secretly banking a bucket of knowledge that I could spaff back in my parents' faces.

It was 1970. And my parents, who were teachers, had taken me into their school for the day. I was an angelic-looking child, all big green eyes and curly blonde hair, so from the minute I entered the staff room I was surrounded by cooing faces.

'Can you tell me a little poem?' said a woman called Pamela, whose wristwatch was being swallowed up by arm fat. 'Do you know "Baa Baa Black Sheep"? Or "Incy Wincy Spider"? Are they your favourites?'

I shook my head. I knew what my favourite was.

'What's your favourite?' she asked, tickling me on my belly and smiling. Her gums looked like they were sweating. 'Can you tell me your favourite poem?'

So I stared at her and recited 'Jabberwocky' from my *Alice Through The Looking Glass* record word perfect. Pam was stunned.

'And can you sing me a little song?' she said, her brow furrowing a little.

I stared at her and thought about what to do. There was only one choice. I'd said my favourite poem. And now I would sing my favourite song.

'Sodomeeeeee' I began, throwing my head back. 'Fellati-o, Cunnarrrrrrrr Lingus, Pederasteeeeeee!
'Mother, why do these words sound so nasty?
'Masturbation can be fun!
'Join the holeeee orgeeee! Karma Sutra!'

(pause)

'EVERYONE!'

THEY HAVE SINCE MADE UP FOR IT

Teaspoons clattered all around me.

'Great,' said my Dad, patting me on the back. 'Just great.'

Pam never bothered me again.

THE SOLUTION

You takes your chances. You makes your choice. There's a lesson to be learned from WDT if you keep a close eye on him. His spine has been shattered with embarrassment, but he masks the anguish by pretending to be quite proud of me. It's a masterly move that operates like a force shield. That said, something died in him that day. Seeing the three-year-old apple of your eye singing about blow jobs is an experience not to be underestimated. Well done, me.

DECLARATIONS OF LOVE

So the day has finally come. You've fallen in love. It's natural in these circumstances to want to run about telling anyone or anything with a pulse. You might want to stand on top of a tall building and shout it out with a megaphone. You might even want to spell it out with discarded orange peel. Who knows? The point is, you can't keep the fizz to yourself, and this means chucking your love guts up all over your parents' soft faces.

Parents tend to respond in one of two ways. They can either express little or no interest (been there, seen it, done it) or they can take the view that you're on the helter-skelter to a crash mat of misery. Some parents might give you the impression that they're delighted for you. They're not. They are merely paying you the slightest of lip services. Even if you turned up and said, 'Hello, Parents. I am in love with a multimillionaire who is the only living person to be canonised by the Catholic Church', they would still turn to you, smile and tell you that while that was all very nice, they still miss the last one you brought home to meet them.

You can't win. Parents always operate on the basis that the last one was the best one, and no top spin you can chuck at it is going to smash that wicket. For some reason, the merest mention of the word 'love' brings out a siege mentality in your parents. They just can't let it lie. Observe.

'I am in love with pineapples !' declared I, throwing my arms into the air. 'There. I've said it, and I don't care who knows it. As fruits go, they are the undisputed King of Razzmatazz. I defy anyone to find a more thrilling fruit.'
'Pineapples?' said WDT. 'No. You're not right there. Very acidic. Pleasant enough. But nothing special. Now take the passion fruit. Now THAT'S a fruit!'
'I disagree,' said I. 'The passion fruit is secretive and sly. It can't

hold a candle to the glory of the high-hatted pineapple.'

'I remember when you loved passion fruit,' said WDT, wagging a finger. 'Happy days.'

'I never did love the passion fruit,' said I, protesting. 'I may have flirted with it, but it wasn't for me. I found it too tart.'

'Well, what about the mango?' asked WDT. 'You were mad about the mango. It was mango this, mango that. You never went anywhere without a mango. And then there was the lychee. That was before the mango. You're fickle with your fruit, Emma.'

'You're talking out your arse,' said I, with a dismissive wave.

'And a pineapple is so flashy. I'll tell you this for nothing, if a pineapple was a car, a hairdresser would drive it and it wouldn't do many miles to the gallon.'

'Look. I didn't ask you for a top ten run-down of fruits I have loved. I just like the pineapple these days. All right?'

'I mean, it's not like it's a new fruit. It's not like when we all discovered coriander. Or hummus. All right, they weren't fruits. But my argument stands.'

'I just like pineapples.'

'In a tin?'

'No. Not in a tin. In the fresh variety. I like to cut the big tufty hat off. And then I like to cut the rind off so you get a heptagon. And then I like to cut it into slices. And then I like to cut the slices into cubes. And then I like to put the cubes in an airtight box and put it in the fridge. And then I like to eat the cold, cold cubes with a cake fork. Around four o'clock. Just before *Deal or No Deal*. Sometimes even during *Deal or No Deal*. That's what I like to do.'

'Well. Great.'

'Yes.'

'So I'm guessing you didn't do much today?'

'I did actually. I did a lot.'

'Hmm. Well. Enjoy your pineapple.'

'Thanks. I will.'

If a pineapple were a car, a hairdresser would drive it

THE SOLUTION

OK. So I've cheated a little. But don't let this fruit-based love anecdote fool you. This lady–fruit love illustrates a universal truth – a parent is physically incapable of accepting that you can make qualitative emotional attachments. The only relationships your parents will unconditionally accept are those you form with a blanky or an imaginary friend. That's it. Note the disdain with which WDT greets the news of my new-found love. That's textbook. Expect it. And the masterly way in which he sows the small seeds of doubt that maybe, just maybe, I don't know what I'm talking about. This is dangerous. I might not think about this now, but three months down the line when I'm sitting, staring at a pineapple and wondering what I ever saw in it, WDT's words will come back to haunt me. He's no Lazy Susan.

AN AWKWARD SITUATION   *yikes*

The following is quite an interesting problem. We've all been there –
what do you do when you find yourself being felt up under a table by a
Polish octogenarian war hero? Can you rely on your parents to get you
out of this morally sticky corner? Don't be stupid. Of course you can't.

'We've been invited to Rhoda's house for dinner,' HMB had announced
a week previously.
'Do I have to come?' said I, because that must always be my knee-jerk
response.
'Well, I suppose not,' replied she. 'But your father will be very disap-
pointed if you DON'T come.'
'Hmm,' said I, eyes narrowing. 'How very underhand of you.'
'Good,' said she. 'So we'll pick you up at seven. And PLEASE wear some-
thing vaguely smart. Would it kill you to use an iron once in a while?'
'Blah, blah,' said I. And that was that.

Cut to seven days later, and HMB, WDT and I are standing in the hallway of their ancient and eccentric friend Rhoda's house.

'I'm glad you came,' whispered WDT, giving me a nudge.
'And you're wearing a skirt,' observed HMB, nodding down in the
direction of my knees. 'Though it would be nice if it didn't look quite
so crushed.'
'Parrrrrrrp!' came a noise from the top of the stairs. 'Parp! Parrrrrrp!'

We all turned round and looked up. It was Rhoda. She was sitting in a
stairlift, wearing a red velvet turban and blowing a hunting horn.

'Parrrrrrrrrrrrrrp!' blew she, as she made her very slow, mechanised
descent.
'I want to be like her when I grow up,' I mumbled in Mum's direction.
'Sshhh,' said she, giving me a poke.
'This is Milos,' said Rhoda, waving a regal hand in the direction of a

crumpled, dusty-looking fellow sitting in an armchair.

'Hel-lo,' said he, with a thick Eastern European accent. 'Wery nice to meet.'

'Where are you from, Milos?' asked HMB, shaking him by the hand.

'Poland!' smiled he, nodding.

'Milos fought in the Second World War,' Rhoda yelled from the other side of the room. 'He's a bona fide War Hero!'

'How lovely,' clapped HMB. 'Well done, you!'

So let's cut to the meal. We're having a starter of cold, greasy avocado soup. It's making me want to vomit out of my ears. Milos is sitting to my left and has been telling me about marching out of Warsaw. HMB is to my right and is cleverly soaking up the cold, greasy, avocado soup with bits of bread, which she is even more cleverly abandoning on a side plate. Suddenly, I feel a wrinkly, shaky hand rest itself on my knee. I freeze. The hand, undeterred by age or withering, starts to make its way North towards my lady secrets.

'Ooooh,' say I, and not in a good way.

What to do? Turn to the doddery, old war hero, call him a dirty old bastard and embarrass him in front of the assembled guests? Or do you ask your mother? Let's sniff it and see.

'Mum,' mouthed I, leaning in to her ear, 'Milos is feeling me up under the table.'

'Oh, just let him,' said she, not even looking at me. 'And pass me your bread.'

THE SOLUTION

And there you have it. Job done. I suppose that HMB's advice is the best in the circumstances. He's really very ancient and, if push came to shove, all three of us could have him in a headlock quicker than you can say incontinence. Add to that the fact that he fought the Nazis, and a sense of obligation creeps in making you realise that this might just be your chance to repay the debt. Thank you, old man, and crack on.

MY SECRET VALENTINE

Ahhhh! It's that time of year when young hearts turn their thoughts to love. Hopes rocket skywards, and expectations leave you breathless. The reason – the Valentine card – holy grail of every budding romantic. But the chilly hand of fear is stuffed down your oesophagus because perhaps you won't get one. Which would make you as undesirable as a tramp's toe. But then you hear it – the thump of post on mat. You've got one and someone, somewhere loves you. Thank God! It's official – you're not a total loser. But all is not as it seems. Because the card has come from your mother, thus making it null and void and, even worse, making you a bigger loser than if you hadn't had one at all. Cue scenes of hysteria and roll on the recriminations.

It's 1982. I'm firmly ensconced in my teenage years. It's Valentine's Day. A card has arrived and it's addressed to me.

'Mum! Dad!' shout I, with all the zing of pinged elastic. 'I've got a Valentine card! Wowzee! I wonder who it's from?'
'It's from me,' said HMB, smiling. 'Do you like it?'
'What?' said I, gasping.
'I sent it to you. I didn't think you'd get any.'
'What?' said I, reeling.
'I didn't want you to be disappointed. I even disguised my handwriting. I used European Fs.'
'There aren't any Fs in "Guess Who?",' said I, staring into the card.
'Well, that shows how brilliantly disguised it is,' pointed out HMB.
'I can't believe you've done this,' said I, shaking the card in my mother's direction. 'What were you thinking of? I mean, honestly?'
'I was sending you a card,' explained HMB, shrugging. 'Because I knew you wouldn't get any. Which you didn't.'
'Don't RUB it in!' yelled I.
'But you DID get one,' yelled back HMB. 'You got one from ME!'
'That doesn't COUNT!' yelled I.
'Yes it DOES!' yelled she.

Happy Valentines Day Emma ... Love Mum x

'No! It DOESN'T! And I can't believe you just assumed I wouldn't get one!'
'But I was right! You didn't get one!' screeched HMB.
'But now you have got one,' pitched in WDT. 'So that's nice isn't it?'
'NO! It isn't NICE! It's AWFUL! I want to DIE!'
'Well!' exclaimed HMB throwing her arms in the air. 'You try to do something nice...'
'Stop saying it's NICE! It's not NICE! It's the worse thing EVER!'

At this point, I threw the false Valentine to the floor and stamped on it. Twice.

'But you wouldn't have wanted not to have one!' pleaded WDT, pointing at the crushed card.
'I'm struggling to decide which is worse,' said I, giving them both a thorough stare. 'The fact you decided there was no way I was going to get one. Or the fact you've TOLD me that you sent it.'
'Yes,' acknowledged HMB, 'that may have been an error.'
'I drove to Letchworth to post that,' said WDT, still pointing.
'The thing is,' began HMB with a sigh. 'You're getting to that age when it matters if you don't get one. And you've never had any.'
'I did!' exclaimed I. 'I got one last year!'
'Hmm,' said WDT, shifting on his feet.
'Don't tell me you sent that one as well?' said I, hand travelling to forehead.
'Wellllllll,' said HMB, with a grimace. 'In a word, yes.'
'Oh my God,' wailed I. 'My parents think I'm a loser! I got twenty-six Valentine cards when I was eight! At Whitehill Junior School in 1977, you had two choices. Me. Or Paula Berryman. Or Jane Atkinson if you were in the mood for racey. She went under a blanket with Thomas Frost. They may have kissed. The reputation stuck. But I got twenty-six! And not just that, but Simon Harwood gave me an enormous padded Valentine's card and what I thought was a box of chocolates. All right, he ate all the chocolates and put a large plastic ring in the box instead, but he was my boyfriend for four years.'
'Yes, but you don't see Simon Harwood any more,' pointed out my mother.

'No,' replied I, shaking my head. 'Because we fell out on the last day of school after he danced with Deborah Hollick in country dancing.'

'Bastard,' muttered WDT.

'Yes. But I got him back by going and looking at Nicholas Hall's penis behind the pegs.'

'Devastating,' nodded WDT.

'Correct,' said I. 'But my point is, some people have, in the past, found me attractive. Therefore, it's not unreasonable to assume that someone might in the future.'

'In the future, yes,' agreed HMB.

'So don't EVER send me a Valentine card again. All right?'

My parents nodded, and at that precise moment the phone rang. It was my best chum Sarah Biggerstaff.

'Did you get any Valentine cards?' asked she.

I thought about that for a second.

'Yes!' enthused I. 'I got one!'

And with that, my mother folded her arms and mouthed those fatal words, 'Told. You. So.'

REALLY annoying.

LOSER!

THE SOLUTION

Revolting. To this day, my mother is still convinced she did the right thing. Damn St Valentine and his love of card-based gifts. And damn even more the fact that I was bothered by it. But know this; every single one of you reading this has received a Valentine from your mother. She may not have fessed up like mine did, but trust me – that card you NEVER found out who it was from – that was from your mother. Yes, it was well-meaning, and they must be given a short, sharp nod of reluctant appreciation for that. But it doesn't make it RIGHT. So feel free to have a backdated tantrum.

THE TROUBLE WITH WOMEN

So you've had a dishonourable discharge from the
Vagina Army. It's Sports Day at Crimson High.
Miss Scarlett's come home to Tara. And Aunt Flo
and Cousin Cramps are in the building. Yes. It's
periods and all that go with them. But there's something worse
than periods, and that's the twilight of your menstruating years. The
menopause is like being gunned down by a freight train. One minute,
you're crackalack for just three days every month, next you're crackalack on a daily basis. Keep knives locked in a safe, cover everything
in padding, and bury yourself in the garden. Because your mother is
about to go quite mad. For the next thirteen years.

it's my hormones

'Hot flush!' yelled HMB, wrestling with her jumper. 'Hot flush!
Window, Tony! Window! Help me off with this! Oh God!'
'I'll stand here and waft air in your direction,' said WDT, who had
indeed opened a window and was now moving the fresh air towards
my mother. HMB was in the evil clutches of the Bad Witch
Menopause, the hormonal devil who possesses all women aged fifty
and over, and whose sole purpose is to bring on turns that would
shame a carousel.
'Oh!' she exclaimed, having divested herself of much of her upper
clothing. 'Damn these hot flushes. Oh wait! Now I'm freezing.
Freezing! Shut the window. Shut it!'

And repeat.

'Have you actually finished having periods yet?' asked I, during a lull
in the madness.
'No! I thought I had, and then boom! I had a period the other day,' said
HMB, with a sigh. 'There's no rhyme or reason to them these days.
And of course, it always happens when you're least expecting it. It's
like being smashed over the head by a dwarf with a mallet .'
'Something I am yet to experience,' said I, crossing my legs.

'So I realise that my period is starting and I've got nothing on me. NOTHING! Because I'm standing on a train platform. And then I remember that sometimes, those little newspaper kiosks do stock lady equipment. So I go up and say, "Can I have some tampons please?" And the lady behind the kiosk picks them off the shelf and then whispers, "Would you like a baaaaaaag?", and I said, "No!" But then, all of a sudden, she throws a copy of the *Evening Standard* down over the box of tampons. So I look at her and say, "No. I don't want a paper, THANK YOU." At which point, she stares at me, proper wide-eyed, and mouths, "There's a GENTLE-MAN behind you!" Can you imagine that? A GENTLE-MAN!'

'What did you do?'

'I picked up the box of tampons, turned round, thrust them in his face and said, "Yes! I'm STILL having periods!"'

'Oh dear,' said I, clinging onto the end of my knees.

'I was quite surprised too,' said WDT, chipping in. 'Because normally your mother makes me go and get her tampons.'

'That is true. Do you remember, when we lived in Broadmead, the woman in the local shop thought you had a disabled wife?' recalled HMB.

'Yes. I was buying sanitary towels, and she looked at me and said it was a shame you were housebound. And I said you weren't, you were just reading *The Guardian*.'

'Very good,' said I, nodding. 'I had a friend whose great aunt came round once and gave her three tampons for her Christmas present. Not even wrapped. Just loose. And when my friend looked at them and then looked at her aunt, her aunt put a hand on her shoulder and whispered, "I don't need them any more." That's some present, ain't it?'

'It's the bloody menopause!' exclaimed my mother. 'It makes you go crazy!'

'Is that a new phone, Em?' asked WDT, who was eying up my recent purchase.

'Yes!' answered I. 'It's got lots of functions. In fact, I can programme it to tell me when my period is due!'

MAN ALERT

'Has it really come to this?' quizzed HMB, throwing her arms into the air. 'That (a) we are living in a world where GENTLEMEN have to be protected from the sight of a box of tampons, and (b) we need mobile phones to send us an alert as to the imminent arrival of our periods? I never heard of such a thing.'

'Although you could have done with that this week,' said WDT, throwing me a wink.

'Oh! Hot flush! Tony! Hot flush!'

And repeat to fade.

THE SOLUTION

It has been proved, under laboratory conditions, that menopausal women have the strength of ten tigers when it comes to snapping people's heads off. Not only that, but if your mother is already erring on the side of eccentric, be prepared for the arrival of the menopause to exacerbate the condition by a considerable margin. It is crucial that at no point do you make light of her menopausal symptoms or suggest that everyone gets a bit hot sometimes and that perhaps she should stop moaning about it. You may as well just tack her onto a spinning wheel, stuff her mouth with fireworks and watch her blow. So tiptoe gently through the maternal tulips, my Parent-Busting friends, and you might emerge (in thirteen years' time) with head still on neck.

strength of ten tigers = 1 menopausal woman

OH GOD, NO! NO! PLEASE GOD, NO!

It's not if, it's when. Parents contain an enzyme that, when in contact with their offspring, oxidises into Embarrassment Concentrate. When it comes to embarrassing you, they can't help themselves. It's what they're programmed to do. They can strike anywhere and at any time. You can't prepare for or protect yourself against it. Let's stroll down Squirm Alley and observe an incident that may leave the more sensitive of you in need of medical assistance. You have been warned.

A certain rail company has gone and got itself some new and improved trains inside which it's installed new and improved toilets. But not for them the humdrum convenience of yesteryear. No. They've gone for a whiff of the space age with a sliding door that has no handle. Imagine being  caught short on the Starship Enterprise or needing a poo on the Death Star, and you're half way there. The new toilet door is so architecturally whizzbang that even a Brainiac with a hundred degrees would be forgiven for mistaking it for a wall.

'This is a wall!' would declare the Brainiac, after years of exhaustive experiments.
'No, Mr Brainiac,' would say the ticket inspector. 'That's no wall. That's the toilet door!'

But let's cut back to the action.

'Hmmm,' said HMB as we stood staring at the handle-less door. 'Is it my imagination or is it impossible to work out how to open the toilet door?'
'This is the problem with space-age designs,' replied I, stepping forward. 'Futuristic aspirations are all very well, but what's the point if you can't comprehend them?'
'Perhaps you have to bang it somewhere?' said HMB, tapping on the door in strategic places.

'It's not like Indiana Jones,' said I. 'Ah ha! Look! There, by the door into the carriage. Press that.'

HMB looked down to her left and pressed the small green square. With a small hiss, the door to the toilet made its slow slide open.

'What is the point,' began HMB, pointing at the green square, 'of having the open button all the way over here? That's very confusing. That looks like it belongs to the carriage door. Not the toilet door. Tsssk.'
'Doesn't this door take ages to open?' said I, observing its snail-like crawl away from us. 'You'd have thought they would have given that a bit more zip.'

And with that, I stepped into the cubicle.

'It's very spacious, isn't it?' commented HMB, poking her head inside. 'You could put a table and chairs in here.'
'Hmm,' said I, looking about. 'How do you close the door?'
'There,' said HMB, pointing. 'Just behind you. By the sink. There's a red square. Try that.'

And so I did, and with an equally slow hiss, the door slugged its way back across the open doorway.

'I'll just wait here,' said HMB. 'Goodness. That door does take its time, doesn't it?'
'Well, it is a very big door,' said I, and with that the massive thing finally settled itself shut.

So I'm inside the toilet. I pull down my pants and get on with what I've come to do. As I do so, I can hear my mother outside the toilet door talking to someone.

'It's VERY confusing,' I hear her say. 'Because you can't work out how to open the thing. I mean, you'd think there would be some sort of sign. But you just press that green button. That one. There. By the carriage door. Here. This one.'

And at that moment, with my pants round my knees, my bottom in the air and urine flowing freely into the toilet, the door made that telltale hiss and slowly, oh so very slowly, began to open.

'No!' screamed I. 'No!'
'Oh dear!' screamed my mother. 'Oh! Oh!'
'No!' screamed I, now running round the toilet cubicle, pants still round my knees.

NO!!!!!

'I just pressed the... oh dear!' said my mother, hand over her mouth.
'No!' screamed I, making a lunge for the red button inside the cubicle. But the door hadn't fully opened. So the red button wouldn't work.

And there I was, one hand covering my lady secrets, the other pressing the red button, and all the time staring at my bloody, bloody mother.

'What a terrible piece of design,' said the man standing in the corridor. 'Isn't it though?' agreed HMB. 'I'll have to send them a letter. Anyway. This is my daughter. She's on television.'

Give me a lethal injection. Now.

THE SOLUTION

Your mother and the future don't mix. But that doesn't even scrape the surface. The problem with introducing your mother to anything remotely newfangled is that she will then become resolute in the belief that it's her responsibility to explain it to any passing pair of ears. But I digress. My mother opened a toilet door while I was urinating. On a train. There is nothing to be done in this situation apart from kill yourself. Bon voyage, cruel world.

THE CUT-OUT-AND-KEEP WHEEL OF EMBARRASSMENT

It's not if. It's when. Your parents will embarrass you. Guaranteed. So how embarrassed should you feel in any given situation? Using the wheel provided, you can work out your Incident–to-Embarrassment Factor to within three decimal points.

1. Cut out Wheel A and Wheel B
2. Make a hole in the centre of both wheels using a skewer, scissors or javelin and use a paper pin to hold the two wheels together
3. Simply rotate the wheel according to your embarrassing specifics and add the numbers to get your embarrassment percentile

For example: Your mother has turned up in a nightgown to pick you up from a disco. Mother = 45, Any Sort of Party = 15, Clothes you wear to bed = 7. Therefore you should feel 67% embarrassed.

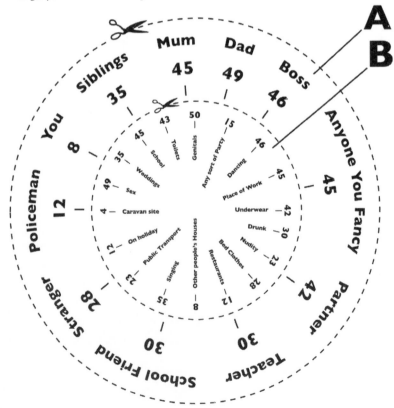

Look at you! You've all growed up! And that means one thing. You've got to get a job. Some of you may have had jobs when you were little. Not serious ones like going down mines; we're not living in 1842. But pocket-money jobs like paper rounds and washing cars. Your parents may have encouraged you to do it. Having a job when you're a teenager instils a respect for money and the working day. Parents love that. And once you've pupated into an adult, every parent, with the exception of the Travoltee and the Marvo, quietly dreams that you'll get a nice, steady job in insurance. They like a job with structure, prospects and pensions, a steady-as-she-goes career in which, one day, you might reach the heady heights of middle management.

How do you deal with parents if, like me, you haven't got a proper job?

I've had loads of jobs. I've worked in a shop, a launderette and a hotel. I wrote adverts in San Francisco and edited books in London. I recruited lawyers and then became one. And then I packed it all in and decided to devote the rest of my life to the tumbledown ruin of acting. It's quite something telling your mother that you're going to give up being a well-paid lawyer to play dressing up and mucking about till the end of your days. Try it now. She'd be happier if you told her you're a paedophile.

This, of course, does not apply to all parents. The Travoltee will have been entering you into talent shows from the moment you could talk. If you don't get a part in a soap or a West End musical, your mother's life will have been a pile of blown-up rocks. If you've got a Marvo for a parent then what's the worry? The hardest thing you're going to do today is decide what cocktail you want the servants to have ready for you as you waft down to your private beach on the island of Mustique. But for most of us, the fact that your parents want you to have a proper job is an inescapable truth. So how do you deal with them if, like me, you haven't got a proper job? Watch with your eyes...

SEPTEMBER THE FIRST

It's a fact well known that mothers think nothing of phoning you at work to chat about nothing. Just because they don't go to work any more means they have developed a veil of oblivion when it comes to acknowledging that you might be busy. If you work in an office, you've got an advantage. You can wave down a colleague and write the words 'HELP ME, MY MOTHER'S ON THE PHONE!' on a Post-it note. They can then wander over and pretend to be Brian, your boss. Even then it's going to be a struggle to get her off the blower because she's going to tell you about that T-shirt she bought from Primark for a pound or die trying. But you've got it easy, my friends. Because if you work at home and you're on your own, you're fucked.

Now I've got a thing about September the first. For me, it's the new January. According to legend, whatever you do on September the first, you will do for the rest of the year. This is true. I'm not making this bit up. So let's have a look at a recent September the first experience. Buckle up. My absolute worst nightmare is about to take place...

It came like a freight train. The alarm went off, I leapt, gazelle-like, and on went the white shirt and socks.

'Come on, Poppy,' said I to My Most Excellent Beagle. 'It's September the first!'

She looked at me, yawned and put her head back down on her paws. How I laughed at her stupidity. For everyone knows that what you do on September the First, you will do every day for the rest of your life. The dog fool.

And then the phone rang.

'Only me!' yelled HMB.

ONLY ME!

'No,' said I, shaking my head. 'No, we can't speak now. It's September the first. I've got to get cracking. Work to be done.'

'So I went to IKEA,' she began.

'No. September. First. I'm not listening.'

'And I wondered if you might like another bedside table ? Because I got myself some lovely boxes from the Marketplace. And Tony got some chopping boards. Didn't you, Tony?'

'Yes!' yelled he in the background. 'They're lovely!'

'No,' said I. 'I've got work to do. Can't have this conversation now.'

'And curtains! Oh! They were only ten pounds!'

'Mum! I'm at work!'

'No, you're not. You're at home.'

'Yes, I know I am AT home, but I am AT work.'

'Yes, but it's not REAL work, is it?' retorted she.

pause to let that one sink in

'OK. Now we're going to have a conversation. It's September the first. I am AT work. Just because I haven't had to leave the house to go my office, just because I haven't stood at the coffee machine and moaned that 'it's always the way... back to work and here comes the sunshine' does not mean I am not AT work. If you want me to, I would be quite happy to stand next to the paper shredder and notice my own tan. I could then ask myself whether "I've been away." I could answer that yes, I had been, but it had been over all too soon. "They always are," I could then say, in response. Then, but only if you wanted, I could stand about drinking coffee and gossiping about myself. But when all that was done, I would go and sit at my desk. Where I WORK.'

'I only wanted to tell you about the bedside table,' said HMB, in a small plaintive whisper.

'OK. That's fine.' said I. 'But perhaps you can tell me later. Or tomorrow. It's September the first, and I'm at work.'

'Hmmm,' mused HMB. 'I would like September as a month, but it's just so smug. Anyway, I can't tell you later because we're going to IKEA again this morning. And then we're going to pop in for lunch.'

'But I'm working!' cried I.

'Oh never mind that,' said HMB. 'Now then, before we go. So I've got the catalogue. They've got Inook – that's VERY nice....'

Bang head on brick wall until I slip into unconsciousness...

THE SOLUTION

There's only one solution. Get Caller ID and don't answer the phone. Ever.

HOPES AND DREAMS

ANY DREAM WILL DO...

If you haven't got a long-held ambition, there's something wrong with you. I'm not talking about achievable goals like losing one pound in weight or buying an underwire support bra; I'm talking about the 'out there' dreams. Like waking up one morning and discovering you've sprouted wings. That sort of thing. I'm talking the out-of-the-box, blue-sky thinking, big stuff. None of your tat.

So let's say you've settled on your dream of choice. It's a proper one, like reinventing milk. This is where your parents step in. A parent's job is to leave you with no doubt that anything you would love to do is probably impossible. This isn't them being mean, it's just their way of protecting you from crushing disappointment. Let's take a look at this in action.

'Sometimes,' said I, with a twirl, 'I like to dance round my kitchen and pretend I'm in a West End musical .'
'You do know that will NEVER happen don't you?' butted in HMB.
'But in my brain I am a brilliant singer who devastates the audience with my sexual charisma,' said I, adding a simulation of a soft-shoe shuffle.
'Yes, Emma,' replied HMB, crossing her arms. 'In your brain. In reality, you can barely hold a tune, can't hit top notes and dance like a drunk aunt at a wedding reception in a room above a pub in Stockwell.'
'That's a bit harsh,' chipped in WDT, frowning, 'but having said that, it is true.'
'Hang on a minute,' protested I. 'I have been in a musical! I was in *West Side Story* when I was at university!'
'Yes,' agreed HMB. 'That's what I'm basing my analysis on.'
'But how can you base any analysis of my talents on that? I didn't even sing one song!' exclaimed I. 'Or dance one dance!'
'Exactly!' declared HMB. 'You were in a MUSICAL and you were the only person in it who wasn't allowed to sing OR dance. Now what does that tell you?'

'Yeah! But I was Anybodys! Who wanted to be in the Jets! I just had to mostly say I had scabby knees!'

'Yes,' said WDT, with an encouraging nod. 'Because they knew you had scabby knee skills. That's what you're good at. You're lucky. You know you've got scabby knees covered. Play to your strengths.'

'But I want to be in a musical!' whined I. 'In fact, I would give anything to be in one.'

'Desperation is not an attractive quality,' noted HMB.

'No,' agreed WDT, shaking his head with a sense of deep-seated rue.

'Blimey, you two,' said I, hand on hips. 'What happened to encouragement and egging on?'

'Well, there's no point is there?' answered HMB, shrugging. 'Where would it get us?'

'Nowhere,' pointed out WDT, helpfully.

'Jeez Loueez,' muttered I, slumping into a chair. 'This is some sort of rubbish. Anyway, the only reason I didn't get to sing or dance was because the director was a bit sensitive and strange.'

'What do you mean?' asked WDT, looking at me.

'She always seemed to be dressed in clothes that looked like alfalfa, and one day, when the lead guy came in with a new haircut, she took one look at it and said, "Henry, your haircut is giving me a pain in my vagina." A phrase I have never forgotten.'

'Hmm,' said HMB, thinking about that. 'Or was it because you can't sing or dance?'

'Probably the last thing,' suggested WDT, giving me a small smile.

I hate my parents.

THE SOLUTION

It speaks for itself, doesn't it? Relentless crushing. That's not to say you can't turn things around and flick them the Vs. I used to be a lawyer. A proper one. I even had a secretary called Madge. When I told my mother I was giving up the law to become a writer and actress, she literally took to her bed for three months with something doctors could only refer to as a 'Victorian illness'. But then, three months later, I introduced her to someone famous off the telly and wasn't she delighted then? So keep dreaming! If parents didn't tell you you couldn't do something, you'd never experience the heady brew of achievement when you can spaff it back in their crying eyes. I think.

A DAILY GRIND

Unless your parents are the landed gentry, chances are they worked for a living. And unless you are blessed with the very rare Marvo parent, chances are your parents had quite a dull job that they stuck at for decades. That's the way it was. This was because aspirational television hadn't yet been invented. They just had kitchen-sink dramas and *Mr and Mrs* to watch and, as a result, were perfectly happy to sell staples for a medium-sized retailer for thirty years. They didn't realise they could jack it all in and become pole-dancers. But don't judge them for it. They didn't know any different. The problem for you is that their employment tenacity means they know for a fact that your attitude towards work is slack and stupid.

'What have you done today?' asked HMB, casting me a suspicious glance.

The staple

'Sod all,' said I, picking my nose. 'Although I did play a lot of Spider Solitaire, difficult level mind, so, you know.'

'How has this happened?' wailed HMB. 'You used to be a lawyer! Are you sure you shouldn't think about going back to it? Because you know you could. You could always go back to it.'

'I would rather scoop out my eyeballs with spoons and sew them to my nipples.'

'I can't understand it,' muttered HMB, shaking her head. 'You used to be capable.'

'Woah there, tiny lady,' protested I, holding up a hand. 'I'm not some flibbertigibbet with soft knees and woe-betide-me ankles. I've got Viv and Verm. I've got the word Dynamic written all the way through me.'

'Have you put any pants on today?' asked HMB, gesturing towards my jim jams.

'No, but what's that got to do with anything?'

'It's the middle of the afternoon! Back in the day, you would have been up at six, dictated twelve memos by seven and saved three sets of children by midday. Now look at you. You just spend all morning playing Spider Solitaire!'

'Difficult level!'

'Do you want your last moments on earth to be lying on a sofa watching *Countdown*?'

'Hmm,' pondered I. 'They probably will be if you think about it.'

'You need goals, Emma! Something to give you a sense of achievement!'

'Like having a go in a hot air balloon?'

'Not really, no.'

'As I am relentlessly having to explain to you,' began I, sitting up. 'I am self-employed. Therefore I can choose when I do work and when I do not. Today, I do not. Think of it as an occasional day.'

'But your days off are hardly occasional. They're more all the time!'

'Oh ho!' accused I, 'says the woman who spent half the year on holiday!'

'Did not!'

'Did too! Teachers get how much holiday? Six weeks in the summer, two weeks at Easter, three weeks at Christmas and then there's half-terms. That's FIFTEEN weeks holiday! And you finished at 3.30!'

'I had marking to do! Marking!'

'Oh boo hoo! Marking! My point is made. You are lazier than me.'

'I'd never not be wearing pants by four o'clock in the afternoon!'

'Then you deserve nothing but my pity,' said I. 'Your life has been a shattered bladder.'

My mother then gave me what many in the trade would call a long and penetrating stare.

LOOK AWAY!

'I can't believe you get paid for showing off,' said she, with a wistful eye.

'I do. Yes,' nodded I.

'I am deeply, deeply jealous.'

'Then take your pants off!' I yelled, with an encouraging wave of my hand. 'Taste the dream! It's never too late!'

'I feel wicked,' said my mother, five minutes later, de-panted and lolloping.

'Lovely, isn't it?' said I and settled back into the sofa.

THE SOLUTION

Unless you're putting on a suit on a daily basis and working in an establishment that has a proper receptionist and filing cabinets, your parents are going to believe that anything you do is as useless as a rocket made of chips. But they can't help it. Their generation were brought up to get a job and stick to it, so our insistence on doing the exact opposite will baffle and confuse. The one thing in your favour is that all parents want their children to have a better life than they did, so if they don't understand what you do, take a page from my book (this one preferably) and get them to wander round your house with their pants off. It will give them a sense of freedom that will thrill.

DRESSED FOR WORK

Let's turn our minds now to the clothes you wear as opposed to the clothes your parents want you to wear. Mums and dads have a clear and definite idea of what you should be wearing, which, because of the earth's gravitational pull, is the exact polar opposite of what constitutes a good outfit. In short, your parents like it best when they think you look 'presentable', which means clean, ironed clothes in acceptable muted colours with shirts tucked in, skirts below the knee and creases down the front of your jeans. And that's just for casual wear. When it comes to work clothes, the angle of requirements sharpens significantly. In short, only a suit will do, shoes need to be polished, and if you can wear a bowler hat , then please carry on. But you like to leave your clothes in a heap at the bottom of the bed where they can accumulate dog hair and extra designer creases, and achieve that special lived-in musk. And this is where the problem arises. Peel back your eyelids and get ready for some learning.

'I know you work at home, Emma,' said HMB, looking me up and down. 'But I do think you might try and make an effort. What if the postman comes to the door? Or an important director?'

'That's not how acting works, Mum,' said I, sitting in a pair of baggy, stained tracksuit bottoms. 'Plus, I regard it as my duty to fly the flag for home workers everywhere. Yet again,' added I, 'I am sans pants. *Vive la révolution.*'

'Well, let's hope the revolution will NOT be televised,' said HMB with a shake of her head.

'Hmm,' said I, raising an eyebrow. 'Excellent referencing of seminal '70s funk songs.'

'Yes, that was quite good,' nodded HMB, looking pleased with herself.

'But I've said it before and I'll say it again,' began I, holding up a triumphant finger, 'it's my duty to get up when I feel like it and sit at my desk in my pyjamas for as long as it feels morally and psychologically acceptable. And I'm allowed to do that, because I spent most of my twenties sitting in strip-lit offices with people with surnames like Barker breathing down my neck.'

'But to work efficiently, you should be dressed efficiently. I think that's physics,' opined HMB, tapping her chin with her hand.

'*Au contraire*,' replied I. 'The output of most businesses would increase tenfold if workers were allowed to come in wearing their jim jams and slipper socks. Just imagine the time you could save every day by not having to get in the shower, do your hair, put your make up on or decide what you're wearing. Imagine if you, like me, could just stumble out of your bed, not even look at yourself once in any sort of mirror, magic or otherwise, and sit yourself at your work station without a second thought. Imagine that.'

'Well, I suppose people WOULD get to work a lot quicker,' said HMB.

'At least one whole hour quicker,' agreed I, nodding. 'And there'd be no chance of people wasting time on office romances. Because everyone would look terrible.'

'Especially if they hadn't brushed their teeth,' added HMB.

'I'm telling you,' announced I, banging a hand on a table, 'this is where British businesses are going wrong. Everyone's spending too long getting ready and not enough time grafting. The British economy would be booming if everyone wandered into work with no pants on.'

'Hmmm,' pondered HMB, 'when you say it like that... but you can't like being like that all the time. Wouldn't it be nice to see you in a gown?'

'A gown?' said I, flinching. 'Who says gown? It's a dress!'

'This is why you'll never be really successful,' said HMB, with a genuine sadness. 'Proper actresses wear gowns.'

GO SHOPPING FOR NEW DRESS

I looked down at my butter-stained tracky botts and the heavy knit slipper socks with cows on the ankles peeping out from under them. My hair was unwashed. I might have smelled.

'Gowns indeed,' muttered I, with a whisper of what could have been. But then came the moment of epiphany. 'Ah ha!' yelled I. 'But I am wearing a gown! A dressing gown! In your face!'

THE SOLUTION

Although I appreciate that many of you reading this will have jobs and that many of those jobs will take place in an office, I think you should join the gang and get pantless. If you're going into work tomorrow, try turning up in your pyjamas. If your boss asks you what the hell you're thinking of, merely wave this book in his or her face and say you're conducting an efficiency experiment that should increase productivity by at least twenty percent. Workers of the world unite!

BRIGHT IDEAS

Because I occasionally work on the tellybox, I am a running target for anyone who has ever had an idea. Although it's perfectly acceptable to sit and listen to strangers tell you their brilliant concept for a sitcom set in a world made entirely from bacon, it's another thing altogether when that stranger turns out to be an immediate family member. When I say 'immediate family member', I am, of course, referring to WDT. When it comes to stunning ideas, this man is the fount of all knowledge. According to him. But we know differently, don't we readers?

'I've had a brilliant idea for a new telly show,' declared WDT, pulling at my jumper sleeve. 'It came to me when I was on a country walk.'
A small sigh squeezed itself out from the side of my mouth. 'Here we go,' thought I.
'I went to try out my new binoculars,' began he, 'because every time I've gone out I've forgotten to take them with me. So I went on a walk specifically to try them out.'
'Hmmm,' said I, because that was all I could commit to at this stage. I didn't want to peak too soon.
'And it was an amazing walk,' continued WDT, smiling. 'Three deer jumped out of a bush. Ran right past me. And I saw a hare.'
'Was it a hare?' quizzed I, suddenly. 'Or was it just a rabbit?'
'It was a hare. I looked at it through my new binoculars. And there was a fox. In the same field. And a dead badger. And that's when I had the idea. Because, at first, I wasn't quite sure if it was a dead badger as it was mostly just a skeleton. And I had to kick it over with my boot. But then I saw a small tuft of black and white fur on the skull, and then I knew. But not just that, but there was a hole in the skull. Like it had been shot or something. And then it came to me. Wouldn't it be brilliant if there was a crime drama about a forensic scientist who specialises in animal deaths? Like *Silent Witness* crossed with *All Creatures Great and Small*? Because people love crime. And animals.'
'Yes,' nodded I, with great reluctance. 'People do like crime. And they do like animals.'

'So Fenulla Drougham, she's the animal forensic scientist, she's called in because chickens are turning up dead all over the county.'

'Chickens?' said I, raising an eyebrow.

'Yes. Chickens. But it's not bird flu. And everyone, including her assistant, Tina Mulgoon, she's a hot head...'

'Of course she is,' interrupted I.

'... thinks it's a fox.'

'Tina Mulgoon's got a lot to learn,' added I.

'But of course it isn't a fox. And Fenulla, after taking one of the chickens back to her laboratory, discovers that one of the chickens is covered in a protein only found in a cow's second stomach.'

'So a cow did it?' asked I.

'No. It's a panther that's escaped from the mansion of a reclusive millionaire who's been trafficking exotic animals.'

'I can see you've thought this through,' said I, folding my arms.

'But Tina Mulgoon can't work it out and wants to know about the protein from the cow's stomach. But, of course, Fenulla is there to explain that the panther had attacked a cow BEFORE the chickens and hence the residue of cow protein had dripped onto the chicken carcass.'

'Even a chocolate Labrador, the stupidest of all the animals, could have worked that out.'

'Yes. Tina Mulgoon needs to realise that she can't go around just blaming the first animal she can think of. Did I mention Fenulla only has one eye?' interjected WDT. 'She wears a patch. A suicidal parrot pecked it out.'

'Are you taking the piss?' said I, smelling the stinkiest of rats.

'No!' protested WDT. 'So that's my idea. Good isn't it?'

'What's it called?' asked I.

'*Crime Zoo*. Might be a good vehicle for Tamzin Outhwaite.'

THE SOLUTION

Commission 32 hour-long episodes immediately.

Miscellaneous difficulties

Some things your parents do can't be pinned down. These are the gob-smacker moments that leave you reeling and breathless. You can't prepare for them because you don't know when they're going to strike. Parents are like stealth bombers, and just when you think you're on a steady, even keel, they'll drop their load. I like to take as relaxed an attitude as I can towards these encounters. Imagine your parents are a python. It's got itself wrapped round you. If you try and wriggle free, it will only grip you tighter. So relax. Give in. And let the madness wash over you.

Having said that, the following Practical Problems are dangerous and should only be read by trained professionals. If you are not a trained professional, please take the following precautions before exposing yourself to them.

1. No one should attempt to read the Practical Problems without having an attendant stationed within a ten-foot radius at all times.

2. All required equipment and supplies for a brain meltdown must be readily available and in good working condition. Equipment should include but is not limited to:
   a. appropriate respiratory equipment
   b. appropriate personal protective equipment; to include items such as hardhats, glasses, boots, hearing protection and gloves
   c. appropriate rescue/emergency equipment such as a safety harness and book tongs
   d. equipment such as barricades, flashlight and tools if reading in bed.

3. In the event of a brain meltdown, the attendant should not attempt to touch, tamper or move the book in any way. Kick it away from the reader with a rubber shoe, evacuate the reader and telephone the appropriate authorities immediately.

Good luck studio!

SWEET NOTHINGS

Sometimes you will find yourself alone with a parent in a confined space for an unnatural length of time. You may have to attempt a conversation. You can usually stick to safe topics like whether or not that cousin who ate pears while they were still on the tree has something wrong with him, or why some supermarkets stock Marmite with gravy when it clearly should be with the jams. But as the hours drag by, the natural parental topics are going to dry up and you're going to have to dig deep. In short, it's time to get quizzical.

'I don't think I've ever seen you eat a biscuit,' said I to my mother, to whom I had agreed to give a lift. My mother doesn't drive, but that doesn't stop her telling me what to do every thirty seconds. 'Traffic light!' she will scream, and 'Look out! Idiot! What an ID-IOT!', to which I will reply, 'He is allowed to turn left. Especially after indicating.' But that's by the by. I had realised that my knowledge of my mother and biscuits was woefully lacking.
'No,' replied HMB, 'I'm not a fan of the biscuit.'

We were driving up the Edgware Road in London and had been in the car so long that not only were the shop signs now all in Russian but the two of us had entered into a conversational impasse. We had covered all the basics including family news and multivitamins, and the reason I had got onto biscuits was because, before we had set off, I had offered HMB a Rich Tea, which is such an inoffensive snack that I was almost aghast when she turned it down.

'You haven't gone wheat-free have you?' I had asked.
'No,' she had said, 'I just don't like biscuits.'

I had let it go at the time, but now, glued into an interminable journey, I felt an idea mulling over in my mind – could I like someone who didn't like biscuits? I mean, could I?

'When you offer me a Rich Tea biscuit,' HMB continued, 'it's like giving me a slice of bread. What's the difference?'

'The difference is that a Rich Tea is a biscuit. And a slice of bread is a slice of bread,' said I. 'You can't equate a Rich Tea with a slice of bread.'

'Yes I can,' said HMB, who was in fighting mood. 'A Rich Tea is a rubbish biscuit. Why would I choose to snack on one? What's the point of it?'

'It's a delicious and multitasking biscuit,' said I, leaping to my best biscuit's defence. 'You can have them nude and straight out of the pack. You can dunk them into tea or even coffee. You can adorn them with all sorts of sweet meats. And cheese. They are very versatile. They do savoury and sweet.'

This fell on deaf ears.

best biscuit

'I hate the Rich Tea and all that it stands for,' said HMB, rubbing her window to clear the condensation.

'Well, what biscuit do you like?' said I. 'You must like one biscuit. Everyone has one biscuit that when they see it, they must have it. Everyone does. If there was a plate of biscuits, what biscuit would you pick? It has to be the biscuit that, when you see it, you have to have it. For me, that biscuit is the pink wafer biscuit. When I see it, I must have it. I also enjoy a plain chocolate digestive. But it must be plain. But the pink wafer is a work of biscuit genius.'

'Emma,' said HMB, which is never a good sign, 'I just don't feel the same way about biscuits.'

'OK,' said I, taking it to the next level. 'You have to have a biscuit. Or die. What's your biscuit?'

My mother sighed. 'Well, that's very silly, but if I had to have a biscuit or die, then I expect I would have one of those biscuits with the pink icing on top and the swirly white bits on it.'

'Would you?' said I, my voice going up an octave. 'Really? A pink iced biscuit with the white swirly bits? I hate them.'

'At least,' said HMB, 'they are like being offered a chocolate doughnut. Not a plain old slice of bread.'

'You're talking rubbish,' said I, incensed. 'The pink-iced biscuit with the white swirls is a flibbertigibbet of a biscuit. At least the Rich Tea is a noble biscuit. It has dignity.'

We then didn't speak to each other for five minutes.

'Mints or Mince?' said I, after a suitable interval.

'Pardon?' said HMB, turning to look at me.

'Mints or Mince?' said I. 'You have to tell whether I'm saying Mince or Mints. So if I said Mints? Or Mince? Then you would say Sweet, then Savoury. But if I say Mince? Or Mints? Then you would have to say Savoury, then Sweet. Do you see? So round one – Mints? Or Mince?'

My mother just stared at me.

'I'll help you out. That was sweet (Mints) followed by savoury (Mince). Round Two – Mince? Or Mints?'

HMB sighed, 'Remind me never to ask you for a lift again. TRAFFIC LIGHTS!'

THE SOLUTION

It was true when you were five and it remains true til the day you die, but whenever you are on a long car journey with a parent (preferably both), it is your duty to drive them slowly mad. Once you can drive, however, the tables turn in your parents' favour because they will use the journey time to beg you not to drive faster than fifty miles an hour and never to overtake lorries. Note then how I stem that tide by pursuing a pointless topic of conversation. The more banal the questions, the more absorbed your parent will become. And that gives them less time to annoy you. See, it's easy when you know how.

SHIT HAPPY

Parents have an inbuilt belief that if only they were in charge of everything, everything would be a lot better than it actually is. Apart from you, the world is, according to your parents, populated by idiots. You could get drunk, steal a double-decker bus and drive it into the Thames and they'd still think you were 'only doing your best', so bask in the immunity. Your parents are the only people living who don't secretly think you're a twat. But when it comes to everyone and everything else, it's a different story. Nothing is out of bounds when it comes to parental displeasure. And, like meteorites, they strike hard, fast and with no warning whatsoever.

'Have you seen that advert?' asked HMB, passing me a cup of tea. 'The one where a bear wanders off into the woods for a shit? And then wipes its arse with that toilet paper?'
'Does a bear shit in the woods?' replied I, nodding. 'Yes. I am aware of its work.'
'Well, yes,' answered HMB. 'A bear DOES shit in the woods. But what bear needs soft toilet tissue to do it? If I owned a soft toilet tissue company, then I would start with a bottom, a HUMAN bottom, show it being wiped, show the dirty paper, with shit on it, not blue liquid, which suggests you have that illness that mad King George III had, which toilet tissue companies have obviously decided is far more common than anyone would previously believe, and then I would go back to the bottom, which was now clean, and reveal the anus, which would bear testimony to the softness of my product because it would not look chafed or red. And then I would have the voice-over artist say "Shit Happy". That's what I would do.'

I was stunned into a momentary silence.

'Not "Shit Happens"?' said I, with a frown.
'That's the expression. Shit happens.'

'No,' said HMB in a very serious tone. 'That would be wrong. That is the expression, you are correct, but it would be a bad idea. Everyone knows that shit happens, because that is what you do when you go for a shit. Although, strictly speaking, the expression is generally used for situations in which things have gone wrong, and in my advert for my product, I wouldn't want people to associate it with a phrase that is resonant of bad luck or something undesirable. That is why I would use the expression "Shit Happy". It is a play on the phrase "Shit Happens" yet it has turned a once sad phrase into one of joy. The actress who had done the shitting would be smiling while holding up the now soiled paper. Having a shit should be a celebration. Not something we are ashamed of or poke fun at. "Shit Happy."'

I paused for a moment.

'Well,' said I, 'I can see this is something you've given a lot of thought to.'
'Yes,' said HMB. 'It is.'
'It's a shame you don't work in advertising, isn't it?'
'Yes. And that I don't own a soft toilet tissue factory.'
'It's terrible when you've missed your calling, isn't it?' said I.
'I can always dream, Emma, I can always dream.'

Shit happy everyone.

THE SOLUTION

Do you think that advert would win prizes? This is strange territory for mothers so watch your backs. When she's in these sorts of mood, anything could happen. She might even declare herself an independent nation state and try to invade the Isle of Wight. And no one wants that. So while it is always in your best interests to indulge the maternal whim, you should never go so far as to encourage it. Contain and restrain. That's what you're looking for.

WEATHER OR NOT?

We all take things for granted. Like opposable thumbs or the mystery of tea made from beef. While it is never a bad idea to stop and contemplate these universal enigmas, sustained philosophical reasoning can be discombobulating for the average parent. Most people know everything they're ever going to know by the age of twenty-one. They then spend the next two to three decades digging their ideas into a hole out of which they will not be dragged for love nor money. So when new concepts present themselves, parents can find themselves in difficulty, especially if those concepts question something they have always taken as read. What to do?

'Is there such a thing as no weather?' said HMB, who was watching the forecast being read by Siân Lloyd, the Welsh weather sensation with the very expressive fingers. WDT, who is Welsh, loves the Welsh Siân Lloyd and her Welsh finger expressions.
'Oooh look at that one, Brenda,' he will say, holding out one arm and extending his fingers with a flourish to copy his heroine. 'A coooollld front! No one does weather hands like Siân.'

He loves her.

'No weather?' said I, to answer the question. 'There's always weather.'
'But what if there isn't?' asked HMB. 'According to that map, there's no weather in the South East tomorrow morning. According to that map, there will continue to be no weather until late afternoon. Plus, while I'm at it, why do we need to know what the weather is like in Norway, Denmark and the Netherlands? Why does the weather map have them? Why?'
'There is always weather,' said I, sensing that a certain someone was getting themselves into a trademark tizzywizz. 'There is no such thing as no weather.'

'Look with your eyes!' said HMB, pointing frantically at the telly. 'According to that map and Siân Lloyd's fingers, there is no weather south of Watford.'

'Perhaps she ran out of clouds and/or sun symbols?' said I, shrugging my shoulders.

'Rain coming up from the Wessssssssstt,' muttered WDT, in a trance.

'It's not that type of map!' said HMB, getting up and tapping the screen. 'It's all done by computer. Siân Lloyd isn't even there. If we were to believe that map, Siân Lloyd is twice the size of the British Isles. She's not. She's just a normal-sized woman with unusually expressive fingers.'

'Mmm,' murmured WDT, miming a particularly impressive hand gesture for fog.

I stared.

don't forget brolly

'What are you talking about?' said I, because yes, it had come to that.

HMB slumped back. 'I just want to know if there's ever no weather.'

'No. There is not,' said I, crossing my arms. 'Don't be ridiculous.' But then I thought about it.

'Hang on,' said I, turning to WDT for assistance. 'What about days that are cloudless and windless? Could they be interpreted as technical weather-less days? What's the definition of weather?'

At the mention of definitions, WDT snapped himself out of his reverie, reached up to the bookshelf and consulted the dictionary.

'Weather,' said he, reading . 'The condition of the atmosphere (at a given place and time) with respect to the heat and cold, presence or absence of rain.'

'Hmmm,' said HMB, 'that complicates matters.'

'How can that complicate matters?' answered I. 'It seems unequivocal. There can never be no weather. Weather, according to the official dictionary definition, is about the temperature, which is inescapable, and whether or not it's raining. And nothing else. Therefore, there is always weather.'

'That still doesn't explain why we have to know what the weather is like in Norway and Denmark and the Netherlands,' said HMB, with a note of bitter rue.

'Maybe it's because they get the BBC,' suggested WDT 'and we want to show willing.'

'Siân Lloyd's not on the BBC,' pointed out HMB.

'Poor Dutch people,' mused WDT. 'Denied Siân Lloyd's weather hands.'

'Perhaps,' said I, 'it's just nice to know it's pissing down in Copenhagen when it's sunny here?'

At which my parents both nodded and went back to being transfixed by a spectacular sweep of Welsh fingers.

THE SOLUTION

Big existential questions like if there is ever no weather need to be treated with kid gloves. Parents believe anything you tell them. There is a temptation to be mischievous in these scenarios, but unless you want your mum or dad wandering about announcing that all clouds are made in a small factory in Jersey, it's probably best to stick to the facts as laid out by your geography teacher. My geography teacher had fingers like crabs' legs and the personality of a gravestone, but she knew her precipitous facts, and for that we thank her. So approach wild questions calmly. And if you're backed into an answer cul-de-sac, cut your losses and come up with something that makes everyone feel a bit superior. Everyone leaves happy. Apart from the Danish.

SMELLING FORTUNES

Sometimes you will find out that your parents have powers you didn't know about. This may be quite shocking. I'm not talking about an ability to weave buildings out of worm's breath, but proper things like playing a trumpet or being brilliant at boomerangs. These are the things they may have excelled at before becoming parents but had to abandon. That's your fault, of course, but never mind. All you can do, when the time for revelations comes, is to arrange your face into a suitably impressed shape and hope that that, on its own, will make up for a lifetime of regrets. It should do. Your parents aren't used to you ever being impressed with anything.

'Did you know your father's got second sight?' announced HMB. 'Or at least he DID have.'

We were sitting reading papers in my parents' dining room. A wood stove was burning in the corner, and the atmosphere was toast itself. I looked up.

'Pardon?' said I. 'Second sight? Dad?'
'Of course I've had no truck with the supernatural,' continued HMB, nose still in a magazine. 'When I was an adolescent and going through my wild phase, I used to wander off to the nearest graveyard and dance round the stones. If there was a big, flat one, I used to lie on it. Nothing ever happened to me. I saw no ghosts. No one went Woo Woo in my ear. Nothing. And I knew then that when you're dead, you're dead.'
'You probably just didn't know anyone in the graveyard,' piped up WDT, who was doing a crossword. 'Just because people are dead doesn't mean they haven't got manners.'
I threw my father an askew glance and narrowed my eyes. 'What is this? Gravestones, dead people, Dad being some sort of wizard?'

'I used to write poems about it,' rattled on HMB, ignoring me. 'I blame the Jesuit priests who taught me. It's their fault. Filled my head with nonsense. Out I'd go, in would come the fog, and there'd be I, forced to have a profound thought about one's place in the universe. Quite exhausting.'

'Yes,' said I, folding my paper onto my knees, 'that's all very nice, but can we get back to the second sight thing? What?'

anyone know the answer to 9 across?

'Your father had second sight,' nodded HMB. 'He used to get terrified. I tried to have a magic mass once. He told me to stop. Not because I was embarrassing him in front of the neighbours but because I might be annoying the spirits. I told him I'd seen a sword of fire in the sky. That shut him up.'

'I was terrified,' said WDT, looking up over his reading glasses. 'But mostly because I didn't know your mother was bonkers then.'

'Tell her about that incident with Grandad,' said HMB. 'Have you heard that story?'

'No,' said I, on the edge of my seat.

WDT put down his crossword and removed his glasses. 'I was eight years old,' he began. 'And my father, being Welsh, used to go and watch Wales playing rugby. He was the treasurer of the Knuts club and they used to go to all the internationals. They'd hire a coach and off they'd go. And that weekend, Wales were playing Scotland, and so my father had gone with the Knuts Club to see them. Scotland won, I remember, and my father was going to come back the next day, on the Sunday. We didn't have television in those days, so that Sunday evening, when my father was due back, we were all sitting round the fire. My sister Marion was upstairs washing her hair. And the dog was sitting under my chair.

'Now, our front door was very difficult to open because over the years the frost had risen the flagstone. So you could just about get the door half open and then you had to push it as hard as you could to give yourself a few more inches, but you could never get it to open fully. It was seven o'clock exactly. And as the clock in our front room chimed out, I was gripped by a terrible icy feeling that so shocked me that I called out for my father. Not only that, but there was a tremendous bang on the front door. Now in those days, you never banged on anyone's doors in Wales. A knocked door meant a death. So we all went to see what it was. And the front door was wide open. All the way, right open to the wall. And at that precise moment, my father's coach had crashed in Liverpool. And my father was the worst injured on the bus. Now then, thirty-five down. Children's Author. Four, six. Begins with E?'

'Enid Blyton,' said I, all agog. 'Is that true?'

'Yes,' nodded HMB. 'See, he's got the vibes. He should open a fortune-telling business. He'd make a packet. Sometimes, when I'm a bit bored, I get him to read my feet. Go on, Tony – show her how you can read feet.'

My mother pulled off a sock and wiggled her toes in my dad's direction.

WDT, having filled in the last clue, peered over the top of his glasses in their direction.

'That line there,' said he, pointing with his pencil, 'represents your brain. No sign of life. Bad luck.'

'Oof, I'll have to put my leg down in a minute,' said HMB with a heave, 'I had too much bread and butter pudding at lunch. Tony! What does that part of my foot say? That bit there?'

'Steely resolve weakened in the presence of milky-based puddings,' said he, not even looking.

'Oh,' said I, very impressed. 'He IS good.'

THE SOLUTION

So there you have it. Apparently WDT is imbued with a gift for voodoo. You'd never guess to look at him. I also found out that he used to play the drums in a marching band and spent his entire childhood thinking a marrow was a banana. He's a veritable man of mystery.

HEROIC GESTURES

Parents spend your entire childhood with the immortal phrase 'I'm not interested in your opinion' rattling on the tips of their tongues. It's true, because they're not. In fact, under international laws, children's thoughts on anything, and yes, this DOES include saving the world from greenhouse emissions, are to be disregarded. The day a parent asks you for advice is momentous. You might want to put up a plaque. Whatever the subject.

'Something's been bothering me,' said WDT, with a sigh. 'And I want your thoughts on the matter.'

I stopped what I was doing. I could smell something peculiar. It was the telltale odour of fear. Time ground to a halt and flies fell dead out of the air.

'Please continue,' said I, settling my hands into my lap. 'You fascinate me.'

'So Spiderman,' began WDT, glancing up to the heavens, 'can shoot webs from his wrists and climb buildings. But if Peter Parker's natural functions are exactly those of a spider, then does that mean that if he impregnated Mary Jane Watson, his babies would swell in a sac that would hang off Mary Jane Watson in a delicate area? And would that sac then burst, sending hundreds of mini Peter Parkers scurrying free?'

A moment of stunned silence passed between us. 'And this is what's been bothering you?' asked I, fixing him with an unblinking stare.

'Yes. This is a problem that is virtually never addressed in the superhero/human love scenario,' said he, with a sense of urgency. 'Superheros have human girlfriends. Look at Superman. He loved Lois Lane.'

'Yes, he did,' said I, with a nod.

'But he couldn't have sex with her. That's why he had to transmogrify into a normal man in *Superman 2*. He was physically incapable of having sex with her while he was a superhero. His sperm could have killed her! If Superman had had sex with Lois before he lost his super-powers, his sperm would have ruptured her womb on entry and shot clear through her bladder, onwards via the lungs and out the back of her throat. If Lois had given Superman relief of an oral nature, the situation would have been reversed, which might, just might, have resulted in a Super Gamete becoming lodged in the shattered hull of Lois Lane's womb. And then, if her human egg had been fertilised (Lois was getting on so it's unlikely it would have happened first time), then the foetus would have killed its mother with the first kick!

'Superman knew this and so did Marlon Brando (RIP), which was why he, like all men, turned in everything he had for a shag. Of course he wasn't to know that Lois Lane was rubbish in bed, which was why he turned back later in the same movie. It had nothing to do with General Zod whatsoever. Although that is what they would like us to believe. The director's cut (only available in Denmark) does have a scene in which Superman tells Marlon Brando that Lois Lane won't do 'that thing, you know, that Suzannah York will do' but it was deleted for the US and UK audiences. Anyway. What do you think?'

'I think you're an idiot,' said I, and went back to reading my book.

THE SOLUTION

take dvd back!!

You've been asked for your opinion so give it. This might be your one chance; spare nothing. Now is not the time for faltering. You've been given an opportunity so grab it with both hands. As you can see, the opinion you give does not need to be lengthy. In fact, the more pithy and precise you can be, the better. Parents are like dogs in that they can only hear a few basic commands – 'Can I have a lift, please?' and 'I'm bringing my washing home' being the most common – so keep it simple and you'll romp home.

BRIGHT AND BEAUTIFUL

As your parents advance in years, you may notice signs of them contemplating their own mortality. This can take various forms – your father might go out one day only to return wearing leathers and riding a Harley Davidson, or your mother might start volunteering at the local hospice. It's not because she has been overwhelmed with philanthropy; it's so she can guarantee herself a bed when the time comes. But mostly, you will find their thoughts turning upwards, to the big Fellah in the Sky. It's a keep-all-your-options-open safety net just in case their lifelong scoffing at all things religious has left them hung dry on the fence called Hell. They're not stupid. Although having said that...

I was standing looking out the window at my parents' house. The weather had been volatile. One minute it was blue skies, the next thunderous rain. Poppy, My Most Excellent Beagle, was perched on top of the sofa next to me. She was particularly busy keeping her eye on a bee that was worrying itself into the top corner of the window pane.

'It's hard to know what to do,' said I, as my mother came into the room, 'when the weather is so changeable. It's difficult to make any sort of qualitative decision.'

'Your grandmother always used to say that strange weather was a sign that God was in a mood,' said HMB, 'usually brought on by me doing something a bit naughty.'

'Such as?'

'Oh, you know, conducting a black mass in the school chapel so we got expelled.'

I shook my head a little. I wasn't quite sure I'd heard right. 'Sorry? What? You had a black what?'

'Black mass. The Archbishop came down from London specially to excommunicate us.'

I stared at her. 'You've been excommunicated?'

'Mmm,' nodded she, quite pleased with herself. 'We drew a pentagram on the altar and all wore hoods. My mother didn't speak to me for a month.'

'How old were you?'

'Eleven.'

'Weren't you terrified?'

'No. We were thrilled. Anyway. You know. Bit naughty.'

I was stunned. 'Blimey,' said I, after a small eternity. 'You're well bad. I can't believe you've been excommunicated. That's proper burn-in-Hell territory. Can't you get re-communicated?'

'No,' said HMB, with a toss of her hair. 'I don't think I can get re-communicated. Although I have found myself thinking about God lately.'

'Twitch upon the thread? Once a Catholic, always a Catholic? That sort of thing?'

'Not really. I found myself wondering why it was that Christians put such an emphasis on marriage when God is a bachelor? He hasn't even had a girlfriend. Mary doesn't count. So here's a God who sends His seed to be artificially inseminated into someone He's never met, He likes beautiful things and He's very creative. On the other hand, He's very opinionated and given to flying off the handle. The point I'm making is this – am I alone in thinking that God might be gay?'

'Oh dear heaven,' said I, slapping a hand to my forehead. 'You're going to fry. Hang on a minute. Aren't excommunicated people damned souls for all of eternity?'

'Hmm,' nodded HMB.

'You're not going to haunt me, are you?'

'Well,' said HMB, thinking about that quite carefully.

'Probably. But just to make sure you're eating enough meat.'

Anyone know a good exorcist?

ghost Mom

THE SOLUTION

This was news to me; let me say that from the get go. There's no two ways about it, it is proper shocking to discover that your own Ma has been branded evil by an entire branch of Christianity. But that to one side, I have heard that having your parents cryogenically frozen isn't THAT expensive these days. Prevents haunting every time. Start saving. Now.

EGGS ARE NOT DAIRY

they aren't!!!

Parents can become very set in their ways. That's old ground that will never be turned over with a new spade. But sometimes the things your parents believe are so totally wrong that, like Custer, you need to make a stand. Although you don't run the risk of dying by an arrow in the ear, this is still dangerous territory. So circle the wagons. This could get ugly.

FRIED

'What did the 0 say to the 8?' said HMB, standing poised in a stairwell.

'I don't know,' said I, stopping to look up at her. 'What did the 0 say to the 8?'

'Like the belt.'

HMB then laughed to the verge of puking. I remained stony faced throughout. That is my job. WDT then entered into the fray by coming out of the downstairs toilet.

'Did you know,' said he, 'that at the end of Act One Scene Three in King Lear, a Chinese waiter comes on?'

'Don't be ridiculous,' said I, falling into the trap, 'there's no Chinese waiter in King Lear.'

'Yes there is,' said WDT, 'Lear calls out for him. He says, "Come hither Ho!"'

There then followed a long and painful silence.

'That might be the worst joke I've ever heard,' said I. 'Anyway, what is this? Open Spot at Kennedy Towers?'

'Why do they keep spiders in reptile houses?' HMB then asked, grinning.

'I don't know,' said I, thinking I was humouring her. 'Why do they keep spiders in reptile houses?'

'No,' said she, pulling a serious face. 'It's not a joke. I mean it. Why DO they keep spiders in reptile houses?'

'I think people have got spiders all wrong,' said WDT, joining in.

'Spiders aren't insects. They might be mammals. They make milk.'

'Don't be ridiculous,' I said. 'Of course spiders aren't mammals. Spiders don't suckle their young. They birth them in a sac and leave them to be stamped on by small boys with thick glasses. Milk indeed!'

'They do have milk. I'm going to look in the Big Book.'

The Big Book is a large, battered encyclopaedia that WDT relies on to end all family arguments by proving himself right.

'There!' said he, tapping an open page. 'Spiders produce the milk and then produce an enzyme that, when mixed with the milk, turns it into silk. It's how they spin their webs.'

'So webs are just spider cheese?' said I, scrunching my face up.

'Sort of,' said Dad, reading on. 'Hmm. Interesting. Spiders AREN'T mammals. They're arachnids. They are a category all on their own.'

'Like eggs ,' said I, with an air of innocence.

'Don't be ridiculous,' said HMB. 'Eggs are dairy.'

'No,' I said. 'You are wrong. An egg is not a dairy product.'

'Yes it is.'

'No. It is not,' I said. 'An egg comes from a chicken. A dairy product comes from a cow. Or a goat. Or a sheep.'

'Or a chicken' said HMB.

'No. Not a chicken. A chicken does not make milk or cheese. A chicken makes eggs and kievs.'

'Yes,' said HMB, 'but an egg is the same consistency as dairy products and you mix an egg with milk to make scramble.'

'Yes,' agreed WDT, 'eggs ARE a bit milky.'

'No. An egg and milk are two separate things. Like beetroot and marzipan. Just because you mix them together does not make them the same. An egg is not a dairy product.'

'But if you go to a farm,' continued HMB, 'then there's milk and cheese. And there's eggs.'

BOILED

'There's also manure,' said I. 'An egg is not a dairy product.'

'But eggs are kept next to the cheese and the milk when you buy them,' said HMB.

'In supermarkets, eggs are next to the sugar' said WDT.

'But that's just to help people who make cakes,' said HMB. 'Of course eggs are a dairy product. Because they are the same colour. Plus, a dairy product is any product of an animal that isn't its meat. '

'Does that make sheep droppings a dairy product? No. It doesn't. An egg is not dairy.'

'Mum's right though,' chipped in WDT. 'If you go to a dairy, you CAN buy eggs. They're very much part of the dairy category.'

SCRAMBLED

'Perhaps we should just ask a farmer?' suggested HMB.

'Am I going mad?' wailed I. 'An egg is NOT a dairy product! Right! That's it! Give me the Big Book! Give it to me!'

WDT handed it over. I thumbed back to the D section.

'There!' cried I, with a sense of triumph. 'Dairy. The department of farming dedicated to the manufacture of milk, cheese and butter. Thank you!'

'But what about cream? And yogurt?' asked HMB.

'Cream and yogurt are by products of milk so they are dairy.' I explained.

'So what's an egg?' asked HMB.

'It's an egg!' screamed I. 'All right! Let's consult the Big Book! Egg! The oval body laid by the female of birds enclosed within a shell or strong membrane! No mention of a cow! Or a dairy! An egg is an egg!'

'You know what you are, don't you?' asked WDT, with a mischievous grin. 'You're an Eggspert!'

'Oh very good, Tony,' exclaimed HMB, patting him on the back. 'That's the best joke yet!'

THE SOLUTION

It's bad enough that your parents think their jokes are funny, but I'm close to losing it in this scenario. Can you blame me? What the frick?

An egg is an egg. End of. In situations like this, you just have to cling to any available surface and hope you don't get swept away by their maelstrom of madness. They still won't believe a word you're telling them of course, but at least you made a stand.

And that brings me neatly to the last piece of advice I can give you:

Love your parents unconditionally because sometimes it's like they've been touched with the simple stick. You won't be able to believe you're anything to do with them. But you are. And always will be. And one day, it'll be your turn.

Good luck.

Conclusion

So, like a sweating sherpa, we have reached the peak of Parent Mountain. Pat yourselves on the back. You've deserved it. And isn't the view lovely? You've learned how to understand your parents' behaviour, set boundaries and bring balance where once there was chaos. Just by reading this book, your life has been improved by at least seven percent*. You've got the power to tame a whirlwind. And you're strangely more attractive. That, my friends, is the power of books.

Like it or not, the relationship you have with your parents is THE most important relationship you will have in your lifetime. It shapes who you are, affects your future and resonates through every aspect of your life. Whether you feel you have lacked your parents' approval or feel crushed by their attentions, you can find a method of constructive communication that works for both of you.

For many of us, the relationship we have with our parents seems stuck in a rut. Some of you may feel as if your relationship with your parents has never moved on since your teenage years and, as a result, you are still in conflict. If you can recognise that this is simply a repetitive pattern of behaviour, you are taking the first steps to moving on. During your teenage years, it is important to establish your own needs and personality and, more often than not, this leads to tensions with your immediate authority figures. In your adult years, there is no longer a need to do this. You are your own person, as are your parents. But for those of you who had difficult teenage years, the vapour trail of that experience can still be visible and, as a result, whenever you are with your parents, you can stumble back into old roles.

* Actual life change percentage may vary.

It's almost impossible to conceive now, but I used to have a terrible relationship with my parents. I resented them for everything, and no visit home was complete without a full-blown row. But then I stopped and asked myself what I was angry about and quickly realised that everything I liked to blame on my parents had nothing to do with them whatsoever. The vast majority of parents do the best they can with what they've got. They're not superheroes, and they can't provide you with an unblemished life. You need to teach yourself how to let go and get on.

So how do you break bad habits? Learning to stop resenting your parents can be like giving up smoking. You know that you hate it but you can't stop doing it. But like any habit, it's all about shutting off the stimuli. If you have a problematic relationship with your parents, try the following;

1. Stop looking at your parents as authority figures. If you can manage this, tension will evaporate.

2. Don't allow yourself to be judgemental: if your parents have different opinions from you, so what? It doesn't matter.

3. Try and look past the Parent and see the person; a person who has their own hang-ups, their own disappointments and their own insecurities. Just like you. So try to be more tolerant.

If you can do all that, you will be well on the way to improving your relationship with your parents.

Before I began writing this book, I set up an online questionnaire about the relationships people have with their families. You can see some of the results of that questionnaire in the Appendix at the back. When I asked you if you loved your parents, a heartening 96.37% of you said you did, with some of you saying it wasn't possible for you to love anyone else more. For the minority of you whose lives have been blighted by terrible parents, you have my sympathies. But for most of us, while the affection is there, it's the tensions we seem to focus on. Clashes with your parents are inevitable but not insurmountable, and when it comes to the relationship we have with our families, we could all do better. If you have an issue, raise it. If you're feeling irritated, ask yourself why. Sometimes, the problem lies with you. It's all about being flexible. Put quite simply, your parents are just different from you. And there's nothing wrong with that. Accept that and you might end up being the greatest of friends.

Who said parents were useless?

Like it or not, the relationship you have with your parents is THE most important you will have in your lifetime

'If there's one thing I've learned from my parents,' one of you told me, 'it's that you can't hide sprouts in a glass of milk.'

See? Who said parents were useless? Now get out there. And start enjoying them.

Some of you may have been raised Mowgli-style by a family pet, some of you will have been surrounded by brothers and occasionally sisters, and some of you, like me, will have walked through the valley of death alone with nothing but a small, mangled mouse for company. He was called Mr Mouse. I loved him.

Everyone's childhood is unique, and because of this it's very easy to feel isolated. But there are common ties that bind us all, and that's what I wanted to explore. When I began writing this book, I wanted to find out about other people's experiences of growing up and their relationship with their parents. So I asked you. And you answered. Dim the lights please, and let's examine the evidence.

Mr Mouse

A massive 88.97% of you grew up surrounded by siblings. Only 8.82% of you are only children, with a tiny 2.2% of you claiming to be in neither category. One of you spent your entire childhood convinced that siblings were *'dried autumn leaves lying in a puddle of stagnant water at the bottom of a wheelbarrow'*. That same person also, rather sadly, told me, *'I think my relationship with my real siblings contained as much warmth as my relationship with those leaves at the bottom of the barrow. They looked on me as someone who stole their mother's affection and I looked upon them as bullies. I couldn't wait for them to leave home and was so pleased when they did.'*

88.97% of you grew up surrounded by siblings

Difficult relationships with siblings seems to be the norm, with only 10.23% of you describing your relationship with your brothers and/or sisters as you were growing up as good. The rest of you spent your childhoods arguing, fighting and going out of your way to make each other's lives a misery.

'When I was first born, my brother apparently called me his "little princess". I don't remember this but it didn't last long. I only remember him punching my front teeth out, chasing me round the house with a sharp plastic sword and trying to set fire to me with a magnifying glass in the garden. For years, a day could not go by without me being given a dead arm or leg, having something sharp or ignited shoved in my face, or just being scared half to death by him trying out judo moves on my terrified anatomy.'

The above is typical of the answers you gave. People with much younger siblings confessed to administering regular beatings, while those of you who had brothers and sisters closer in age experienced feelings of competitiveness and mutual hatred. Fighting was what you did best, with an astonishing 67.35% of you having a permanent scar because of something done to you by a sibling.

67.35% of you have a permanent scar

'I have a scar on my back from when my sister pushed me onto her Sindy wardrobe. And she has a scar on her face from where I bit her (I do not remember doing this but it only shows up when she's had a few drinks).'

So that's all right then, although I would quite like to see that with my own eyes. It's like those mugs with pictures of naked men that only show up when they're hot.

It also came as something of a relief that only 4.78% of you wanted your siblings to die a horrible death. And only three of you actually tried to kill a sibling. Alarmed that the vast majority of you spent your formative years in constant battle, I asked you to name the worst thing you ever did to a sibling. The punishments can be divided into two clear categories. The first just involves being disgusting. There's the gross-out classic:

'*I put worms up my brother's nose.*'

Poo on
a stick

Then there's the more disturbed:

'*I made my sister eat dog poo off a stick when we were playing prisoner of war.*'

And then there's the systematic and methodical determination that comes with the need for slow-roasting revenge:

'*I urinated in my brother's bath water. Twice a week. For seven years.*'

What the above person didn't tell me was whether he or she was able to do this because they shared their bath water and the unfortunate brother always got second dibs, or whether the perpetrator had to make a special effort to go and urinate into the brother's bath water when he wasn't looking. We will never know. Whichever the answer, you have to admire the tenacity.

But my favourite, by a country mile, is this one:

We've all done things that seem like a good idea at the time

'*When I was nine, I tried to let out a sneaky fart down the side of my top bunk in the direction of my brother. Unfortunately, I ended up pooing on him. In the morning, he got all the blame for his dirty sheets.*'

There are so many things that are terrible about this that it's impossible to know where to begin. We've all done something that seemed like a good idea at the time, but surely, SURELY, you can sense when a fart is turning into a poo? What this aptly displays is the dogged determination so prevalent in all your answers. You wanted to hurt your siblings. And sometimes shit on them. From a height.

The other category accounts for 72.12% of your answers. These were the more subtle, psychological tortures designed to disturb and sometimes guarantee a lifelong phobia. One of the more baffling answers was this one:

'I once told my sister that her massive front teeth caused my brother's epilepsy. She cried.'

The desire to emotionally scar a sibling is a common one, with cruelty being cited by many of you as your tool of choice.

'I made up a song about my sister that made her cry. I didn't stop singing it for ten years.'

the desire to emotionally scar a sibling is a common one

'We used to go on long car journeys over to France with the caravan. We would play games and as my younger sister was only a toddler she would always fall asleep in the car. We used to put sweets in her open mouth as she slept. When she woke up we would tell her that we had been on the holiday and she'd slept all the way through and we were now going home. That always made her cry.'

Pretty straightforward stuff. But some of you displayed a gift for twisted genius:

'I once bit the chocolate coating off a Milky Way and left the filling on the floor. I then pointed out the "poo" to my brother, picked it up and proceeded to eat it. He was extremely traumatised.'

Breathtaking in its simplicity yet oh so very brilliant. Not quite as simple as this one though:

'I just told my sister she was adopted.'

Excellent. But there will always be room for some plain, old-fashioned violence:

> *'I stabbed my sister in the leg repeatedly with a pencil and then threw mayonnaise all over her just as she was leaving for the school disco.'*

Weapons of mass destruction

Or this one:

> *'I put a pin under my sister's pillow so that when she lay down it would go into her head. That looks terrible written down.'*

the pencil

the pin

Yes. It does. But that's nothing compared to the lengths of subterfuge that some of you would stoop to:

> *'I once convinced my sister that a Laxative was a Swedish chocolate.'*

the chocolate laxative

And:

> *'When we were very small, I told my little sister that, if she were to jump out of the upstairs window, she'd fall into a flying sleigh that would take her to Chessington World Of Adventures.'*

Which is pure evil, is it not? But many of you were also the victims. There were the physical tortures:

> *'I was hung out of a window by my brother, after showing his new girlfriend his collection of pornographic magazines. It was not a crime that my brother felt comfortable informing my parents about, so punishment was enacted without trial.'*

> '*My sister unscrewed the brakes on my bike, and once hid in the dark and hit me over the head (unconscious) with a hockey stick.*'

And there were the psychotic:

> '*My brother decapitated all my Barbies' heads with a vegetable slicer.*'

> '*My older sister used to terrorise me by telling ghost stories with a particular twist – like the one where the ghost would put pencils in the victim's bed before a haunting – then a couple of days later, she would put a pencil in my bed.*'

But nothing, not even a sleeping bag full of scorpions, could beat this childhood trauma:

> '*My middle brother just used to play Chris De Burgh records. Really loud.*'

A horror that only a lifetime of therapy could solve.

That said, you've also shown incredible kindness to your brothers and sisters. Four of you have saved a sibling's life, 54.92% of you have admitted to sticking up for a brother or sister who was being bullied by someone outside the family and 24.31% of you have stood by a brother or sister during an unwanted pregnancy. When asked about the best things you have ever done for a sibling, the majority of you went for the big, noble stuff like looking after a sibling in a coma or helping a brother with a drug addiction, but it was good to see that at least one of you thought the following was the greatest thing ever:

> '*I taught my brother how to play* Feeling Groovy *on the guitar.*'

But even that is nearer the button than:

'*I gave my sister some hair straighteners.*'

Which sort of misses the point but hey, hair straighteners are GREAT! In the main, your idea of good things you've done for a sibling involve bravery and concepts of selflessness. But when it comes to recalling acts of kindness towards you from your siblings, an astonishing 74.59% of you, chose small, random acts of tenderness that you've never forgotten:

> '*When I was eleven and broke my arm, my brother spent the whole evening at home holding my unplastered hand and reading me stories, instead of going to the sleepover party he was meant to be going to.*'

> '*When I left home every one of my siblings arrived on my doorstep during the week to see how I was and to offer support. The ages ranged from 8 to 21 years old and they all turned up separately, and although it was a little awkward (we're not that good at showing emotions) it was of tremendous help to me and was the beginning of my reappraisal of my role in the family.*'

> '*During one of my darkest depressed phases, my younger brother came into my room silently and sat holding my hand in the dark for about five minutes. It was an extraordinarily kind thing for a teenager to do.*'

> '*I'd just been dumped by a girlfriend. My brother, to cheer me up, sat with me for twelve hours playing Civilisation II. This is the geek equivalent of all that unsightly crying, watching mushy films and loafing around snottily in pyjamas that Bridget Jones did in the film.*'

But there's always room for the practical:

> '*My sister did her best to ensure I knew the value of a manicure.*'

The thrilling:

random acts of kindness

> '*My sister let me use her black eyeliner. I'm a male.*'

And my personal favourite:

> '*When I was sixteen my girlfriend once turned up unannounced while I was on the toilet. My brother spotted her and warned me. Phew.*'

Imagine that being the best thing you could ever remember someone doing for you, saving you from being caught half way through a shit. Actually, that is QUITE good. I bow.

The other area in which you seemed to excel was playing games. Those of you with larger families tended to favour games that involved kidnap and torture, while those of you with one other sibling seemed to have been slightly more inventive:

> '*We played Maureen and Margaret. We were housewives who lived either side of the bed. Our babies slept in shoe boxes.*'

I might be going out on a limb here, but I'm guessing they weren't boys. Unlike this lot:

> '*Our favourite game was Dead Man Hanging. One of us would hang by one arm from the branch of a tree whenever we saw a car coming. When the car stopped and came back to check, we would run off.*'

But then there were the purely joyous:

'We loved rollerblading to the Call My Bluff theme tune.'

'It was called The Spaceship of NooNoo. It involved a blanket. And being spun around.'

And then there were the stranger ones:

'I liked naming the cows in the field next door. And seeing how close I could get to a cow before it dribbled on me. Mainly cow based.'

'I pretended I was a dog for two years.'

And then there's the game that seems to speak fathoms:

that's just plain weird

'We just pretended we were orphans.'

So let's move onto your parents. A total of 86.24% of people questioned were brought up by two parents, with the rest of you being raised by one. One individual claimed to have been raised by six people in some sort of Charlie Bucket-style domestic arrangement, but other than that your familial structural arrangements were pretty similar. For 60.99% of you, your parents are still together, while 26.95% of them are divorced; 8.5% of you have one parent who has died, and 3.54% of you no longer have either parent. Even though the majority of your parents are still together, this doesn't mean they don't have their problems. This was my favourite response:

'My parents have been married since 1960. About five years ago my Dad came to stay with me on his own. He was grumpy for several days. Eventually, we took him down the pub, upon which he announced he wanted to divorce my mother. My Dad is eighty this year and has cooked twice in the past forty years. It turned out the problem was that my mother wouldn't let him look at internet porn.'

Which is strangely great, isn't it?

As far as your relationship with your parents as you were growing up goes, the majority of you (59.06%) were happy to go on record as describing it as 'good'. The rest of your answers followed a predictable pattern in that you seemed to get on just fine until you hit your teenage years, and then all hell broke loose. 'I never felt like they understood me' was the most resonant response, while many of you felt as if your parents were just 'figures in the background' who stopped you doing what you wanted; 22.72% of you felt as though you had a terrible relationship with your father, while a much smaller 5.68% of you cited the relationship with your mother as being extremely difficult. The rest of you were on a pretty even keel with both of them. For those of you who acknowledged a strain, 67.42% felt compelled to make a stand and rebel. Some of you started younger than others:

> *'I went through a phase when I was seven or eight when I insisted on believing that I was an adopted Romanian refugee. This was not helped by the fact that on Sundays, after he'd drunk too much, my father would laugh at me and call me Olga.'*

But most of you saved your fight back for your teenage years, with a heavy emphasis on sitting alone in your room and playing loud music. Some of you went for the sartorial approach:

> *'I began religiously wearing a bowler hat'*

While one of you took your role as a bad teenager extremely seriously:

> *'I stole cars and set the school on fire.'*

59.06% described their teenage relationshp with their parents as 'good'

Good. Because that's doing it properly isn't it? But how do you even start to turn bad when you've got parents who (whisper it softly) are quite cool?

'It's quite hard to rebel against laidback parents with massive collections of Beatles, Stones and Hendrix records. So I did what I had to. I got into bagpipe music.'

A massive 91.07% of you were subject to parental rules. There were the hardy favourites like not eating between meals and elbows not being allowed on the table, but one of you moaned that during meal times you weren't allowed to 'play with yourself', which must have been a terrible inconvenience. Others included being home before dark, not talking back, tidying your room, answering your father, not running in the kitchen, not standing in the kitchen when mum's cooking, not playing with the fish pond, not playing football near the flower beds, not standing on the rockery, not kicking a football up against the house, not kicking a football IN the house, not jumping on the beds or sofas, ringing if you're going to be late, not using the phone without asking, not pushing your bed up against the wall as it blocks the radiators and makes the mildew worse, not picking at the flocked wallpaper, and NOT looking in the drawers in mum's bedside cabinet.

That was the more usual stuff, but some of your parents had specific rules that made you quite indignant:

'They would never let me draw on slices of bread with my felt tip pens. This struck me as being very unreasonable.'

While others suffered a fate worse than death:

'We were never allowed to interrupt The Archers. If we did, our punishment was having to listen to The Archers.'

I might be speaking out of turn, but that's bordering on child abuse.

But one of you had such a stand-out parental rule that it had to be saved till last.

'Never look a mallard duck in the eye.'

That was a rule. I can't even BEGIN to imagine the incident that brought that one into play, especially as it is so breed specific. Is it all right to look other types of ducks in the eye? And what about geese? They're almost ducks. And what happens when you do look a mallard duck in the eye? Everyone knows swans carry guns, but mallard ducks? Who knows? Don't try and find out for yourselves. Rules are there for a reason.

The biggest problem for you, as you were growing up, was being embarrassed. Top of the agenda – sex. For a staggering 100% of you, the thought of your parents having sex was, and still is, as repulsive as a sludge smoothie. But even worse was catching them at it. You might want to pour yourself a stiff drink…:

the thought of parents having sex was, and still is, as repulsive as a sludge smoothie

'I once walked into the bedroom with all my friends behind me. Mum was giving Dad a blow job.'

'I was eleven. I heard noises and thought Dad was having a fit. I rushed into their bedroom and ran round to his side of the bed. I asked if there was anything I could do. Mum, who was on top, politely declined my offer of assistance. It still makes me blush twenty-six years later.'

'I was fourteen and we were on a caravan holiday in the Lake District. My parents gave us a map and a destination and told us to go out and find it. Shortly after leaving I slipped and hurt my elbow so we went back, casually flung open the door to the caravan and there they were on the floor. Having sex. Hideous. Hideous. Hideous. It makes my toes curl just thinking about it.'

Yuckadoodledoo. But if you thought that was bad, what about this:

WARNING!
Do not read if prone
to weak stomach

'My mum and dad had a hot tub and my mother happily explained to a friend of mine that yes, they had had sex in it and yes, semen does float.'

That's the sort of thing that makes you want to emigrate.

Not all your parental embarrassments are about sex though. Here's one that's verging on the horrific:

'My mum and dad's room was at one end of a big, open landing. The spare bedroom was at the other end next to the bathroom. Dad would always walk naked to the bathroom in the morning. Once there, he would proceed to fart thunderously for about five minutes. That was fine unless a friend was staying. Dad would make no concessions. If the friend emerged from the bedroom at the wrong moment, Dad would just engage them in early morning chit chat. Then he would wander into the bathroom and blast them out with his bloughs.'

But it's not all just genitals and essential bodily functions. Another disastrous combination was your parents and restaurants: 32.87% of you had embarrassing stories about going out for meals, nearly all of which involved plain, old-fashioned rudeness.

'My parents were visiting me in my new flat. We went to a local family run Italian restaurant. It's the end of a delicious meal.
WAITER: "Would you like anything else?"
MUM: "I'd like a cappuccino."
WAITER: "One cappuccino..."
MUM: "No. I don't want it here. I want to go home and have one of those ones from a sachet."'

HOW TO BRING UP YOUR PARENTS

To be honest, you were pretty much embarrassed by everything to do with your parents. You were embarrassed by your parents' clothes, their dancing and their taste in music:

> *'When I was about twelve I had a sleep over. My dad asked my friends if they'd like some music to dance to. My friends all yelled "Yeah!" and began leaping around. He put on 'Hall of the Mountain King' from the Peer Gynt suite. My friends took the piss endlessly.'*

While having to concede that that one is appalling, it is pretty clear that your parents' mere existence embarrassed you. But, according to your answers, they seemed to really crank up the stakes as soon as you started dating. The statistics speak for themselves here, with your dads committing 76.53% of the worst offences:

> *'My dad showed my boyfriend a knife and told him he knew how to use it.'*

> *'My father shook my boyfriend's hand, nodded towards me and said "So. Boned her yet?"'*

> *'My boyfriend was standing in the kitchen. My dad turned to him and said, "You may as well fuck off mate. The only pair of bollocks going up them stairs tonight is mine."'*

That's a world of pain. Mums aren't out of the woods though, not by a long chalk. They seemed to concentrate on quietly hating whoever you brought home, although some of them weren't so discreet:

> *'Mum took me to one side when my boyfriend was in the toilet to warn me that he "minced when he walked."'*

And for one of you, it wasn't the parents that were the problem:

> *'As my boyfriend and I were leaving the house, he turned to my*

mum and said "Don't worry. I won't rape her."'   Oh dear…

That must have set her mind at rest no end.

For those of you who are gay, the main issue was telling your parents. With very few exceptions, coming out was a source of great anxiety:

> *'Before I told my parents I was gay, I told them I had killed someone, as a joke, to see what they'd be like with a shock. It wasn't a good idea.'*

A surprising 43.17% of you relied on a brother or sister to tell your parents you were gay so you didn't have to, while an uplifting 87.26% of the gay respondents told me that their parents knew anyway and it came as nothing of a shock. Having said that, 64.9% of you felt your parents still took it quite badly and that your relationship with them has been permanently damaged as a result.

So how do you get on with your parents now? The overwhelming majority of you (92.57%) believe that your relationship with your parents has improved since you left home. A lot of you put this down to simply not having to be with them on a daily basis. Only a very few of you (6.12%) think your relationship has deteriorated, with a tiny remainder of you (1.31%) making a conscious decision to have no further contact with any living parent. The following are indicative of the answers you gave.

> *'Since I've had my own children and my dad has retired my relationship with him has improved no end. I think the day I told him I was pregnant he sort of let me go and has been supportive and kind at every point. I've come to realise that he was a grumpy old sod because he was doing a job he hated to give his family the financial lifestyle he wanted us to have. My relationship with my mum has remained pretty much the same – although I could do without all the unsolicited advice on*

bringing up children and how to keep my house clean. Other than that, she is still very lovely.'

'Cautious with long stretches of silence.'

'It is still quite close. I should phone them more often. My mum still worries about us all even after we have left home, e.g. she hardly ever let us take a day off sick as children even if we were actually a bit ill but now if I have the slightest sniffle she nags and nags at me to go to the doctor. I have to censor things very carefully if things aren't going completely well in my life, in case she picks up on the negativity and frets about me. She's very canny though, so it's difficult. My dad is much more laid back, but I know he still worries under the surface. I have to say that I am getting more worried about my parents as we all get older and I would like to move close to them, but that's not possible right now. It's rare that the whole family meets up but it's fantastic when we do, we get very giddy and there is much jollity.'

'I see them as people in their own right now, not just as parents. I do feel that they are still slightly too involved in my life for someone who is over thirty and owns her own home, though.'

plug, plug

So there it is: a short potted snapshot of you and your parents. Thanks to everyone who answered the online questionnaire. Without you, this book would have been at least 54% worse.

If you enjoyed reading my book then please feel free to visit me at my website **www.emmakennedy.net**. If you want to contact me, you can email me at emmak@globalnet.co.uk

And if you liked my book and think I can be trusted, let me recommend another blog-based book by Greg Stekelman. It's called *A Year in the Life of TheManWhoFellAsleep* and it's hilarious. Greg also has the best website I've ever seen. So visit him at www.manwhofellasleep.com.

worth a look

ABOUT THE AUTHOR

Emma Kennedy is an actress, presenter and writer who has appeared in many comedy shows including *People Like Us*, *The Smoking Room* and, most recently, *Suburban Shootout*. She was also in the film *Notes on A Scandal* for two whole seconds. She has won several prizes: a Comedy Lounge Award and a British Television Advertising Craft Award for Best Actress. She has written loads of things for Radio 4 including the multi award winning *Sunday Format* as well as the acclaimed documentary series *Who Wears The Trousers* and the popular radio adaptation of *The Papers of AJ Wentworth*. She has also written *Tracey Beaker* for CBBC and has provided the scripts for several documentaries on Channel 4. But her greatest achievement was being the World Runner Up Conker Champion. She would have won. But was let down by a soft nut.

THE

END